CAROL ANNE DAVIS

SADISTIC KILLERS

PROFILES OF PATHOLOGICAL PREDATORS

summersdale

SADISTIC KILLERS
Copyright © Carol Anne Davis 2007

Summersdale Publishers Ltd
46 West Street
Chichester
West Sussex
PO19 1RP
UK

www.summersdale.com

Printed and bound in Great Britain

ISBN: 1-84024-581-6
ISBN 13: 978-1-84024-581-3

Cover photographs show Irma Greese and Neville Heath.

About the Author

Carol Anne Davis was born in Dundee, moved to Edinburgh in her twenties and now lives in south-west England. She left school at 15 and was everything from an artist's model to an editorial assistant before going to university. Her Master of the Arts degree included criminology and was followed by a postgraduate diploma in Adult and Community Education.

A full-time writer since graduating, her crime novels *Kiss it Away*, *Noise Abatement*, *Safe as Houses* and *Shrouded* have been described as chillingly realistic for their portrayals of dangerous sex and death.

She is also the author of the true crime books *Couples Who Kill: Profiles of Deviant Duos*, *Children Who Kill: Profiles of Preteen and Teenage Killers* and *Women Who Kill: Profiles of Female Serial Killers*.

Carol's website is located at www.carolannedavis.co.uk.

Acknowledgements

I'm grateful to Dr Bob Johnson for providing me with information about his work with sadistic killers. During his years as a consultant psychiatrist at Parkhurst Prison – and as Head of Therapy at Ashworth Maximum Security Hospital – he treated numerous violent men.

And I'm deeply indebted to Lynn Paula Russell for giving what must be one of the most honest and detailed interviews on consensual sadomasochism ever to appear in a mainstream publication. As the artist behind *The Illustrated Book of Corporal Punishment* and numerous similar works, she brings courage and humour to a subject that is frequently misunderstood.

Many thanks to Mark Ramsden for sharing his insight into the psychological forces driving many sadomasochists. Mark wrote the text for the photographic book *Radical Desire* and is also author of several novels including *The Dungeonmaster's Apprentice* and *The Sacred Blood*.

I'm grateful to the publishers of *Master Detective* magazine for providing me with additional information about the largely forgotten murder of British teenager Suzanne Capper. I'd also like to acknowledge the Home Office for clarifying the legal position on sadomasochism and for suggesting other sources worthy of research.

For Ian

CONTENTS

Introduction..9

Part One – Nowhere to Go: British Sadists
Neville George Clevely Heath..15
Patrick Joseph Byrne...30
Victor Glenford Miller...39
Anthony Paul Anderson...45
Colin John Ireland..50
Sadistic Diversity...63

Part Two – Moving On: American Sadists
Robert Ben Rhoades...96
Rex Allan Krebs..105
Dayton Leroy Rogers..117
Robert Christian Hansen..133
John Joseph Joubert..162
Jesse James Cummings..170
Richard Francis Cottingham..181

Part Three – The Wilderness Years: Australian Sadists
Christopher Bernard Wilder...198
Ivan Robert Marko Milat...218
Paul Charles Denyer...232

Part Four – Everything Under the Sun: Sadism Worldwide
Sadists Who Kill Men...242
Sadists Who Kill Women..255
Sadists Who Kill Children..270
Sadists Who Kill Indiscriminately..279
Female Sadists...286

Part Five – Boundaries
Safe And Sane: Consensual Sadomasochism.................................306
Changing Things..319

Appendix: Useful Addresses...327
Select Bibliography...329
Index...332

INTRODUCTION

'Life being what it is, one dreams of revenge,' wrote the artist Paul Gauguin in the nineteenth century. It's a sentiment echoed by many sadistic killers. Most are working class males in their twenties and thirties, but the chapter on female sadists explores murders committed by women as young as 19.

Sadistic killers differ from most murderers in that they love to control their victims and make them suffer – witnessing such pain and fear brings the sadist immense sexual satisfaction. They also want to prolong this controlling phase for as long as possible. This is in stark contrast to the man or woman who kills for profit, to eliminate a love rival or during a domestic argument. Such non-sadistic killers try to annihilate the other party as quickly as possible, often stabbing them through the heart or bludgeoning them about the head. Similarly, the murderous parent hurriedly smothers their baby's cries and the necrophile kills swiftly in order to have access to dead flesh.

To the sadist, this shoot-to-kill approach is a complete anathema, as it leaves him (or, less commonly, her) with a dead body. In contrast, he needs a live, sentient victim who will respond to his commands. If he can transport his victims to his home or to a hotel, as Robert Rhoades and Richard Cottingham did respectively, then he can train them to satisfy his every desire. But if a sadist inadvertently kills his victim too quickly, he will often try to hurt or humiliate the corpse, extensively mutilating the flesh in his desire for revenge. His rage, which has invariably built for years during his unhappy childhood, has to go somewhere so he attacks the cadaver.

Details of what the sadist did to his victim (and, in some instances, how the victim responded) have often come from the sadist himself as he confided in close friends, a tape recorder or a diary. In other instances, this information comes from pathologist, police or psychiatric reports.

The British sadists profiled in this book were often on low incomes so lacked a safe house to take their victims to. Consequently they killed in hotels, hostels or the victim's own home. In contrast, the American sadists had customised vans in which to transport their victims and one of the sadists even owned a small plane. Similarly, the Australian sadists often utilised the great outdoors, attacking their victims on secluded beaches or taking them deep into the woods. I chose these cases from the many available because of their variety: every type of sadist, from a teenage boy scout to a wealthy building contractor to an unemployed cross-dresser, is portrayed in detail here.

Sadism isn't new, but it was once the province of the comparatively rich – as Maslow's hierarchy of needs delineates, you have to be well fed and comfortably housed before you can begin to feel sexual. But in our industrialised society, even the unemployed sadist has his basic requirements taken care of and can find the energy to lure victim after victim to a secluded forest, safe house or modified van.

Broadly speaking, there are three types of sadists – the sadistic killer, the sadistic criminal and the consensual sadist. The profiles in this book obviously concentrate on the killers, with the majority of them killing serially. But it also covers the second category by default as almost all of the killers were sadistic criminals earlier in their offending careers. That is, they abducted and harmed various victims but did not kill them, either because they came to their senses or their quarry escaped.

The third category, that of the consensual sadist, should ideally be outside of a study of criminality, but law enforcement agencies and the general public don't always make the distinction and, as a result, the man who whips his consenting sexually-submissive girlfriend is confused with a genuine abuser and may even be charged with actual bodily harm. Yet many of our most lauded literary figures and artists have been recreational sadists – and ten per cent of the general population has an interest in sadomasochistic exchanges – a subject explored in the penultimate chapter on consensual erotic punishment.

The final chapter explores how we can prevent sadistic killers being formed and how we can potentially treat those who already exist. It's followed by a *Useful Addresses* section for anyone who wants to know more about sexual power play, child protection and criminal violence.

Doubtless the occasional Pollyanna figure will dismiss this book as gratuitous, but, as former FBI agent John Douglas pointed out, it's only by studying a man's actions that we can know what kind of person he truly is. More importantly, without this knowledge we can never change anything.

PART ONE

NOWHERE TO GO: BRITISH SADISTS

CHAPTER ONE

NEVILLE GEORGE CLEVELY HEATH

Heath's obsession with flagellation began during his childhood in England. By adulthood he had bankrupted himself by paying prostitutes in foreign climes to let him cane them again and again. Returning to Britain and purchasing several riding switches and dogwhips, he sadistically murdered two young women.

Formative influences

Neville was born on 6 June 1917 to Bessie and William Heath, a housewife and barber. Bessie was described as much more domineering than her significantly older spouse. The family lived in Ilford but soon moved to Wimbledon where Bessie gave birth to a second son. Neville was always much closer to his mother and brother than to his father.

When Neville was five, his parents enrolled him at a mixed gender convent school which was just down the road. Unfortunately the school believed in caning children and – like many other English schoolboys – Neville became terrified of receiving a painful beating. However, watching other children being caned, he began to fantasise about flogging them himself. At six years old, he grabbed one of his female contemporaries in the classroom and wildly applied the rod to her until a passing teacher intervened. The little girl was so upset that she had to be sent home.

It's likely that he was expelled for this incident – leastways he now moved to Rutlish public school which only catered for boys. But the damage had already been done and his sexuality was now sadomasochistic to the core.

By his early teens he'd developed a fetish for handkerchiefs, probably because they featured in his fantasies about tying girls' wrists, and began to steal them from the neighbourhood women. It was the start of an escalating pattern of sexual offending that is still prevalent in today's criminals: many young men graduate from stealing knickers from washing lines to peeping through windows to indecent exposure and even rape.

At 15, Heath was at a party playing a parlour game called 'Murder' and, alongside another boy, locked a teenage girl in a room and began to kiss her. The girl became upset and the other boy backed off but Neville grabbed her by the throat to hold her head in place, his fingers leaving deep red marks on her neck. He only let go when she became hysterical and he feared that other partygoers would intervene. Her father was concerned at the level of aggression that the teenager had shown but decided that it was merely horseplay which had gone too far and let Heath off with a warning not to do it again.

Sadly, this failure to recognise early criminal sadism is all too common, with onlookers dismissing a child's cruelty towards younger children, or even to animals, as just a phase. Granted, at this stage, juvenile sadism can fade if the child is removed from the influence of a brutal parent or sadistic schoolteacher; but, without such intervention, his inhumane tendencies will invariably increase.

Early thefts

Neville left school at age 17, became an office boy and soon found out that he hated mundane work. Desperate for instant gratification, he joined the Territorial Army, which offered status and physical exercise, both important to the teenager. Soon he enlisted in the air force cadets and was variously posted to Cambridgeshire, Sussex and London, his male comrades finding him a superficially nice young man. Young women also liked him and he went to bed with lots of them, but none offered the sadomasochistic experiences he craved.

However, in London he found prostitutes who would allow him to whip them if the price was right – and it was rumoured that he whipped some of the girls so hard that he actually drew blood. (Most consensual sadomasochistic encounters involve a great deal of ritual and stop far short of bloodshed or lasting damage, but Neville Heath was intent on causing maximum pain.)

Desperate for cash to fund his prostitution costs, he soon began to steal and was questioned by the army authorities. Facing arrest, he made one of his very rare visits home to his mother – this was technically desertion – and was subsequently discharged.

By now he'd matured into a handsome and well-built young man with wavy fair hair, bright blue eyes and a propensity for laughter. Only the sometimes cruel set of his mouth belied his underlying pathology. He continued his life of crime, often reinventing himself and forging cheques to fund his club- and pub-based lifestyle. Again, the authorities caught up with him and he was soon facing jail. But his good looks and good family name worked in his favour so that he was given probation instead.

Not one to learn from experience, the 21-year-old robbed a friend's flat, purchased clothes by forging a banker's order and attempted to obtain a car by false pretences. This time he was sent to borstal where the staff found him condescending and sly.

£50 whippings

Released from borstal in October 1939 to help in the war effort, Neville Heath was drafted into the army. Like many psychopaths he did well there, being completely fearless. He also found numerous females willing to go to bed with him. But one girl sarcastically refused him and he immediately pulled her hair back and began to beat her about the face until she broke away.

He was posted to Cairo and soon discovered the Amazon Room available in most of the brothels, where a customer could whip reluctant young girls for £50 a night. (At the time, a visit to a 'vanilla' – straight sex – prostitute in London only cost a pound.) He paid handsomely to thrash a pair of 15- and 16-year-old sisters, using a cat-o'-nine-tails. He later told an acquaintance that he liked to leave a minute between each stroke of the whip for the full pain to be realised, and for the hellish anticipation to build again. He also found that several female sadists from the upper classes had paid large sums to whip and cane the girls.

On other occasions he lashed a 20-year-old female sex worker with a slender leather switch and on yet other occasions used a whip on an 18-year-old female. He told his fellow officers that he liked to hang a girl upside down from the brothel's pulley system before choosing the whip which he would use on her for an extended period of time.

Heath also paid to watch one young girl whip another in his favourite Cairo brothel. Later he joined in, bending one of the teenagers over a wooden bar and binding her wrists together with handkerchiefs before tying her hands above her head to a ceiling post – handkerchiefs formed part of his fetish so he often introduced them to a sadomasochistic encounter. The brothel keeper encouraged him to whip the girl as hard as he wanted, providing he didn't draw blood.

When the young officer couldn't afford another session he would go to bed and have regular sex with someone he'd picked up at a bar, but whatever he did it failed to rid him of his demons and he began drinking heavily. He would later tell a friend that he once got so drunk and out of control that he feared he'd beaten a belly dancer to death – and there would later be conjecture that he'd stabbed another girl to death whilst posted abroad.

Spending beyond his means on whipping prostitutes, the young lieutenant soon got hopelessly into debt and once again began to pass bad cheques and forge more. Drummed out of the army for these offences, he fled to South Africa and joined the air force under the pseudonym James Robert Cadogan Armstrong. He became a pilot instructor and was valiant when facing death.

Marriage and fatherhood

Whilst in Johannesburg, the 25-year-old introduced himself as Bruce Lockhart to Elizabeth Pitt-Rivers, an 18-year-old from a good family. He was so eloquent and well read that she soon fell madly in love with him. But her parents discovered that Bruce Lockhart was not his real name and demanded an explanation. He then said that his birth name was James Robert Cadogan Armstrong but that the Armstrong family had died and it was too emotionally painful for him to use his own name.

Unsurprisingly, the Pitt-Rivers raised an eyebrow or two but young Elizabeth was determined to stand by her man and promptly eloped with him. Seven months after their marriage she was proud to bear his son.

The next two years were the most stable in Neville Heath's life. He was promoted to the rank of captain in the South African Air Force and also proved to be a charming husband (and doting father to little Robert) who made no unusual sexual demands on his wife.

But, sent to the RAF in Britain for a few months, he returned to his criminal ways, making money by getting engaged to girls from wealthy backgrounds then selling the engagement presents. Moved to Belgium, he quickly sought out brothels where he could whip female teenagers for a price.

Returning to South Africa and his doting wife, he started to write bad cheques, some of which were honoured by his embarrassed father-in-law. Eventually Heath was arrested for fraud. More and more evidence of his criminal ways came to light and his wife reluctantly began divorce proceedings, unusual in those till-death-us-do-part conventional times. He agreed to the divorce, which seems to have involved his unfortunate father-in-law paying off more of his debts, and it became final in October 1945.

Deported from South Africa, the newly single captain arrived back in England on 5 February 1946. He immediately borrowed money from his father, saying it was to take flying lessons (in reality, he was already a proficient pilot), but instead moved to London and began to drink and socialise in the capital's hotels.

He found a club where he could pay to watch prostitutes being bent over naked and caned before an audience. At first he took a group of friends along but it was obvious to them that he was obsessed by the spectacle and this made him poor company. Soon he returned to the club alone. Interestingly he paid to watch women whipping men, suggesting he may have had a masochistic side as well. He also bought a whip from the club – one of four whips he owned – which would later be used on his first confirmed murder victim. But prior to this he'd use it on sexually-submissive girls…

Flagellation

On 23 February 1946, Heath took one of his acquaintances to a hotel for what was initially a consensual sadomasochistic experience. The woman – who was married – stripped and lay face down on the mattress, allowing Heath to spreadeagle her and tie her wrists and ankles to the posts of the bed.

He began to cane her at the level they'd agreed, but soon increased the severity of the strokes till she began screaming. Someone in the corridor overheard her pleading with Heath to stop and the assistant manager was summoned and unlocked the door. They found Heath standing over his partner and wielding the cane, her buttocks a scarlet testament to the degree of punishment he'd applied.

Embarrassed, the woman refused to press charges and quickly left the hotel. Despite this close call, three months later Heath did the exact same thing with another woman, who again understandably declined to involve the police. That same month – May 1946 – he met 32-year-old Margery Aimee Brownell Gardner and was clearly impressed with her, enjoying a consensual sadomasochistic session and telling a friend that she was 'a little scout'.

Margery, who had film star good looks, had tried to make her living as a freelance artist, but like most freelancers she had financial problems. She sometimes made extra money by working as a film extra and was happy to accept meals and gifts from various bohemian friends including known criminals and pimps. Margery was sexually submissive so the couple were superficially a perfect match.

They enjoyed several dinners together and probably an equal number of sadomasochistic sessions throughout that month, but during one encounter Heath whipped her so hard that her screams persuaded the hotel staff to intervene.

The first murder

On 16 June 1946, Heath spent the day in a pub frequented by Fleet Street journalists, offering to fly them abroad in a private plane. One hack gave him 30 pounds for a proposed trip to Copenhagen and the con man left the pub while he was ahead of the game. By now he had been drinking for 12 hours and may have had up to 28 beers, a dangerous amount for a psychopath who already has lowered inhibitions. Flush with cash, he met up with Margery Gardner in West London and asked her to accompany him to the Pembridge Court Hotel.

At first, the punishment was excitingly consensual. Heath gagged Margery and tightly bound her wrists and ankles as she lay naked on her stomach. He began to whip her with his dogwhip (used so often that the tip had worn away, exposing the metal underneath), its diamond-mesh pattern leaving its telltale marks on her naked flesh.

But he began to whip much too hard and when Margery flipped herself over to protest, he whipped at her face, the strokes cutting her eyelids. He whipped her an unknown number of times, 17 of the strokes leaving clear weals on her alabaster flesh as she screamed into her gag.

His cruel lust building, the 29-year-old bit into his lover's nipples, almost severing them. He also pushed an object – possibly the handle of the whip – into her with such force that it caused internal injuries. At some stage during this assault he pushed Margery's face into the pillow, suffocating her.

Psychologists would later speculate that the amount of alcohol he'd drunk made it impossible for him to get or maintain an erection and that the humiliation of this had caused him to go temporarily mad with rage. Heath was a superficially pleasant man from a non-criminal family so they explained the crime by blaming alcohol rather than exploring the sadism which had emanated from his school days and which now formed the core of his sexuality.

When Heath recovered, he moved Margery's lifeless body to the other bed and washed her face, perhaps hoping to revive her. Realising that this was impossible, he left the hotel. He had entered the room with Margery shortly before midnight – and by 1.30 a.m. he had fled.

An unlikely alibi

Neville Heath now travelled to Worthing where he had a recent girlfriend called Yvonne who strongly resembled a younger version of Margery Gardner. When he was relaxed in her company, he told her a bizarre story, saying that he'd lent his hotel room in London to a friend, and that his friend must have killed Margery. He said that she'd died by having a poker stuck up her. In reality, the young woman had sustained horrible internal injuries but there wasn't a poker in the room and no one had ever seen Heath with a poker. It's much more likely that he violated her with the whip handle but that his sexual fantasies included hurting women with pokers so he substituted this in his imagination and in telling the tale. The girl was shocked and asked what kind of man would do such a thing and Heath airily replied 'A sex maniac.' Yvonne, being young and naïve, believed his story and, when he proposed, still agreed to marry him.

When the maid entered the west London hotel room five days later, she found Margery's naked body tucked up in bed, blood still smeared over her face, body and vagina. Heath had booked the room in his own name – and Margery had told several of her like-minded friends that they were going to enjoy a flagellation session with his dogwhip – so he immediately became a wanted man.

The second murder

Heath now fled to Bournemouth and booked into a hotel under the pseudonym Group-Captain Rupert Brooke. He loved Rupert Brooke's poetry and had copied some of his verses into his notebooks and diaries.

At first he contemplated suicide and asked to be moved to a room with a gas fire as he planned to gas himself. He also wrote to his parents saying 'life doesn't mean a thing', but he didn't post the note. As the days passed without police interference, he realised that he might literally get away with murder, and his spirits revived.

Whilst out for a stroll, he met a girl he knew and was introduced to her friend, Doreen Marshall. Doreen had been ill so her parents had sent her to Bournemouth to enjoy the sea air. Her doting father had bought her a return train ticket. Sadly the return portion would never be required.

Heath invited the 19-year-old out to tea and they met up again that evening, dining at his hotel then sitting in the lounge bar with Heath hastily downing numerous beers, gins and brandies. It was evident to others in the lounge that Doreen was increasingly wary of him and at 11.20 p.m. she asked the porter to order her a taxi home.

Moments later Heath cancelled the taxi and insisted that he'd walk her back to her hotel. He told the porter that he'd be back in 30 minutes but Doreen corrected, 'He'll be back in fifteen.'

When they reached the comparatively sheltered area of Branscombe Chine, Heath turned on the luckless young woman, punching her in the face and knocking her to the ground.

Whilst she lay there semi-conscious, he tied her hands in front of her with a handkerchief, kneeling on her so hard in the process that he broke one of her ribs. He removed his own clothes and stripped hers off, ripping her underwear from her struggling body, then attempted to rape her. When he failed, he took his large pocket knife and sliced at her throat. He also cut from one breast to the other and threw himself across her, biting her nipples savagely. Then the stabbing continued – marks on her bound hands showed where she'd tried to defend herself from the agonies inflicted by his slashing blade. But another stab wound to her throat, which partially severed her vertebral column, provided the fatal blow.

When she was dead, Heath fell on her again with his knife, slashing one of her thighs then pulling the blade upwards to cut deeply into her pubis, stomach and breasts. When he was happy with his handiwork, he took Doreen's ring and watch from her still-warm corpse and untied the bloodstained handkerchief from her wrists to keep as a souvenir. He dragged her body by the feet to some nearby rhododendron bushes, cutting further branches from nearby scrub to cover it up.

Rifling through her bag, he removed her money, return rail ticket and a small penknife, before throwing the bag behind a bathing hut. Realising that he was covered in blood, he washed himself in the sea, disposing of the murder weapon there, before dressing and walking back to his hotel.

A hastily created alibi

Heath didn't have a viable explanation for what he'd been doing for the past few hours, so rather than go past the reception desk, he fetched a ladder from the hotel yard and used it to climb into his window. When the porter, unsure if he'd returned or not, peaked into his room at 4 a.m. he was fast asleep. Waking the following morning, the sadist found scratches on his neck and covered them with a silk scarf. He also pawned Doreen's watch and ring, having pocketed her cash.

Meanwhile the manager of the Norfolk Hotel became alarmed that Doreen Marshall had not returned. Knowing that she'd planned to have tea at the Tollard Royal Hotel with Group-Captain Rupert Brooke, he phoned and asked what had happened. Heath denied knowing Doreen and said that he'd meet her anguished parents at the police station to confirm this. The newspapers at the time saw this as Heath surrendering to the authorities – but in likelihood the young sociopath thought that he could talk his way out of it and pretend to aid in the search.

But his fingerprints had already been found in the hotel room where Margery Gardner died and police were looking for him throughout Britain. And when he saw what he thought was Doreen's ghost (it was her older sister who bore a remarkable resemblance to the murdered woman) he went white and began to shake.

Arrested, he eventually admitted to being Neville Heath. A ticket in his coat led them to a left luggage locker which contained the bloodstained scarf which had tied Margery Gardner's hands and the other which had muffled her screams. The locker also contained the steel-cored whip which had so cruelly lacerated her flesh. Moreover, a pearl found in his pocket had been torn from a necklace around Doreen Marshall's throat. His guilt a foregone conclusion, he was remanded in custody in Brixton prison.

Body discovered

On 8 July, a girl out walking her dog found Doreen Marshall's body hidden under some cut branches and bushes on Branscombe Chine. She was naked apart from one shoe, though her clothes had been piled on top of her body. Her throat had been cut to a three quarter inch depth.

The police now began to investigate Neville Heath's past, going through the six hundred names in his address books. Understandably, given the ignorance about consensual sadomasochism which existed at the time, few of his lovers told the truth. For example, the married woman who had screamed when caned too hard told the authorities that she'd only gone to Heath's room for a friendly drink and that he'd grabbed her arm and twisted it behind her back, telling her that he hated women. She further lied that when she refused to strip for him, he threw her against the wall so violently that she passed out.

When she regained consciousness, she told police, she found that she was naked and that he had tied her hands behind her back with a handkerchief. Beating her with his fists, he knocked her out again. In reality, Heath's biographer Francis Selwyn would later note that they'd had a consensual caning session but he'd probably caned her harder than they'd agreed upon. Nevertheless, she'd voluntarily left the hotel with him rather than ask the manager to order her a taxi to take her home.

A crowd puller

Heath had cheerfully admitted both murders to the police but his counsel urged him to plead not guilty by reason of insanity for the sake of his family. Shrugging, he entered a not guilty plea.

Questioned by a psychiatrist, he would only say that whipping a girl gave him the kind of sexual release that sexual intercourse gave to most men. He subsequently suggested that he'd recovered from a blackout to find Margery Gardner lying dead next to him. He was so indifferent to the suffering which he'd caused, and so fearless regarding his own imminent fate, that it was evident to the psychiatrist that he was a psychopath.

Newspaper accounts of his flagellation fetish made the case the most talked about of its day, and women flocked to Neville Heath's trial, coming to blows outside the courtroom in their desperation to reach the public gallery. Some had queued for 14 hours, his sadism clearly having strong appeal. That said, there was no suggestion in the newspapers at this stage that Margery Gardner and previous partners had consented to being tied up and chastened, so the public's impression was of a man who had forced all of his partners to submit to the whip.

There had, of course, been British sadists before Neville Heath, but they lacked the clear sadistic symbolism of the whip and handcuffs. Jack the Ripper, for example, evidenced sadism in his slashing and cutting gestures and especially in excising the breasts and uterus of some of his victims. The true identity of Jack the Ripper remains unknown: he may have been the gentleman James Maybury or the mentally ill scavenger Aaron Kosminski beset by voices. He may even have been a medical student called John Sanders who went insane and was shipped off to a sanatorium in Weston-super-Mare. Coincidentally, the bracing seaside town also featured in Neville Heath's life story for he borrowed a large amount of money from an aunt who lived there and never paid it back.

But, whoever Jack the Ripper was, he lacked Neville Heath's controlled cruelty, for as mentioned earlier Heath would wait for one minute after lashing a prostitute, enjoying her anguished writhing to the full before applying the next merciless stroke.

Now the public wanted to know exactly what he had done to his two victims. Many female members of that public also wanted to attract his attention, dressing in their most fashionable clothes and self-consciously combing their hair as they sat in the Old Bailey's gallery.

A psychopath

The trial opened at the Old Bailey on 24 September 1946. Heath pleaded not guilty to murdering Margery Gardner. The prosecution gave the impression that she'd been tied and whipped against her will and the defence tried to suggest that she was promiscuous – but, even if she had been, it hardly excused violating her with a whip handle and suffocating her to death. The girlfriend who Heath had proposed to in Worthing took the stand and described him as a gentle and considerate lover then the prosecution detailed the injuries he'd inflicted on his naked victim. Another doctor testified to the injuries received by Doreen Marshall. The trial lasted for three days.

Unsurprisingly, it took the jury only an hour to find him guilty of Margery Gardner's murder. Asked if he had anything to say, he replied 'Nothing' and was duly sentenced to death. The authorities decided there was no point in having a separate trial for Doreen Marshall's murder as her killer was already condemned to die.

Afterwards the popular press gave the impression that men enjoying sadomasochism today would become murderers tomorrow. But, as Heath's biographer Francis Selwyn perceptively noted: '… no one had suggested that the teachers and workhouse masters who flogged their way through generations of the young were likely to die on the gallows.'

The hanged man

Awaiting execution, Heath let his mother visit him once then he refused to see her or the rest of his family and friends as he felt ashamed of the prison uniform. He wrote to his mother saying, 'My only regret at leaving the world is that I have been so damned unworthy of you both.' He wrote again the following day, hours before he was to be hanged, to tell her that he would stay awake to see the dawn for the last time, adding 'Well, it wasn't really a bad life while it lasted… Please don't mourn my going… and don't wear black.'

Just before his execution on 16 October 1946 he was offered a glass of whisky and joked to the warden, 'You might make that a double.' He was equally unconcerned as the hangman led him to the scaffold, saying, 'Let's get it over with.'

Afterwards the jury asked to see his body, as did several curious females, a request which was curtly refused. That lunchtime he was buried in an unmarked grave by Pentonville Prison's wall.

CHAPTER TWO

PATRICK JOSEPH BYRNE

Patrick Byrne committed one of the most horrific sex murders of the late 1950s – and immediately tried to commit a second. His sadistic acts sparked one of the biggest murder hunts in British history.

Early trauma

Patrick was born to Elisabeth and Joseph Byrne in Dublin in 1932, the second son of what would ultimately become a large family. He was much closer to his mother than to his father, and would remain so throughout his life. This preference for the mother is common in boys who grow up to become sadists, as the father is often so overbearing that the child cannot identify with him. In contrast, the mother tends to be pathologically overprotective, sometimes keeping the child away from possible playmates and making him reliant on her company. Beaten by one parent and emotionally suffocated by the other, the child retreats into a sadistic fantasy life, fantasies that he may later act out.

Psychiatrists would later note that Patrick had sexual abnormalities of the mind when still a child, a trait invariably formed by nurture rather than nature. But they were unable to find out about his formative experiences. It's merely known that he was small for his age, had curly hair and sparkling eyes, but was extremely nervous and shy.

When he was eight, his mother brought him to hospital in an unconscious state and he remained unconscious for three days. She said that he'd been playing outdoors when a wall fell on him, breaking one of his legs and battering onto his head.

Patrick already had a slightly below average IQ and very poor literacy skills which would have made him unpopular with his teachers. And Irish teachers in the 1930s and 1940s were often disciplinarians who beat their little pupils mercilessly. In class he remained a passive-aggressive loner; though, like many disturbed children, he was creative, being good at art in particular.

As Patrick moved into his teens, he found it impossible to talk to girls, though he fantasised about having sex with them. And as he matured, his fantasies became increasingly cruel.

At 14 he left school and found a factory job. Soon he was drinking heavily. He remained desperately shy, and, even when dragged out to social events by relatives, sat in a corner and refused to dance.

But at 17 he lost his virginity to a much older woman who had recently been widowed. His religious upbringing may have caused him to see this sexual relationship as abusive and wrong – in any case, he would later state erroneously that it was the start of all his problems. He hinted to a friend that he'd told his mother but that she'd refused to intervene. He had sex with the widow many times but believed that she'd put a spell on him and that she'd ruined him for girls his own age. He increasingly hated younger women who he saw as the source of his nervous tension, and he had masturbatory fantasies of putting helpless females through a circular saw.

Early crimes

Like many murderers-to-be, he started with lesser crimes which involved trespass, being convicted of three separate counts of housebreaking in Dublin. In retrospect, he may have been looting these houses for women's clothing – some of society's cruellest killers have been cross-dressers who have identified on one level with women due to their strong bonding with their mothers, but who, on another level, despise this supposed weakness in themselves and want to obliterate it. He may also have been hoping that the female occupant would return home, giving him access to a victim in a safe house.

Byrne later spent two years in the Royal Army Ordnance Corps but they saw nothing untoward about his behaviour as he remained quiet and shy.

When he was 26 his mother relocated him, his brothers and three sisters to England. The Byrnes now settled in Warrington and Patrick found a job as a labourer, though he was unreliable and often reported for work in a drunken state.

The voyeur

Patrick Byrne was still living with his mother and had never had a steady girlfriend, but in his fantasies he raped and mastered every girl he came into contact with. This is a trait that's especially common in embryonic-stage sadistic killers: unable to begin or maintain loving relationships, they spend endless hours developing a rich cruelty-based fantasy life.

It's unknown when his peeping Tom activities began, but he was definitely an active voyeur when he found work in Birmingham and moved on his own to a lodging house there in the mid 1950s. His nickname by then was Acky and someone had written 'Acky Byrne The Window Peeper' on a wall close to his home.

Byrne found erotic satisfaction in watching unaware women undress. His favourite venues included the Birmingham YWCA hostel a mere half mile from his lodging house, the hostel where he would eventually kill. On one occasion he was caught on the stairs there and on another occasion he entered a young teacher's room, the sound of her door opening waking her. He stared at her breasts through her nightgown and walked towards her but she remained calm, explaining to him that she was engaged to another man. He seemed to respect this (it made her a 'good woman' in his eyes), apologised and agreed to leave. She then led him out of the front door, locked it and phoned the police.

Patrick was introduced to an 18-year-old girl at a social club and met her there weekly, though he never made a pass at her. He insisted on walking her home because he warned that 'bad men might rape or hurt her'. He talked of such potential attacks again and again. But many women were naïve about criminal psychology in the 1950s and they simply believed that Patrick was a gentleman who was looking out for them. In truth, he was projecting his own sexually sadistic fantasies onto other men and imagining they were as deviant as he.

Prison

Byrne now began to show his true colours, assaulting a policeman in January 1958. He was sentenced to two months in prison. A few months later he was drinking in a Warrington pub when the landlord refused to serve him again as he was clearly drunk and disorderly. 'Give us the drinks or I'll knife you,' Byrne screamed, so his friends tried to eject him from the building, but he was holding onto the bar top so tightly that it took three of them to prise him loose.

The murder

On 23 December 1959, he drank heavily in a Birmingham pub at lunchtime and into the early afternoon. When he belatedly returned to the building site where he was working, his foreman ordered him to remain on the ground rather than risk him climbing the scaffolding. Shortly afterwards, Byrne decided to go home. He was walking along the road when he saw a girl going into the YWCA hostel in Edgbaston, one of his favourite peeping Tom locations. He went to the back of the hostel, peeped through a window, and saw another girl in a red jumper and underskirt combing her hair.

Deciding to get a better look, Byrne entered the hostel through an adjacent open window and stood on a chair so that he could peep through the glass partition above the door. After a few minutes it became obvious that the occupant – Sidney Stephanie Baird, who was always known by her middle name – wasn't going to undress further, so Byrne got off his chair. Seconds later Stephanie, who must have heard a noise in the corridor, opened the door and asked him what he wanted. When he said that he was looking for someone she offered to get the warden, whereupon Byrne attempted to silence her with a kiss.

He put his hands around the 29-year-old's waist and pushed her back into the room, making her scream in terror. During the desperate struggle which followed, the contents of the room were strewn all over the place. The 27-year-old then put his hands around her throat and she fell to the floor with him on top, whereupon she sustained a fractured skull. Byrne continued to squeeze her throat whilst kissing her, then he bolted the door and undressed himself.

He removed Stephanie's jumper and committed various sex acts upon her body. By now she was dead or dying. He'd later say, 'I seemed to be in a hurry to do everything to her and hadn't the patience.' He undressed down to his shoes and socks then rolled all over her and entered her corpse. The fantasy had been to make girls scream by putting them through a circular saw – but now that he'd inadvertently killed his victim, he wanted to defile her body as much as possible, an extension of his sadism.

When he tired of necrophiliac sex, he went into her cupboard and fetched a table knife, carving around her right breast until it was fully excised. He then scored her chest with the blade and cut her back. He also attempted to cannibalise one of her breasts after putting sugar on it, and sawed her head off – an act which took between 15 minutes and half an hour.

Halfway through these mutilations, which doubtless brought him to orgasm, Byrne scribbled a note on an envelope which said: 'This was the thing I thocht (sic) would never come.' He would later say that he thought he might rape a girl but didn't believe the day would come when he would murder for sex.

He left her body on the floor but placed her head and the knife blade on the bed. He seemed confused at his own motivation for removing the head, later telling the police 'It's been puzzling me since why I took the head off. It's not connected with sex in all the books I've read.' It's likely that his hatred was aimed at another woman, and he was only able to depersonalise Stephanie's body by removing her face.

Attempted murder

Byrne now dressed but he had the desire to kill another female victim, specifically an attractive one. With this in mind, he went into the hostel's garden and took a bra from the line, wrapping a heavy rock in it. Thus armed, he made his way to the YWCA's ironing room where he found 20-year-old Margaret McDonald Brown. He switched off the light then struck her on the head, but when she screamed loudly (her thick hair had cushioned the worst of the blow) he ran away. Margaret Brown collapsed and another resident phoned the police.

They began to search the hostel for the attacker, finding, to their horror, the decapitated body of Stephanie Baird. Her headless corpse was so horribly mutilated that one of the two policemen who found her vomited and the other went into deep shock and remained off work for many weeks.

Meanwhile, Byrne hurried back to his lodging house a mere 400 yards away, changed out of his bloodstained work clothes and wrote a suicide note to his mother which said 'I am very sorry youse will have to receive this horrible letter.' He went on to suggest that he had a split personality but that the real him was good. Then he remembered that it was Christmas, a time of year which was incredibly important to his religious mother, so he decided to live and tore up the note.

He went out drinking with his cousin but was so shaken by the murder and attempted murder that he was afraid to sleep alone and so slept in his cousin's room. The next morning, he took the train to his mother's home in Warrington.

Manhunt

Meanwhile the police began one of the biggest manhunts in British history, employing bloodhounds and setting up roadblocks. Every sexual offender in the area was rounded up and interviewed. They also checked 4,000 handwriting samples against the note, painstakingly pieced together by the police, that Byrne had left behind.

By January, the Birmingham police were cooperating with half a dozen other British forces, ranging from York to West London. When this still didn't bring in their killer, they got in touch with their European counterparts asking if they had any unsolved sex crimes with a similar signature.

Meanwhile they were also interviewing every man who lived or worked within a three-mile radius of the YWCA. During these interviews, Patrick Byrne's landlady told them that he hadn't returned from his mother's after the Christmas break, which seemed suspicious, but his cousin gave him an alibi for the night of Stephanie's murder. Luckily, the police went to his mother's house in Warrington anyway and she explained that he'd now found a labouring job near her home so had moved in with her and wouldn't be returning to Birmingham.

Asked to attend Warrington police station on Tuesday 9 February 1960, he arrived and nervously denied any knowledge of the crime. But he looked stunned when they asked if they could take his fingerprints. The detective had a feeling that the somewhat immature labourer was holding something back and added, 'Is there anything else you would like to say?' Byrne hesitated then blurted out, 'Yes, I want to tell you about the YWCA. I had something to do with that.'

He went on to give full details of the mutilations carried out on Stephanie Baird, details which hadn't been made public. He said: 'I cannot get it off my mind.' He added that he'd had an equally strong urge to kill Margaret Brown – to kill all beautiful women – but that he'd panicked when she screamed and the stone swung out of his hand.

Trial

Byrne pleaded guilty to the murder of Stephanie Baird at Birmingham Assizes in March 1960, so only his degree of culpability had to be decided at the trial. Three psychiatrists testified for the defence, saying that Byrne was a sexual psychopath who was aroused by sexual perversion, their term for sadism. He was also sexually immature and partly insane – but at the time of the offence he'd known that his actions were wrong. The prosecution said that he was fully aware that he was killing his victim and mutilating her body so deserved to be found guilty of murder rather than manslaughter.

The all-male jury took only 45 minutes to find Patrick Joseph Byrne guilty of murder, and he was sentenced to life imprisonment. He appealed and the sentence was changed to manslaughter on the grounds of diminished responsibility, but the court confirmed that the sentence should still be life.

Freed

Patrick Joseph Byrne spent the next 33 years in prison, then was released in 1993 on licence, aged 61. But his subsequent behaviour concerned the Home Office and he was recalled as a precaution in 1999.

CHAPTER THREE
VICTOR GLENFORD MILLER

Victor Miller was responsible for one of the cruellest child murders of the mid 1980s. His desire to hurt young boys sent him out into the Herefordshire countryside again and again.

Early beatings

Victor was born in 1956 to a Jamaican father and a white mother in England. The couple had three sons, but when one died, his mother deserted the household. Victor was distraught, but his father's solution was to beat him with increasing severity and he became a deeply disturbed little boy.

The authorities removed him from his home and sent him to a residential school in the village of Bodenham. (He would later take one of his victims to a field a mile away from this locale.) His family rarely visited him during the next eight years.

Failed by the adults in his early life, Victor took to cycling for hours through the countryside, lost in his fantasies. Back in the school, he was desperate to control his environment and would tidy his few possessions and fold his clothes again and again. If anyone invaded his space he became alarmingly aggressive but on other occasions he retreated under his bed and would lie there, curled in the foetal position, for hours.

At 15 he had a nervous breakdown, after which he became a ferocious bully. He was moved to a state school but they were unable to cope with him. By his later teens he was before the courts for possessing a weapon, for burglary and for attacking other teenagers. In hindsight, it is clear that he was a fledgling psychopath. In the early 1970s he was sent to borstal where he continued to lie, steal and bully other inmates, becoming increasingly sadistic and frightening.

Sexual assaults

In 1976, he attacked a younger man at knifepoint and sexually molested him. Convicted of indecent assault, he was sent to prison for four years. The police were privately convinced that he'd sexually assaulted other young men but that the victims had been too afraid or ashamed to report the molestation or rape. (Most sexual offenders are only convicted for one out of every five assaults.)

In jail, Victor Miller was segregated from the mainstream population and served his time with other sex offenders. Like most sadists, he was an exemplary prisoner and earned parole after two and a half years. Sadists, who have suffered repeatedly in their chaotic childhood homes, often do well in a structured environment such as prison where the authorities are watching them and giving guidance. But, left to their own devices in the outside world, their rage builds, their cruel fantasies take over and they look for a victim to hurt and dominate.

A few weeks after Victor Miller's release, he attacked a 16-year-old boy but evaded justice by moving to Wolverhampton, where he attacked two youths at knifepoint, stabbing one of them. This time he was sentenced to seven years.

A sort of love

Victor now met a paedophile called Trevor Norman Peacher and for the next few years they were prison lovers. (Trevor Peacher had brutally attacked a paper boy and imprisoned him in his flat for several hours.)

When their sentences ended, they bought a small flat together in Wolverhampton but their love affair was frequently argumentative, particularly as Trevor liked to drink and Victor detested alcohol.

Abduction

Victor continued to fantasise about torturing boys. By now he was working as a van driver, a job which gave him time to dream and an opportunity to trawl for prey.

Early one morning in 1985, he grabbed a boy who was delivering Sunday papers in a village on the outskirts of Wolverhampton and bundled the teenager into his white van at knifepoint. He drove to the isolated hamlet of Catstree near Bridgnorth and indecently assaulted him. The boy promised he wouldn't tell anyone what had happened, and Miller let him go. The child kept quiet for some time but eventually told his mother, who decided to honour his pleas that they not involve the police. (She would inform the authorities later in Miller's offending career.)

A torture victim escapes

The week leading up to 15 January 1988 was a particularly stressful one for Victor Miller as he had a violent argument with his lover Trevor. As a result, both men took the week off work and Trevor remained in a drunken stupor in the flat, being vaguely aware of Victor coming back occasionally for a change of clothes.

At teatime on Friday the fifteenth, Victor Miller drove to Hereford in search of a suitable victim. Soon he saw 18-year-old Richard Holden cycling home. A small, slender teenager, he looked younger than his actual years and probably resembled the 14-year-olds that Victor most desired. (It's likely that Victor himself was sadistically assaulted when he was this age – after all, he had a nervous breakdown at 15. And killers often seek to destroy a younger version of themselves.)

Miller stopped the teenager and asked for directions, then drove around in a circle so that he was waiting for the youth when he cycled downhill. He grabbed Richard's handlebars, pulled him off the bike and put a knife to his throat. He then dragged the youth to his car where he chloroformed him.

The sadist then drove at speed through the countryside, before parking, blindfolding the youth and carrying him into a field. Richard revived somewhat and was marched through an orchard at knifepoint, then he lost consciousness again.

At some stage he revived and Victor Miller beat his back with a broken stick and possibly with a branch of gorse, implements he'd brought with him for the purposes of flagellation. The boy was so shocked by this deliberate cruelty that he blocked the details out, and would only remember them later under hypnosis. But his flesh showed the marks made by the stick for many days.

As the effects of the chloroform wore off, Richard became aware that he was sitting down and stripped to the waist with his abductor unzipping his flies. Terrified, he tore off the blindfold and kicked out at his attacker, managing to throw him backwards so that he fell. Jumping to his feet, Richard ran and hid in a nearby field waiting for the car to leave, then raced through the countryside until he found help.

A lucky escape

The following day, Victor Miller again went out in search of a boy to torture. This time he stopped a 14-year-old in Broome and asked him for directions to Birmingham. But the boy noted that the dark-complexioned young man didn't follow the instructions he gave – and he became increasingly alarmed when he saw that the man appeared to be circling the area and staring at him in a predatory way. He hid in the garden of a house until he saw the reassuring presence of the local post van and began to cycle alongside it. To his relief, Victor Miller drove swiftly away.

The murder

But Miller was determined to get himself a victim, and on Sunday he went to Hagley and drove around until he saw 14-year-old Stuart Gough who had just finished his Sunday paper round. Miller abducted Stuart at knifepoint, blindfolded him and drove him almost 40 miles to the Herefordshire woods. The details of what he did to the boy have never been disclosed, the police stating that the public and press did not need to know.

After murdering the teenager, Victor Miller drove 80 miles to the Staffordshire moors where he buried the child's clothing, his newspaper sack and asthma inhaler. He also buried his own knife.

A false alibi

Victor Glenford Miller was a suspect from early on in Stuart Gough's disappearance as several witnesses had seen a round-faced mixed race man in a silver-coloured car acting suspiciously in the area, and Miller fit the bill with his silver Colt Sapporo. He lived within easy driving distance of the abduction location and had previous convictions for attacks on young boys.

Miller said he'd been working with Peacher at Manders Paints all week (Miller had a job as a warehouseman there in Wolverhampton) but when the police checked their alibi, they found that neither man had been at the firm for the last seven days.

The evidence against Miller began to mount up. Gorse needles were found in the boot of his car – and gorse branches had been used in Richard Holden's torture. Tyre marks in the orchard matched the tyres of his car. And Richard identified the vehicle's customised loudspeakers.

The body

Victor Miller was charged with Richard Holden's abduction and injury, but he still refused to admit that he was responsible for Stuart Gough's abduction and suspected murder. But Trevor Peacher now admitted that he'd given his lover a false alibi and the police let Miller know that they were aware of the earlier Catstree assault.

Eventually, two weeks after Stuart Gough had disappeared, Miller agreed to take police to the body and directed them to a remote part of the Herefordshire woods. There they saw a foot poking out of the leaves. The killer was too distraught to look at the body and backed away before police could begin unearthing it. This type of behaviour isn't unusual in sadistic killers – confronted with their actions after the rage and lust have subsided, they are capable of shame. But it's a fleeting emotion which doesn't prevent them from going on to offend again and again.

Returned to the police station, Victor Miller admitted causing the child's injuries. He also admitted sexually assaulting a total of 29 boys over the previous few years. He asked his solicitor to request that the courts give him the maximum possible sentence for Stuart Gough's death.

On Thursday 3 November 1988, he got his wish as he was sentenced to life imprisonment. The judge described him as a 'sadistic sexual psychopath' and suggested that he should never be released.

Trevor Peacher said that he still loved Victor but that he couldn't forgive him for murdering Stuart Gough. He was subsequently sentenced to three years in prison for giving Miller a false alibi.

CHAPTER FOUR
ANTHONY PAUL ANDERSON

Most criminal sadists abduct strangers or victimise their own spouses and children – but Anderson brutally murdered his violent grandfather, his grandfather's common-law wife and two neighbours, all within five days.

Rejected

Anthony was born in Sheffield in 1967, the third child of Zoe Velt and Richard Anderson. The couple went on to have a total of five children but their relationship was increasingly dysfunctional. Zoe had been left traumatised after being sexually abused by her father and found it hard to show love towards her children, and Richard suffered from clinical levels of depression.

When Anthony was only four his mother deserted the family. His father couldn't cope and was admitted to a mental hospital and all of the children were taken into care.

It's likely that by now Anthony was already an embryonic-stage psychopath, for the staff found him hard to connect with and they noticed that he lied compulsively. He managed to disrupt both the care home and the school environment and never learned to read or write. No one wanted to foster him and he remained in the orphanage until he was 16.

Shortly after leaving care, Anthony was sent to borstal on an aggravated burglary charge. Released after a year and a half, he was given a job through the National Association for the Care and Resettlement of Offenders and went to live with his mother, but after a few months she couldn't stand his paranoia any longer and he was so agitated that he had to be heavily sedated by his GP. He then went to live with his father, who rented a council house nearby.

The teenager was soon returned to prison for another six months for thieving, after which he again lived with his father. During this period he was also convicted of arson, which – when not connected with insurance fraud – can be regarded as a form of sadism. Indeed, there have been documented instances of sadists starting a fire then remaining at the scene to hear the victims' anguished screams. Some have also been known to orgasm whilst watching the destructive power of a fire.

A belief in demons

Anthony Anderson remained lawless and disturbed as he moved into his late teens, living off the proceeds of his burglaries and supplementing this with casual black-economy work at scrapyards. He also revelled in frightening people, welcoming visitors to his flat then jumping out at them whilst wearing a devil mask. He believed that demons actually existed and that he could make demonic energy work for him, a relatively common way for a powerless young man to feel in control. But Anthony was determined to make what he saw as powerful gestures so, whilst drinking heavily, he told his fellow pub goers that he had murdered two men at a disco and he threatened to kill more.

He began to terrorise one of his neighbours, former schoolteacher Raymond Faversham. The latter had taught in

Africa but had contracted malaria and returned to England where he found it impossible to find work. Sinking into a deep depression, he'd turned to alcohol for solace and had become something of a recluse.

Raymond also had crippling arthritis in his hands and in his legs which meant that he walked with a limp – he was the perfect victim for an increasingly deranged sadist. Anthony Anderson took to regularly threatening him, burgling him and even throwing a dustbin through his window late one night. He also jumped out at the older man whilst wearing his devil mask, causing Mr Faversham to lose control of his bowels.

The first and second murders

On Thursday 25 August 1987, he broke into Raymond Faversham's house, overpowered the sleeping man and bound him. He pulled down his underpants and probably sexually assaulted him with his penis or with a weapon. The sadist also tortured the former schoolteacher, stabbing him with two knives a total of 500 times. He pulled Mr Faversham's intestines from his abdominal cavity and draped them over the bed. One of the knives Anderson used was buried so deep into the victim's body that it remained there until discovered by the pathologist. The other knife was left sticking out of his back. When his victim was dead or dying, Anthony Anderson covered his body with clothes, stole a clock and a microwave and left the house.

The following day or the day after, he broke into neighbour Marcus Lamont's house. The two men had been enemies for a long time and now Anderson would have his revenge.

Binding the other man with his own clothes, he began to torture him with a knife, making a total of 70 insertions. He cut his victim's stomach then rammed Lamont's own genitals into the cut. He also inserted cigarettes into his mouth and his rectum. During this sadistic onslaught, Marcus Lamont died from shock or loss of blood.

The third and fourth murders

Anthony soon made his way to his domineering grandfather Stasys Petrov's allotment. (He would kill all four of his victims between 25 and 29 August 1987.) The older man had been born in Lithuania but had eventually moved to Yorkshire where he served a prison sentence for committing incest with his daughter, Anthony's mother. Having heard about this incest, Anthony thought that his grandfather might actually be his father, though this wasn't the case.

Now Anthony Anderson gagged and bound the older man in his allotment shed and beat him to death with a sledgehammer, later telling acquaintances that the man's brain had looked like baked beans. He locked the shed door before he left.

The fourth victim was Stasys Petrov's common-law wife, Elsa Konrad. She was ironing in the kitchen when Anderson attacked her, battering at her body again and again with an axe. Afterwards he covered her body with a sheet, stole numerous items – including a flick knife – from the house and bizarrely left his tie in the toilet bowl.

Arrest and trial

Anthony Anderson's bizarre behaviour continued when he was taken into custody. He claimed that he had psychic powers and told the officers, 'You know fuck all about black magic!' Asked to talk about the murders he said, 'They are just too horrible to describe.' Later he justified his grandfather's murder by explaining, 'He raped me mother,' adding falsely that his mother had committed two of the homicides. Later still he said that he had 'a personality disorderment'. He also went on hunger strike for four days, though no one could figure out why.

The sadistic psychopath remained terminally bewildered, telling detectives that 'the only judge in the world is God' and 'I heil Hitler. Hitler was a Catholic and so am I.'

At Sheffield Crown Court he was found guilty of multiple murder and sentenced to several terms of life imprisonment with the proviso that he serve at least 25 years. After his trial he said, 'I want to write a book about my life and how I've been tret.' His mental health continued to decline and he was transferred to a mental hospital from which he's unlikely to be released.

CHAPTER FIVE

COLIN JOHN IRELAND

This killer is notable in that he killed five gay men in 1993 but isn't homosexual. He also said that his motive wasn't sadistic pleasure but the need for publicity.

Endless upheaval

Colin was born on 16 March 1954 to 17-year-old shop assistant Patricia Ireland. His father ended the relationship during the pregnancy so Colin was initially reared by Patricia, her brother and her parents who all lived in the same house in Dartford, Kent.

But by the time Colin was five his mother understandably wanted her independence from the family, so she and Colin moved to a flat in Gravesend. Unfortunately, supporting them both from a part-time shop job proved impossible, and within a year she'd returned home. A year later she moved out again, this time taking six-year-old Colin to Sidcup. Again, the move was a disaster and, evicted, they moved into a homeless shelter which Colin would later describe as 'cell-like' and miserable. After three months she admitted defeat and took Colin back to her family's council house.

By the following year, she'd found herself a husband and the trio set up home in Dartford. But they still struggled to pay the rent so moved often to evade their mounting debt.

School bullying

As a result of the frequent house moves, Colin attended six primary schools in the next five years. He was always the new boy who was picked upon for being shy, very thin and useless at sport. His parents couldn't afford to keep replacing his school uniform so it was sometimes too short for him, yet another reason for the other children to mock. Colin began to arrive late to avoid the worst of the teasing and was frequently caned for this. Around this time, he began to have increasingly sadistic fantasies.

His sense of being an outsider was amplified when, due to serious financial arrears, he and his mother had to return to the homeless shelter for several months. (The shelter was for women and children so he was separated from his stepfather.) He also felt different because his mother had raised him as a Mormon and none of his acquaintances shared his faith. His religion forbade the drinking of tea and coffee and was against homosexuality.

Further trauma

Colin's stepfather eventually left the marriage – which had been dysfunctional for some time – and was replaced by another. Some true crime writers have reported that he was frequently beaten by this second stepfather whilst others say that the man was kind. The boy definitely became increasingly disturbed and the NSPCC became involved, giving him Christmas gifts.

He also later told a journalist that he was put into care when he was ten as his mother had given birth to his brother and couldn't afford to feed two children, but that when her finances improved she took him back.

What's certain is that after years of a lack of security the youth simply stopped trusting adults. He was particularly angry when his mother remarried, and chose to revert to his mother's maiden name of Ireland rather than take his second stepfather's name.

Paedophile advances

As a lonely and confused boy, Colin was a magnet for paedophiles. At age 11, he took a holiday job with a fairground and one of the older male employees lured him to a caravan and pulled down his trousers, but he left before the paedophile could take the situation further. At 12, he was using a public toilet when a man offered him money for sexual activity. Colin remained in the cubicle for some time, tempted at the thought of the money and vaguely curious, but when he left the cubicle the man had gone. Shortly after this he was offered sweets by a paedophile at the local cinema and a few weeks after that an older male acquaintance offered him money in return for sex. Ireland would later say that he rebuffed all four offers and was disgusted by them – but psychiatrists believe that he was sexually ambivalent, hardly surprising given the raging hormones of adolescence and his long-term loneliness. The bullying at school continued, making him feel increasingly sadistic and he fantasised about destroying the entire world.

Animal abuse and arson

By 13 he'd begun to catch and torture cats, eventually killing them. This gave him more pleasure than masturbating over lingerie catalogues and vanilla porn. He learned how to make a garrotte and would slowly strangle small animals to death.

At 16 he stole a few pounds and made plans to run away but was caught and sent to a school for disturbed teens. There he was mocked by another boy because of his poverty and got his revenge by setting fire to the clothes he found in the teenager's room. Luckily a social worker found the fire and put it out quickly before the building caught alight, but it was a clear arson attack and Ireland was asked to leave the school that day. He left with one 'O' Level, no future plans and a heart filled with hate.

Early criminality

Colin now fled to London and got another fairground job where he saw boys of his own age and younger being abused by paedophiles. To support himself, he took to burglary, was caught and sent to borstal. He quickly escaped. He was caught and sent to a stricter borstal where he remained until he was 18. He now began to read Nazi propaganda – as did Moors murderer Ian Brady when he was in borstal – fantasising that he was part of a cruel master race.

Ireland continued to offend throughout the remainder of his teens and was sent to prison again aged 21 for stealing a car and burgling two properties. Released at age 22, he moved in with a workmate, a West Indian woman with four children. They slept together and he at last lost his virginity.

But all too soon he went back to prison for demanding money with menaces. He served 18 months, was out for a few months then went back inside for two years for robbery. The following year he committed the crime of deception. He was also violent towards various girlfriends. Employees would initially like Ireland as he was polite and helpful. But his antisocial side would quickly resurface and he lost or quit various jobs – everything from a bouncer in a gay club to a volunteer fireman – because of his changeable moods.

Survivalism

Colin wanted recognition yet wasn't prepared to put in the work necessary to get himself a good education or a work-based skill. So he turned to survivalism, joining other macho men who were determined to live off the land, albeit only at weekends. Unfortunately his fellow survivalists noticed that he often sneaked into town for fried chicken – when perfectly good berries were on the menu – and they began to call him Chicken Colin. Desperate to win their approval, he took to sleeping outside without even a sleeping bag and told them that he'd served in the French Foreign Legion, but the Legion have no record of this.

First marriage

Then, at 27, he met a 36-year-old disabled woman called Virginia. He was kind to her and unfailingly gentle with her five-year-old epileptic daughter – doubtless he remembered the fear and isolation of his own childhood and wanted to improve hers.

The couple married in 1982 but Colin was constantly in and out of prison and Virginia noticed that he was becoming increasingly erratic with violent mood swings. Four years into the marriage he had an affair with another woman and the relationship broke down irreparably. In 1987 they divorced.

Second marriage

Colin continued to go on survivalist weekends and one of them involved a trip to Devon. He went into a pub there called The Globe and immediately started a whirlwind romance with the owner, Jan.

Jan was seven years his senior and a single parent with two children – Ireland seemed to be attracted to ready-made family units where he became the stepfather, recreating the family of his youth. He married Jan after three months, though many thought them an unlikely match.

Four months later they went to visit Jan's mother in Margate, but after dropping her off Colin returned home in his wife's car. Back in The Globe he ransacked the till, stole cash and electrical goods and disappeared. Jan contacted the police when she returned to Devon but Colin had assumed an alias and wasn't traced.

Alone again, naturally

He now fled to Southend-on-Sea and claimed unemployment benefit under the name of Colin Williams. He was homeless for a while then settled into modest accommodation provided by the Department of Health and Social Security, the other tenants noting that he was a loner who didn't bring friends back to his room. Many people are loners by choice as they find too much company tiring, but Colin was actually lonely. He just didn't know how to connect to other people.

He eventually found himself a girlfriend but soon beat her up – damaged men like Ireland often beat up women who are getting too close to them. She called the police and he was accused of causing actual bodily harm. But, like many domestic disputes, it eventually ended in an acquittal and he was free to hurt other men and women. It's unlikely that the sadism of his teens had abated, and he doubtless found some sexual pleasure in inflicting pain on his luckless girlfriends.

However, his fortunes improved markedly in 1992 when he volunteered to work at the town's night shelter. He was so hardworking and polite that he was soon made a deputy manager. He'd known homelessness so wasn't judgemental towards his clientele.

For the first time in years, Colin Ireland had stability. He had a roof over his head and employment status and was kept well occupied. Compared to the alcoholics and mentally ill people residing in the dormitories he felt like a winner. But all that was about to change.

Just before Christmas 1992, some staff members who didn't like him made unspecified allegations. They were unfounded but frequent and eventually he became so incensed that he resigned, devastated because the job had meant everything to him. (Most reports erroneously state that he had a violent fight with a gay homeless man and was sacked.)

The next ten weeks, leading up to his first sadistic murder, were spent in increasingly vengeful fantasies. He read books on serial killers, noting that one FBI agent had said that you had to commit five murders to be considered a modern-day serial killer. (Technically a serial killer 'only' has to commit two murders but such double killers are sufficiently common that many law enforcement agencies only consider a man or woman to be a serial killer when they've committed at least three homicides with a cooling-off period between each.)

The first murder

On 8 March 1993, Colin Ireland made his way to the Coleherne pub in Earls Court that at the time was frequented by gay sadomasochists. He wore a handkerchief of a certain colour which indicated to the other men there that he was a dominant male. With his heavy build and somewhat stern expression he looked the part. Forty-five-year-old theatre director Peter Walker accidentally spilled his drink on him and half jokingly said that he deserved to be beaten. It was the invitation Ireland was waiting for and he agreed to take a taxi to the man's Battersea flat to beat him there.

Unfortunately for Mr Walker, Ireland wasn't interested in consensual erotic bondage, domination and sadomasochism (BDSM). Back at the flat, Walker took off his clothes and Ireland handcuffed him, gagged him with condoms and bound him with rope to the bed. He then beat Peter Walker with a dog leash and a leather belt.

But Ireland wanted the ultimate control, the power over whether someone lived or died, so, leaving his victim trussed helplessly on the bed, he went into the kitchen and fetched a plastic bag, putting it over his victim's head. He watched the man fight for breath, removing the bag just before Peter Walker lost consciousness. When he removed the bag, Mr Walker gasped 'I'm going to die, amn't I?' and the sadist agreed that he was.

We'll never know how long Ireland toyed with Peter Walker, but eventually he left the bag in situ and his victim suffocated. He then held his lighter to the dead man's pubic hair. He would later tell police that he only did this out of curiosity, but, given that he went on to torture a later victim by holding a lighter to his testes, it's likely that testicle torture comprised part of his fantasy.

Searching through the man's personal papers, he found proof that Peter Walker was HIV positive and was incensed – after all, Walker had planned to have sex with him.

Colin stayed in the flat all night, then went home and watched the news but didn't see details of the killing. Disappointed, he phoned the *Sun* newspaper and told them that he'd carried out his new year resolution to murder a man. He also phoned the Samaritans and asked them to feed Peter Walker's two dogs.

Further madness

Ironically, the following day the Law Lords ruled that sadomasochistic practices between *consenting* adults could lead to them facing lengthy jail sentences. This made it impossible for the consensual adults who'd been in the Coleherne to come forward and tell the police who Peter Walker had left the pub with. After all, they themselves might now face prosecution. It also made British law look increasingly ridiculous for it was legal – at the time – for a man or woman to beat their vulnerable child yet they faced imprisonment for chastising their sexually-submissive partner for their erotic pleasure.

The second murder

March and April passed with Ireland happily reliving the murder, then on 28 May he struck again, returning to the same pub as before and engaging 37-year-old Christopher Dunn in conversation. The librarian admitted that he was submissive and they went back to his flat in Wealdstone, London where they watched a sadomasochistic video as foreplay and shared a meal. Later Ireland handcuffed his naked and willing victim. It was only after he'd cuffed Mr Dunn's wrists and tied his feet that he demanded the librarian's bank card number, which Christopher Dunn gave to him.

Ireland later claimed that he'd had to torture this information out of Christopher, which seems unlikely – but what's definite is that the killer burned his victim's testicles with a cigarette lighter and beat him with a belt before suffocating him to death.

He stayed in the flat until daylight, then merged with the people going to work. He also used Christopher Dunn's bank card to withdraw £200.

Two days later the body was found by a friend. Unfortunately, the police thought that Dunn had died during an act of auto erotic asphyxiation or a consensual sex game gone wrong so they didn't connect his death with the murder of Peter Walker. (Consensual gay sadomasochistic sex tends to be more severe than consensual heterosexual sadomasochistic sex so the police didn't associate the man's burns with a criminal act.)

The third murder

Only six days passed before Colin Ireland returned to the BDSM pub. This time he met up with Perry Bradley III, a sales director from Texas. The two returned to Bradley's flat in Kensington but he initially refused to be tied up as he was aware that there was a bondage killer on the loose. The two men enjoyed a meal together and a couple of drinks and Mr Bradley suggested they have vanilla sex. Colin Ireland demurred, explaining that he could only get off on BDSM, so the businessman eventually agreed.

When he was trussed up on the bed, Ireland said that he only wanted the PIN number of his bank card. Perry offered to go with him and withdraw the cash, but Colin said that he didn't want to be seen acting suspiciously in the early hours of the morning. The businessman gave the criminal the number and tried to be as helpful as possible in a desperate attempt to save his own life.

Colin Ireland waited until the man was asleep – or pretending to be – then strangled him with a rope, enjoying his terrified struggles. Afterwards he put a doll on the body because he hoped this would demean his victim further. Again he spent the night with the corpse and left the following day.

The fourth murder

The need to kill was accelerating, so Ireland returned to the Coleherne on 7 June and chatted up 33-year-old Andrew Collier, the warden of a sheltered housing complex. They returned to his flat in Dalston and were having a drink when there was an altercation in the street. Both men hurried to the window – and Colin Ireland unwittingly left his fingerprint on the window sill.

The men then went over to the bed and Ireland handcuffed Andrew Collier's wrists and bound him to the bed. Eventually he strangled him with a rope. He then went through the man's wallet looking for cash, only to find a card stating that he was HIV positive, Ireland's second such victim. Enraged, he singed part of the corpse with his lighter, and, determined to wreak further havoc, strangled the man's cat. He put its mouth around Collier's condom-clad penis and put its condom-clad tail in Collier's mouth. Remaining with the bizarrely-posed body for the next few hours, he left in the morning, taking away the crockery he'd used.

In the days which followed, he boasted to acquaintances that he'd be famous one day, that he'd done something remarkable.

But he'd lied about being in the Foreign Legion so they didn't pay much attention to his boasts.

He also phoned Kensington police and anonymously admitted all four killings and warned them he'd kill another man. Shortly afterward he phoned Battersea police station and asked them if they were still investigating Peter Walker's death. In his own mind Ireland was now a powerful figure – but to the rest of the world he was a twice-divorced, unemployed and uncharismatic man.

The fifth murder

Back for a fifth time to the Coleherne on 12 June, Ireland picked up 41-year-old Emanuel Spiteri. He'd been born in Malta but now worked in London as a chef. Ireland himself had been a chef's assistant and this made it easy for the men to find common ground. Mr Spiteri lived in Hither Green so they had to travel via Charing Cross Station. Unknown to Ireland, they were caught on the security camera there.

Back at Emanuel Spiteri's flat, Colin Ireland bound him and tortured him, but he refused to reveal his PIN number. Ireland eventually strangled him with a nylon rope. He set fire to the bedroom before he left, but the flames quickly went out.

Seeking publicity

The killer kept watching the news for details of his handiwork, but Emanuel Spiteri's body hadn't been found, so four days after the murder he phoned the police again and gave them the details. He also talked about the first four murders, saying that he'd 'done five now' so was the serial killer he'd set out to become. He added that he probably wouldn't offend again.

Keeping control

Colin Ireland now saw that the CCTV photo of himself and Mr Spiteri was in all the papers, which meant that the police could arrest him at any time and he'd lose control of the situation. Determined to remain in charge, he contacted them via his solicitor and said that he'd been with Spiteri but had left the man safe and well. It was a calculated bet: after all, he didn't think that he'd left his fingerprints at any of the murder scenes and he'd even taken away the plates and cutlery he used in the murder houses so that he didn't leave any forensic clues.

The evidence

But the police were able to link him forensically to Andrew Collier's flat, thanks to the fingerprint he'd left on an inner window sill. And his voice had been found on a police tape dating back from 1991 when he'd been charged with domestic violence. They were able to prove that it was the voice of the man who had phoned the police admitting to being the gay killer and threatening to 'kill one a week'.

Ireland was arrested and charged with all five murders but he said nothing in custody, simply folding his arms and regarding officers with a faint half smile.

Confession

He remained silent for the next three weeks then realised that he'd have to talk in order to show the world how clever he'd been. He subsequently confessed to all five of the murders, explaining that he'd bought each pair of handcuffs from a different shop in order to evade suspicion. He'd worn gloves so that he wouldn't leave fingerprints (barring the one left on the window sill) and had taken all of his personal possessions out of his pockets so that he couldn't unwittingly leave proof of his identity at a scene. He'd also stayed in the murder houses overnight so that he could merge with commuters in the morning as they went to work.

Ireland told the police that he thought he'd be better off in a restricted environment such as prison as he'd be unlikely to kill again there, whereas he'd remain a risk if he could still target masochistic gay males in the outside world. He said that he'd taken no sexual pleasure from torturing the men; that they merely disgusted him.

Trial

The trial was held at the Old Bailey in December 1993 and the killer pleaded guilty to all five murders. He remained unrepentant, sending Christmas cards to friends containing messages which urged them to read the papers on 20 December, his sentencing day.

His motive for the five murders was discussed in court. He'd apparently told the police that he'd read several true crime books and decided that serial killing was something that he could be good at. As he was sadistic – though, he said, not *sexually* sadistic – he wanted the murders to be cruel, and he knew that the easiest victims to ensnare would be masochistic homosexual men. (Psychiatrists still suspect that Colin was bi-curious but in denial about this.)

The defence could offer no mitigating circumstances, simply noting that he'd pleaded guilty to all five murders which saved the nation a prolonged and costly trial.

The judge described the murders as grotesque and cruel and described Colin Ireland as 'exceptionally dangerous'. He was sentenced to five life sentences with the recommendation that he never be released.

Given his need for notoriety, Colin John Ireland will remain a risk to other prisoners: he has nothing to lose by taking further lives as he's already been given life imprisonment.

CHAPTER SIX
SADISTIC DIVERSITY

The British sadists in most of the previous profiles had distinct sexual preferences – Neville Heath, active in 1946, liked to whip young females. In contrast, Patrick Byrne, who murdered in 1959, fantasised about using a circular saw on girls. Victor Miller, whose crimes spanned the 1970s and 1980s, preferred to beat his teenage male victims with a stick, and Colin Ireland, active in 1993, favoured slow suffocation of homosexual men. Only the deeply disordered Anthony Anderson seems to have lacked a signature, using everything from picquerism (cutting for erotic purposes) to bludgeoning with a hammer and an axe.

But the following case studies illustrate just how wide-ranging sadistic fantasies and actions can be. One sadist maimed and killed his victims from a distance with nail bombs, another favoured ligature strangulation whilst a third had a razor fetish. These cases also show the various mental disorders which can accompany criminal sadism, as one was diagnosed as schizophrenic, one was a necrophile and most were sociopaths.

PAUL BEART

Convicted of a horrific torture murder in 2002, Paul Beart illustrates the difficulty of treating an adult psychopath.

In 1997, he was jailed for a violent sexual attack on a young woman. Whilst incarcerated, Beart took part in a sex offenders rehabilitation course which he was deemed to have passed with flying colours. Intelligent and well read, a university drop-out, he was bright enough to give the authorities the answers they required.

Beart was freed in 2000 after serving just over half of his six-year sentence, a report saying that he'd 'addressed his offending behaviour' and was safe to be released on licence. He would kill within five months.

In April 2001, he left his home in Boston, Lincolnshire and travelled to Newquay in Cornwall, booking in to a beach resort where he knew there would be young women. For the first two days he stalked three such women, and on his third day he assaulted two teenage girls in the street.

Shortly afterwards he saw Deborah O'Sullivan walking home from a nightclub. Pulling her behind a wall, he tortured her for the next hour, burning her with his cigarette lighter and ripping her skin open with his bare hands. The 31-year-old woman begged for mercy but her 26-year-old attacker told her, 'I'm going to kill you.' He continued with the attack, sexually assaulting her and battering her with a litter bin. One of the blows broke her arm but the sadist still wasn't satisfied and attempted twice to strangle her.

Beart then left the unconscious woman and gave himself up to the police saying, 'I think I've killed her. This country should have the death penalty for people like me.' Having achieved what he wanted from the assault, he was indifferent as to whether his victim lived or died.

Police rushed to the scene and found Deborah alive but unrecognisable. She died in hospital three days later without regaining consciousness.

Paul Beart pleaded guilty on 5 November 2001 at Bristol Crown Court. The following day he was sentenced to life imprisonment with the recommendation that he never be released. He has now been assessed as an untreatable sexual sadist and psychopath.

DAVID JAMES COPELAND

In April 1999, David Copeland bombed residents in Brixton, Brick Lane and Soho, causing death and horrific disfigurement. Public interest centred on his racist agenda and, as a result, his underlying sadism was completely ignored.

Small in stature, David (born 15 May 1976) was bullied at school. His dyslexia went unrecognised and he was put into a remedial reading group. His genitals didn't develop at a normal rate so they had to be examined by clinicians, something which deeply embarrassed him. By 12 he was having sadistic fantasies about torturing his classmates and burning down his school.

His sense of inferiority deepened when it became clear that his younger brother had a high IQ and his older brother was street smart. Believing himself unable to compete, he locked himself away in his room playing heavy metal music for hours at a time. Contrary to popular belief, this music tends to calm down its listeners, who feel that the bands understand them. Professor Jeffrey Arnett interviewed dozens of such teens for his book *Metalheads: Heavy Metal Music and Adolescent Alienation* and found such music 'purged their angst'.

But it was going to take more than a few tunes to relieve David's loneliness and inferiority complex, so by secondary school his sadism had deepened. He was one of only two boys who watched what they believed was a snuff video in which people were extensively tortured, probably the well-known fake snuff movie *Faces of Death*. He also began to self-medicate by inhaling glue.

At 16 he got drunk with a few friends and vandalised a building in Aldershot. He was so drunk when his mother came to the police station that she was afraid to take him home to his father, and instead sat with him for several hours in the car. A year later he and his older brother assaulted a neighbour, and Copeland was given community service. In the same time period he began to have sexual fantasies in which he was a powerful SS officer who enjoyed raping numerous female sexual slaves and torturing men.

His parents asked him if he'd met a nice girl yet and, paranoia possibly setting in, he believed that they thought he was homosexual. He began to carry a knife when he went out at night and wondered what it would be like to use it on a gay male. Though heterosexual male sadists prefer to hurt girls and women, they will single out boys and men if these are easier targets. Their strongest motive is to cause pain and fear, so any sentient partner will do. Animals are the third category targeted but they are less desirable as, though they can show signs of suffering, they obviously can't respond verbally to the sadist's commands.

In 1995, David's mother left his father. Apparently this didn't affect 19-year-old David very much as he'd seen his parents grow apart for many years. He remained living with his father, sometimes signing on and sometimes doing casual labour work. The two men continued to argue interminably.

The following year Copeland was pleased when a bomb exploded at a rock concert in Atlanta after the Olympic Games. He later admitted that he was excited by the suffering.

At 20 he moved into a bedsit close to his work, a move which increased his loneliness and isolation. He began to neglect his personal hygiene, one of the many signs of depression and low self-esteem. Once a month he visited a prostitute, always choosing a different woman. He wanted to ask them to tie him up but he didn't have the courage and settled for vanilla sex. Ashamed at his own shyness, he constantly thought about suicide, though fantasies of drugging girls and doing what he wanted with them would temporarily cheer him up.

At 21 he joined the British National Party with its keep-Britain-white ethos, and suddenly had meetings to go to and a social life. Later he joined a religious movement called Christian Identity which identifies the chosen race as white. Now Copeland was no longer the girlfriendless semi-literate man without a purpose – instead he was the chosen representative of an omnipotent deity.

Unfortunately a belief in this deity didn't quell his sadism and he began to collect photographs of bomb amputees, war atrocities and mutilated murder victims. He was particularly thrilled to find a photo of a starving African baby and would later tell police that he 'got off' on such images. He also loved the movie *Henry: Portrait of a Serial Killer*, which represents the aimless life and supposedly daily violence of the late serial killer Henry Lee Lucas. He became equally enamoured of the Arkansas religious group Kingdom Identity which believes that homosexuality should be punished by death.

Deciding to kill and maim the various societal groups which he despised, Copeland turned to the Internet and learned how to make explosives. He began to have panic attacks so returned home to his father for a few months but stabilised after being prescribed sleeping pills. He resumed his rambling talk to acquaintances about wanting to hurt black people and remained generally aggressive. The rows at home continued and eventually his father threw him out.

In January 1999, David Copeland moved into a bedsit in Farnborough and found a job doing engineering work on the

Jubilee Line. A sympathetic co-worker befriended the boy, later describing him as 'immature, unloved and insecure'.

But 22-year-old David found a source of affection when he bought a white rat for company. He doted on his pet and would later pay for it to have the best veterinary care. (Though many sadists torture animals, a few – such as Christopher Wilder – are genuinely fond of them. After all, an animal can offer unconditional love, something that many sadists have never known.)

Every night the young man returned to his bedsit and communed with his rat then spent hours making bombs, testing them on a quiet stretch of wasteland. He would later say that he wanted to be remembered.

On 17 April 1999, he set off for Brixton carrying a bag with a pipe bomb inside. The bomb nestled within a sandwich container which was packed with thousands of nails which he hoped would lacerate human flesh.

Brixton bomb

Copeland travelled by train and cab to Brixton Market and put the bag with the bomb down by a busy bus stop. He then returned home to watch the news.

At teatime the bomb exploded, sending nails into people's heads, limbs and groins. Two people lost an eye and a two-year-old boy had a nail penetrate his brain. Ironically, given that the bomber wanted to hurt black and Asian people, 24 of the 42 victims were white.

But the young man with the bag had been captured on CCTV so Copeland's freedom was limited. Later, when the photos were printed in national newspapers, one of his colleagues would recognise him and give his name to the police.

Brick Lane bomb

Excited by the carnage which he'd caused, the dispossessed young man now focused on the Asian market at Brick Lane in the East End of London. He planned to cause as much carnage as possible before he was identified. He arrived on Saturday 24 April, only to find that the market was now held on a Sunday. He also saw several white people, the so-called chosen race, in the vicinity. But sadism is no respecter of colour, so he set the bag containing the ticking pipe bomb down beside a car and left the area.

The subsequent explosion blew the vehicle apart and damaged nearby shops and restaurants, perforating several shoppers' eardrums. Others had glass from nearby windows embedded in their heads.

Visions of torture

David Copeland would later tell police that he felt nothing at the carnage he'd caused, but he continued to seek out cruel images, going to Soho and renting a video which he believed featured bondage and torture. He was incensed to find that it actually showed coprophilia (defecation for erotic purposes, one of the least popular fetishes.)

Whilst returning the video, he heard on the shop radio that the police had video footage of the bomber. Determined to cause one final act of mayhem, he fetched the bomb-making equipment from his bedsit and took it to a hotel.

The pub blast

On Friday 30 April, he travelled to Soho and left his bag containing a bomb in a pub favoured by gay men, the Admiral Duncan. The bomb exploded, tearing the skin and flesh from nearby revellers. Over a hundred men and women were burnt by the intense blast and lacerated by the flying nails.

Andrea Dykes and her unborn child were killed instantly and her husband remained unconscious for three weeks. One of their friends, who had just agreed to be their child's godfather, died of his injuries the following day. Three men lost a leg and a fourth man had to have both his legs amputated. The scene resembled the horror of a wartime battlefield.

Meanwhile David Copeland travelled back to his bedsit, well pleased with his handiwork. He loaded a crossbow and put it beside his bed so that he could shoot one of the arresting officers he knew would call.

But when the constabulary arrived, he gave himself up without a fight. Asked why he'd planted the bombs, he said 'to terrorise people'. Questioned about his choice of targets, he said that Brixton was a black area, Brick Lane an Asian area and Soho frequented by gays.

During interviews, the police asked him 16 times why he had planted the bombs and he gave incoherent replies but finally said that he was 'totally shot away, a loner'. When they asked why, he added, 'My family fucked me up.'

They asked the 23-year-old if he realised the implications of what he'd done, including years of imprisonment. He nodded and said, 'I had no life anyway.'

He talked at length about his philosophy, completely failing to see the irony in his own words. He told police that 'white people were the best mentally'; this from a boy who wrote about being a 'profit' when what he meant was 'prophet'. He added that he hated homosexuals because 'the whole point is to breed'. But he'd never bred, only briefly having a girlfriend.

Belated voices

At first Copeland was on remand in Belmarsh prison but he became increasingly tearful and suffered from insomnia, plus there were fears that he was schizophrenic, so he was transferred to Broadmoor, a prison hospital for the mentally ill. There he went on hunger strike, protesting at the drugs he had to take. An insightful psychiatrist noted that Copeland had 'significant sadistic elements to his thoughts and behaviour'. It was a sadism which had previously been ignored, the bombings being labelled as racist and homophobic crimes.

At the Old Bailey, he pleaded guilty to causing the three explosions and guilty to manslaughter rather than to the murder of the dead victims. The defence said that he was schizophrenic but a psychiatric nurse who had examined him when he was first taken into custody noted that he was sane.

Copeland himself told doctors that he'd originally faked symptoms of mental illness in order to get 'nutted off' to Broadmoor, but now he found the mental hospital much worse than a regular prison.

The prosecution noted that, though he had a personality disorder, it was not strong enough to impair his judgement. He'd known exactly what he was doing when he'd planted all three bombs. On 30 June 2000, he was given six life sentences and returned to Broadmoor indefinitely.

Copeland remains in the maximum security hospital, doubtless disturbed that the notoriety he so desired is already fading. In 2003 he was attacked by another patient whilst in his room.

JOHN TAYLOR

John Taylor was cruel towards animals from an early age, but as he matured into manhood he extended this cruelty towards his female lovers. In time, he became predatory towards young girls then committed at least two particularly savage rapes. In

2000 he abducted a teenage girl and took her to his home where he sadistically murdered her.

He was born in 1956, the first child of Margaret and Frank Taylor. They went on to have another two children, a girl and a boy. His introduction to lawlessness came early when an unnamed adult in his life took him poaching and encouraged him to kill animals and birds. At nine, he joined the Boys' Brigade and enjoyed going camping with them in Lindley Woods.

John didn't do well at school and left at age 15 without any qualifications. Thereafter he drifted from one unskilled job to the next. At 18 he became a Boys' Brigade officer at Armley United Reformed Church, but he horrified one young boy during a countryside outing by snatching a fox from the hounds and stabbing it to death with a knife. On other occasions he would catch a rabbit, torture it then kill and mutilate it.

Whilst carrying out his Boys' Brigade duties one day he met Janet, who ran the Girls' Brigade from the same church and worked as a nursery school teacher. They married when John was 21.

Three years later they had a son and two years after that a daughter. They then bought a family home – a terraced house – in Bramley, Leeds. The four Taylors lived there throughout the early 1980s and John Taylor eventually set himself up as a dog breeder, but he failed to house-train the animals so the house became increasingly dirty and smelled foul. He also began to keep owls and bought 2,000 baby chicks to feed them on, chicks which he stored in the family freezer. It was the final straw for the marriage and his wife left him, taking the children with her. Later the couple divorced.

By now Taylor was selling pet food and pet accessories from the house and sometimes from a market stall, but they didn't attract a sufficient number of women into his life so the 30-year-old began to advertise for partners in contact magazines, travelling throughout Britain to meet those who replied. He met at least 25 such women – and had sex with some of them – but the relationships usually ended after only one or two dates as he was often unwashed and his general appearance was unkempt. His sadistic fantasies were much stronger in his mind than his day-to-day reality, his need to dominate increasing as his social life declined.

Animal abuse

Taylor now began to abuse and neglect his animals for kicks, eventually murdering four dogs and 30 ferrets. He often left the animals locked in a room for hours at a time and he didn't clean the house so it was saturated with animal urine and excrement. He continued to torture rabbits, foxes and other animals he ensnared in a nearby woodland, becoming aroused by their anguished screams and agonised writhing, but what he really wanted was a woman to control.

The first rape

On a pleasant afternoon in October 1988 he donned a balaclava, armed himself with a knife, then hid in Houghley Gill, a large wooded area near his home, and waited for a victim. When a woman walked past, he grabbed her from behind, pulled her into the bushes and ordered her to lie down. He raped her, using a great deal of violence, and repeatedly threatening her with the knife. The woman, who had been on the way to her young daughter's school to collect her, was left badly bruised and deeply traumatised.

The second rape

Rapists are essentially using rape – a sexual act – to meet non-sexual needs. Therefore, the act rarely satisfies them and they go in search of a more 'perfect' rape victim who they hope will bring them peace. And so, a mere four months after the rape in Houghley Gill, John Taylor made his way to an estate near his home in Bramley, where he'd previously identified a potential victim. Again he donned his balaclava and produced his knife before entering the unlocked back door of a house. He ordered the woman upstairs where he bound, blindfolded and gagged her. Ignoring her screaming child, he brutally raped her and was excessively controlling and aggressive throughout. Even judged alongside other violent rapes, Taylor's cruelty was notable and a judge would later describe these rapes as the most depraved he'd known in his entire career.

Unsolved murders

Four years later, in 1992, a prostitute called Yvonne Fitt was found stabbed to death in Houghley Gill, John Taylor's favourite hunting ground. She had been hastily buried. She had last been seen 12 miles away from her final resting place.

Then, on 7 November 1994, 13-year-old schoolgirl Lindsay Jo Rimer disappeared from the West Yorkshire district of Hebden Bridge. Lindsay had gone to a club where her mother was having a night out and asked her for money to buy breakfast for the following day. She went on to the local Spar to buy cornflakes and was captured on CCTV. Shortly afterwards she disappeared.

The following April two canal workers found her body in a canal, near an area where Lindsay and her brother had once lived in a caravan. (Their father had lived in an adjacent caravan.) She had been strangled and the body had been weighed down.

In 1996, the burning corpse of 17-year-old Deborah Wood was found on Burley Park Railway Station embankment. She had been suffocated within 24 hours of leaving a pub, where she'd had a drink with her father and a few friends. Her body appeared to have been kept in a freezer for some time, before being wrapped in plastic bin liners and bedclothes, doused with petrol and set alight. Police would later investigate Taylor for these homicides.

In 1998, Taylor was taken on by Parcelforce as a delivery driver, a job which gave him freedom and the chance to find out who lived where.

Another relationship

By early 2000, John Taylor had answered a classified ad from yet another single mother who had advertised through a lonely hearts column. She saw how much he loved hunting rabbits and shooting game in Lindley Woods, but as she too loved the outdoors she saw this as a plus. Within weeks he had asked the 34-year-old and her two teenage children to move in with him and they agreed.

The woman, Deborah, found that the house was filthy and she spent untold hours cleaning it. But, rather than seem grateful, Taylor began to demand that she dress up for him.

More alarmingly, she began to realise how little he cared for the nine dogs, 20 ferrets, and various birds he shared his house with. One day his Alsatian puppy attacked his pet duck and he shot the puppy. Bizarrely, he went on to kill his 40 pet chickens and hung them up in the kitchen with bags over their heads.

His behaviour in the bedroom became increasingly sadistic. At first the bondage, blindfolding and gagging were consensual but soon he began to whip Deborah's inner thighs with a switch. She protested that she didn't like it, so during their next sex session he tried something different, binding her hands behind her back with cable ties and then tightening other cable ties around her breasts until she began to scream. He then whipped her breasts with a branch, only stopping when she burst into tears.

This behaviour is the complete opposite of the consensual, or recreational, sadist who wants to give his partner pleasure from an erotic whipping. Such men will ascertain which level of pain is pleasurable to their lover and will keep the stimulus within agreed boundaries. But Taylor didn't care about his girlfriends and didn't see their sex sessions as being about mutual orgasm. Instead, he wanted to cause maximum distress.

After Deborah ended the relationship, he began to stalk women at Houghley Gill, a beauty spot near Bramley. At least one woman saw him there with his dog, hanging about for three hours at a time and acting suspiciously. He was hoping that a suitable young female victim would come along.

On Sunday 26 November 2000, he rose as usual and walked his dogs. By late afternoon he'd taken up a position at the Gill where he could see whoever walked by without being noticed. Then he took out his knife and waited for a lone female to arrive.

Murder

Unfortunately, in the same time frame, 16-year-old Leanne Tierney decided to take a short cut home. Leanne had had a nice day, going to church in the morning and doing some Christmas shopping with her best friend in the afternoon. Now, keen to get back for her evening meal after a tiring shopping trip, she cut through the wooded valley of Houghley Gill.

There, John Taylor grabbed her and marched her to his house where he bound her hands behind her back using three cable ties. When he tired of his victim – or when his rage reached its zenith – he strangled her with a ligature, possibly with further linked cable ties or with a grey scarf which he had double-knotted around her neck.

Meanwhile Leanne's family had alerted the police and it was obvious from the start that she wasn't an unhappy runaway. She was very close to her mother and her older sister and was doing well at school where she was studying for nine GCSEs.

Everyone described her as a happy, bubbly teenager who loved spending time with her friends.

Frozen corpse

The police now launched one of the biggest ever searches in West Yorkshire, using helicopters, police dogs and underwater search teams. They searched hundreds of local houses, outbuildings and a nearby industrial unit. They also searched local canals and waterways. Meanwhile, several psychics phoned the family and told them that Leanne was still alive. But her body was in John Taylor's freezer – or a freezer that he had access to – and police would later surmise that he remained obsessed with her corpse and returned to it frequently.

Nine months after murdering the 16-year-old, he wrapped her body in plastic bin liners and a floral duvet cover, drove to Lindley Woods near Leeds and began to dig a grave. But his spade soon hit numerous tree roots and he gave up and left Leanne's corpse only partially covered in soil. This was his undoing as the duvet cover and bin liners were later traced to his home.

John Taylor isn't the first British killer to keep a teenage female victim in a freezer. On 30 December 1957, 17-year-old Anne Noblett was cutting through a field near her home in Wheathampstead, Hertfordshire, when she disappeared. When her strangled body was found a month later in woods five miles from her home, it had been kept in a freezer or similar cold storage unit from the time of her death. Detectives said that there was a sexual motive for the abduction: they believed she'd been abducted by two men but they didn't have enough evidence to make an arrest.

Still predatory

After murdering Leanne, Taylor began a new relationship with a woman he met through a lonely hearts column. But within weeks he was trying to ensnare her 15-year-old daughter, touching her in inappropriate ways. He then subjected her to a series of obscene phone calls in which he threatened to bind and whip her. She was doubtless at serious risk.

Thankfully, when the girl's mother went to Taylor's house for the first time, the neighbours told her that he had women visiting at all hours. She also saw how filthy the house was, and found the bedroom was stocked with whips, handcuffs and nipple clamps. Perturbed by her new boyfriend's promiscuity and lack of hygiene, she promptly ended the relationship.

Body found

In August 2001, a man walking in Lindley Woods discovered a large package wrapped in a floral duvet cover. He called the police and they cut open the cover to find a decomposed body wrapped in plastic bin liners. It was later identified from its fingerprints as Leanne. Her loving family, who had never given up hope that she would be found alive, were devastated. Her mother had even left the back door unlocked for months in the hope that the teenager would return.

Thankfully the duvet cover and plastic bin liners yielded numerous clues – the cover was matted with dog hair and the twine used to tie the bin liners matched twine at Taylor's home.

Leanne's body also yielded various clues. Taylor had left the cable ties in place which he'd used to bind her wrists, cable ties which were mainly used by Parcelforce. The dog collar that he'd fastened around her neck was traced to a batch of six that he'd purchased by mail order the month before Leanne disappeared. He'd also left a paper trail as he'd paid by credit card.

The police ran his name through their computer and found out that he was already on their database – one of his ex-girlfriends had phoned in suggesting that he might be Leanne's killer. His behaviour had become increasingly sadistic and she knew he was very familiar with Lindley Woods where the teenager's corpse had been found.

They searched the filthy house and were initially disappointed to find that John Taylor had removed all of the carpets and burned them. But a few shards remained on a carpet nail and these fibres perfectly matched the carpet fibres found on Leanne's jumper. They also found pieces of burned burgundy carpet hidden in the garden's long grass.

The garden was also a cemetery for the animals which the sadist had maimed and murdered. One border terrier had been beaten with a meat cleaver and an Alsatian had been shot, but it's unclear how the other dogs and ferrets met their deaths.

Arrest and trial

Taken into custody, Taylor at first said that Leanne had brushed against him in the woods and that he'd acted on impulse by grabbing her and warning her not to make a sound. She'd screamed once (this part is true – locals reported hearing one scream) then he'd bound her wrists behind her back with his dog leash and thrown his coat over her head. He'd then forced the girl to walk the half mile to his house, a journey which would have taken over 20 minutes. This strongly suggests that it wasn't his first murder, that he'd controlled other victims for shorter periods and that this had given him confidence.

Back at his house, he claimed that he'd taken off Leanne's coat, blindfolded her and bound her with cable ties. He said that he'd been cutting up a pair of trousers to make a hood to conceal his identity when the teenager's blindfold slipped. He'd lunged at her to replace the blindfold, they'd struggled and she'd fatally struck her head.

Most of this scenario was doubtless a lie. Taylor had fantasised for months about exactly what he'd do to a female victim, months in which he'd have made himself a hood or mask if he genuinely wanted to conceal his identity. The reality was he knew that he was going to kill his victim so was happy for her to see his face. And Leanne hadn't died of a head injury, but from ligature strangulation which is up close and personal, the sadist's choice. John Taylor also suggested that after the supposed head injury he'd left her corpse alone till the following day – but a man as sexually obsessed as John Taylor would hardly have ignored a nubile female body. The pubic hairs found on the scarf around her neck suggest that he got close to her corpse then put it in the freezer before it began to decompose.

Taylor pleaded guilty at Leeds Crown Court to kidnapping and murdering Leanne Tierney. Psychiatrists noted that he was a sexual psychopath and a danger to all women, and Mr Justice Astill described him as a 'dangerous sexual sadist' who had abducted the girl for depraved sexual purposes. The 46-year-old killer stared straight ahead as he was sentenced to two life terms.

Further sadistic crimes

Aware that a crime of this magnitude – abducting a girl on foot at teatime in a popular beauty spot – was unlikely to have been his first offence, police began to re-examine other unsolved sexual assaults in the area. As a result, they found that sperm samples taken from the rape victims at Houghley Gill and Bramley estate matched John Taylor's DNA. He eventually pleaded guilty to both rapes and was sentenced to a further two life sentences on 4 February 2003.

Scottish police subsequently said they planned to question the killer about the unsolved murder of six young women aged from 21 to 31 as he regularly drove to Glasgow for sexual liaisons and allegedly visited a brothel there where one of the murdered girls worked.

Taylor is currently incarcerated at Wakefield Prison in Yorkshire and is unlikely to ever be released.

WILLIAM FREDERICK IAN BEGGS

Born in Moira, County Down in Northern Ireland in 1964, William Beggs tortured several young men in England before committing his first sadistic murder in 1987. Freed on a technicality, he went on to commit a second even more horrific homicide in Scotland and was re-imprisoned in 2001.

Early shame

William was attracted to same sex partners from an early age – but this put him into conflict with his strict Protestant upbringing. His deeply devout parents were politically active and he followed them into politics. By college, he had became the chairman of a right-wing group, even supporting Ian Paisley's 'Save Ulster From Sodomy' campaign, but he was expelled from a loyalist paramilitary organisation for loitering outside schools and fled to Scotland to escape their wrath.

However, Beggs couldn't turn his sexuality off, and by the time he attended Paisley University in Scotland, he was showing his predatory nature. He made advances toward straight male students after parties – and one was concerned to find that the razor in the bathroom had been broken and the blade removed. Beggs, who had a razor blade fetish, had doubtless planned to cut him with it but there were too many other revellers about.

Throughout his early twenties, the attractive dark-haired Irishman lured various gay men back to his flat where he plied them with drink and drugs before cutting them with razor blades, his preference being to slash a sleeping victim. In this he was unusual, as sadists normally relish an awake victim's increasing terror and pain. But he liked to cut deeply and possibly feared the level of struggle that a conscious victim would make. As it was, his bleeding bedmates awoke in agony and fled the scene but chose not to go to the police for the 1980s were still homophobic times.

On other occasions, Beggs could be a charming companion and intelligent conversationalist. He often went walking in the countryside with one gay male friend called Richard who said that 'Beggs was like many gay men with a strict religious upbringing who consequently can't cope with their sexuality'. He recognised that Beggs was deeply conflicted, but didn't realise that he was dangerous.

The first murder

In 1987, William Beggs (who often introduced himself as Ian Beggs) went out cruising and picked up 28-year-old Barry Oldham in a Newcastle gay nightclub. The mature student thought he had no reason to fear his well-spoken and articulate new friend.

The men went back to Beggs' flat and had sex. No one knows the exact sequence of events, but at some stage Beggs slashed Barry's throat from ear to ear. He attempted to decapitate the student and also tried to cut off his legs. Eventually he disposed of the badly-cut corpse on the North Yorkshire Moors.

Beggs, who had been observed leaving the dump scene in his car, was soon arrested for the murder. He admitted it, was convicted and given life imprisonment but walked free two years later on a technicality. The judge had mentioned some of Beggs' previous razor attacks on other youths, and this had prejudiced the accused's case.

Attempted murder

The police were alarmed to hear that William Beggs was a free man, as they were convinced that, by getting him jailed for his first murder, they'd stopped a potential sadistic serial killer. And their concern was justified for, in 1991, just two years after being freed from jail for Barry Oldham's murder, Beggs took another gay man called McQuillan back to his Kilmarnock flat. McQuillan fell asleep and awoke to find himself lying in agony on the bed, with his right leg badly cut and his left leg held over William Beggs' shoulder. He felt a terrible pain as Beggs took a razor and cut his leg to the bone. The youth looked into his torturer's eyes and knew that he was about to be murdered. He wrestled with the sadist and jumped through the glass window of Beggs' first floor flat in a last-ditch effort to save his life.

Knocked unconscious, he lay on the grass then revived to hear a woman saying that she'd called an ambulance. He saw Beggs hovering behind her then he lost consciousness again. Medics later noted that Beggs had cut the youth so viciously that his wounds were worse than those caused by shark bites and that McQuillan was fortunate to survive.

Beggs was sentenced to six years for this horrific assault, years in which he learned more about the legal system and helped other prisoners with their appeals. Released in 1994 for good behaviour having only served half his sentence, he took up a computer consultancy. He began to study for a PhD at Paisley University and also undertook some tutoring work which doubtless let him get close to attractive young men.

Throughout the rest of the 1990s, he lured various youths back to his flat, got them drunk and hurt them. He told friends that he particularly liked cruising the streets in the early hours of the morning, looking for drunk young men. But raping and cutting terrified victims wasn't enough for Beggs. He wanted to kill again.

By now he was in his late thirties and had put on weight. His looks had also coarsened so it wasn't so easy for him to attract beautiful youths to his Kilmarnock flat. Perhaps this is why he decided to ambush a straight young man who just happened to be in the wrong place at the wrong time.

The second murder

On 5 December 1999, Beggs went to a party in Edinburgh where he stood out as he was one of the few revellers who wasn't in fancy dress. He left the party before midnight and drove the 90-minute journey back to Kilmarnock where he encountered 18-year-old Barry Wallace who'd been dropped off by friends only a mile from his home. Barry, who worked for Tesco, had been on a Christmas work night out and had had several drinks.

The 38-year-old cajoled or forced the teenager (who wasn't gay) back to his flat where he handcuffed his wrists and ankles and brutally raped him. Barry struggled so violently during the assault that the cuffs bit into his flesh, leaving deep cuts. The rape itself was so savage that the police later said that Barry possibly died of shock. An alternative explanation is that he suffocated from having his face pushed into the bed or floor.

At some stage during the assault, Beggs got out his razors and knives and cut off Barry's head and limbs. Driving to Loch Lomond to dispose of some of the body parts, he phoned a friend and told him that he'd enjoyed a sexual conquest with a young man last night. Beggs kept the head for another day then took a trip on a ferry and disposed of his grisly parcel in the sea off Troon.

Body parts discovered

Shortly afterwards, police divers on a training course at Loch Lomond found one of Barry's hands and part of one of his arms wrapped in a bin bag. Nine days later a woman walking her dog on Barassie Beach, near Troon, found a package containing Barry's severed head.

It was obvious that the body had been cut with a razor, so police looked at similar murders and found that William Beggs had attempted to decapitate and remove the legs of his first murder victim. They checked and found that, not only had Beggs been freed from that charge, but he now lived in Kilmarnock where the victim had lived.

The police's luck now briefly ran out, for William Beggs was working in an Edinburgh call centre when he heard on the radio that the limbs in the loch had been found. Knowing he'd be the prime suspect, he immediately went on the run.

He fled to Amsterdam and lived as a fugitive for a fortnight – but the police had published his photograph in numerous newspapers so he decided to give himself up and fight extradition to Scotland. As a result, he managed to remain in The Netherlands for a year. In the meantime, in January 2000, the police found more of Barry Wallace's body parts in the loch.

Beggs' flat also yielded several links between himself and the murdered teenager. The key to the handcuffs used on Barry were found in his house as was a kitchen knife with Barry's blood on it. Other tiny spots of the 18-year-old's blood were found in the kitchen and the spare room.

Even more tellingly, the house was filthy and overrun with rubbish – but the bedroom had been recently and extensively redecorated. The floor had been varnished and the wallpaper changed.

In January 2001, Beggs was returned to Scotland under police escort. On remand in Saughton Prison, he demanded to be given the gay porn which a friend had sent to him. (Pornography is only allowed at the governor's discretion in British prisons.)

In September, Beggs went on trial at Edinburgh High Court. The court heard from various acquaintances how he liked to pick up men in straight bars, get them drunk and offer them a bed for the night. Beggs claimed that Barry Wallace was gay and had attacked him. But there was nothing to support this and Barry had a girlfriend.

The court heard that at least 20 drops of blood – four of them Barry's – had been found in Beggs redecorated flat and that the teenager's blood had also been found in the grooves of a large kitchen knife.

In October 2001, William Beggs was sentenced to 20 years for Barry Wallace's razor blade mutilation and murder. He showed no emotion as the verdict was read out – but he was upset when he later heard that he was going to be put on the sex offenders register.

Parents' legal action

William Beggs' parents and aunt now launched a legal action against Strathclyde police, claiming that they had been wrongfully arrested and interrogated on 4 January 2000. The police suspected that the Beggs had helped their youngest son redecorate his flat after the murder of Barry Wallace (he'd phoned them several times after the murder) so had questioned them for six hours and taken their fingerprints and mouth swabs. As a result, the couple were seeking 'aggravated and exemplary damages'.

But later the compensation claim was dropped, with a Strathclyde Police spokeswoman confirming that 'the civil action for damages raised against the Chief Constable of Strathclyde Police by the father, mother and aunt of William Beggs has been dismissed in favour of the chief constable.'

Beggs' legal action

Subsequently, William Beggs – now in Peterhead Prison – launched a legal action against the prison claiming that their failure to provide him with secure computer facilities was a breach of his human rights. He argued that his correspondence should remain private: the prison had provided him with a portable computer but he had to save his work to a hard disk. He lost his case, but the judicial review cost the British taxpayer at least £15,000, hardly the best use of resources. And, as an intelligent but bitter jailhouse lawyer, he is expected to make other expensive appeals.

Beggars belief

Recently a Scottish newspaper reported that William Beggs was to enter into a civil partnership with his prison lover, a 43-year-old man imprisoned for having sex with minors. The authorities admitted that they were powerless to stop the ceremony, but said that they would not allow the two men to share a cell. But Beggs has allegedly told friends that he may take court action over this.

In April 2006, he asked Edinburgh High Court to free him, pending an appeal against his conviction, but his request for interim liberation was denied.

GRAHAM COUTTS

In 2003, Coutts was found guilty of murdering a female friend, an act he had committed out of a desire to assuage his asphyxiation fetish. But the Law Lords subsequently agreed that jurors should have been given the option of bringing in a verdict of manslaughter.

Born in Leven, Scotland (though, by the time he murdered, he lived in England), Graham Coutts began to have sexual fantasies about strangling women when he was aged 15. As he matured sexually, he satisfied himself with consensual sex – but as he moved into his twenties he began to put his hands around girls' necks during intercourse, asking them to feign unconsciousness. He also liked to bind their hands behind their back with tights. Later this wasn't enough for him and he asked a girlfriend if he could strangle her until she passed out. He also liked to take the submissive role and asked one girlfriend to strangle him until he lost consciousness.

He told another girlfriend that he had an increasing urge to rape and strangle a woman and she persuaded him to see a psychiatrist. But Coutts quickly stopped treatment and instead began to frequent websites such as Hangingbitches, Necrobabes and Deathbyasphysixia. (These sites were shut down after details of his reliance on them came to light.) He searched for further images of sadism and necrophilia by entering the terms 'strangled women' and 'dead women' into a search engine.

As the years passed, Graham Coutts' behaviour became increasingly misogynistic. When one of his girlfriends wept because of a family problem he told her that the tears were a turn-on and he began to masturbate. On another occasion he completely depersonalised her by putting a pillowcase over her head before they had sex.

Graham had originally hoped to be a full-time professional musician but he'd settled for playing the guitar in a pub band. It was respectable creative work but a far cry from the worldwide fame he'd longed for and his sense of frustration doubtless intensified his fantasies of being sexually in control.

The victim

Graham Coutts now began to fantasise about a specific victim – 31-year-old Jane Longhurst who taught English and music to children with special needs. Jane had been friends with Graham's girlfriend, music teacher Lisa Stephens, for the past five years and was delighted that the couple were expecting twins. Jane and her boyfriend Malcolm spent time with Lisa and Graham at their Brighton flat, and Jane, who loved keeping fit, sometimes went swimming with Graham.

She tended to see the best in people: she came from a close family, had met Malcolm in church and was adored by her pupils. She had no reason to think that her friend's partner was fantasising about slowly strangling her. Sadists often choose strangulation as a method of torture and eventual death as they can tighten then loosen the ligature pressure, enjoying their victim's struggle for breath.

The obsession deepens

Meanwhile, Graham Coutts' fetish was getting worse. He'd now downloaded over 800 images of women being raped, hung and strangled. Many of the images he downloaded also involved necrophilia, either real or staged. Coutts wanted a woman whom he could rape and strangle and a body which he could return to again and again.

Power and control were becoming increasingly important to this prematurely-balding man. His guitar playing didn't bring in a sufficient wage so he'd become a part-time Kleeneze salesman – delivering catalogues door to door and taking orders for cleaning products – to make ends meet. In a few weeks he'd be responsible for twins; yet more stress.

He told his girlfriend to change the password on their computer so that he could no longer use the Internet to access the asphyxiation-oriented sites as he thought this was inconsistent with fatherhood. But trying to ignore his desires only made them stronger, and on 13 March 2003 he spent two hours downloading images of strangled women and masturbating over them.

The following afternoon Graham Coutts engineered events so that he had Jane to himself. All that's certain is that she phoned her friend Lisa in the morning as Lisa had been off work for several days with morning sickness. But she'd gone back to work that day and Jane spoke to Graham instead. He probably asked her to go swimming with him – her costume would later be found at his storage unit along with her clothes and mobile phone.

Raped

When Graham Coutts had Jane alone in his flat (Lisa wasn't due back for several hours) he overpowered her and tightly wound a stocking around her throat. He raped her as he strangled her – the strangulation would have taken approximately three minutes and it left the nylon deeply embedded in her neck. He then hid her body in an empty upstairs flat to which he had the keys, probably returning to it frequently and re-enacting his strangling fantasies. In any case, he'd later bound a green scarf around Jane's neck.

Eleven days later, knowing that the new tenants of the flat were about to arrive, he rented a storage unit under the pseudonym of Paul Kelly and drove the body there, returning to it ten times for sexual pleasure, making a visit every three to four days.

Body found

By mid April the decomposing corpse had begun to give off a noticeably rank odour so on the nineteenth he removed it from the storage company: the company noticed that when he took away a large box from his unit, the foul smell which had permeated the area disappeared. Coutts then drove to a bird sanctuary at Wiggonholt Common near Pulborough, West Sussex and set fire to Jane's body, using petrol from a can that he'd bought at a service station in Hove. But he'd covered her head with a box marked 'Fragile' – and there was a very similar box at his home also marked with this word. Furthermore, unknown to him, his movements at the storage unit and at the service station had been caught on CCTV.

Semen

Interviewed by police, he initially denied everything. But when he was shown the evidence they'd found in his storage locker – a used condom and Jane's blouse smeared with Coutts' semen, her bloodstained trousers and a bloodstained rope – he began to rock back and forth. Becoming tearful, he said, 'I can't talk about it. I just don't know what happened.'

Blaming the Internet

As word of Coutts' interest in misogynistic websites became public knowledge, various individuals and groups blamed the Internet for Jane Longhurst's murder. But there were lust murders long before the Internet was available, with would-be killers finding source material in everything from the Bible to lingerie catalogues. Paedophiles can even become aroused by toy and baby catalogues. There have also been instances of killers with a hanging fetish taking ordinary photos of women from newspapers and drawing nooses around their necks. Admittedly the sites Coutts visited were particularly misogynistic, but they wouldn't have driven the average man to kill.

Arrest and trial

On Monday 28 April, Coutts was arrested and remanded in custody. Appearing at Lewes Crown Court in November 2003 he pleaded not guilty. Taking the stand, he claimed that he and Jane had had consensual breath-restricting sex using a stocking and that her death by strangulation had been an accident; in his words 'a tragic and totally unforeseen blunder'. In reality, Jane had been very happy with her live-in boyfriend Malcolm and they had been talking about getting married. Malcolm was devastated by her death.

But the prosecution's case was stronger, for they argued that if Jane had died during a consensual session leaving Coutts horrified, why would he debase her corpse again and again?

Coutts wept as he watched video footage of himself buying petrol at a garage and removing the box containing Jane's body from the storage unit. He was so upset that the court had to briefly recess. He admitted that he'd had a fetish about women's necks since he was 15 and said that his strangulation fantasies also hailed from that date.

The judge said that the strangler had been seeking perverted sexual gratification and, on 4 February 2004, sentenced him to a minimum of 30 years, ensuring that he'd be 65 before he could apply for parole.

In 2004, Court of Appeal judges rejected his appeal against conviction but reduced his 30 year minimum jail sentence to 26 years. But they added that his case raised issues of 'general public importance' fit for consideration by the House of Lords.

Coutts' legal team then approached the House of Lords, arguing that there was insufficient evidence of intent and so alternatives to a murder conviction should have been offered to the jury. In June 2005, five Law Lords agreed that the jury should have had the opportunity to bring in a manslaughter verdict. They referred the matter back to the Court of Appeal. There is now a possibility that Graham Coutts will be retried for Jane Longhurst's death, with manslaughter – rather than only a murder conviction or acquittal – as one of the options available for the jury to select.

PART TWO

MOVING ON: AMERICAN SADISTS

CHAPTER SEVEN

ROBERT BEN RHOADES

Rhoades abducted an unknown number of young girls throughout America from the late 1970s to 1990. Though only convicted of murdering one teenager, the police suspect him of up to 50 unsolved homicides. He was finally caught with a naked and bridled young woman in his truck.

Formative horror

Robert was born on 22 November 1945 to Betty and Ben Rhoades. Ben was a 32-year-old army man, whilst Betty was a 31-year-old housewife. Robert was their third child and they would go on to have a fourth.

The family lived in a small house in County Bluffs, Iowa. Initially, Ben Rhoades was stationed overseas but when he came home he found a job as a fireman. He was a strict disciplinarian and an obsessive paedophile.

It's known that Robert's formative years were deeply unhappy, writing of his sadism, his biographer commented that 'Rhoades's childhood marked him to become what he was'. Robert would later hint to his third wife that he'd been sexually abused and admit that he'd had a terrible upbringing but he couldn't bring himself to go into further detail about what had taken place. (Decades later he would still remain mute about what he'd endured, when admitting to being an abuse victim might have warded off the death penalty.)

Outwardly, he did reasonably well at school, joining the choir and the French Club. But he got into trouble with the police for tampering with a car and for fighting. In retrospect, these might have been cries for help.

Just before Robert graduated from school, his father was arrested for paedophilia, having sexually assaulted his 12-year-old niece. He received a suspended sentence. But he went on to sexually molest his 12-year-old nephew, was caught and committed suicide rather than go to jail.

Three failed marriages

By now Robert had joined the Marine Corps, but the following year he was arrested for robbery and discharged from the service. He returned to Iowa and married, the marriage producing a son. But after four years the relationship broke down and he took his two-year-old boy on a road trip in order to keep him away from his mother, the actions of an immature and very angry man. Forced to return the child, Robert then spent his life savings on prostitutes. His second marriage also failed and he married for a third time, but within six months he was bored with the relationship and introduced his wife to a swingers' club.

When he wasn't evidencing his sadism, Rhoades displayed a strong masochistic streak. He persuaded several of his lovers to urinate on him, and he took the slave role when he went to a fancy dress party. He also gave his wife a male slave he'd contacted through an advertisement, and whom he clearly identified with.

But he remained sadistic, and this showed in the way that he increasingly humiliated his third wife. She'd had a previous failed marriage and he preyed on her fear of being alone again. He did what the classic sadist does, choosing a woman with low self-esteem then isolating her from her relatives. Soon she became his figurative whipping boy, as he told her that virtually everything she did was wrong. But after a particularly vicious argument he raped her anally and vaginally and she found the courage to walk out on him.

Rhoades now had the freedom to victimise young girls, something he'd probably done before – the police would later surmise that he was actively abducting and torturing hitch-hikers throughout the 1980s, no doubt killing some and terrorising others into keeping silent. Superficially charming, the long haul truck driver could quickly persuade vulnerable young women to enter his vehicle.

Shana's abduction

In January 1990, he ate at a truck stop in San Bernardino, California – but his mind wasn't on his meal as he had other appetites he wished to satisfy. He offered 18-year-old hitch-hiker Shana Holts a lift, she accepted and soon fell asleep in his cab.

Shana awoke to find the truck driver pulling in to the side of the deserted highway. Frightened, she tried to get out of the cab but he slapped her across the face and pushed his pistol into her ribs. He then forced her, at gunpoint, into the sleeper compartment where he handcuffed her to chains which hung from a ceiling bar. He also cuffed her ankles and adjusted her until she was spreadeagled on the bed.

Rhoades removed the terrified girl's blouse before forcing a horse's bit into her mouth and buckling it around her head. Her suffering still not complete for him, he tortured her with pins. Her ordeal would last until the following month. Later, he chained her to the outside of the truck and cut off her long hair before whipping her with a leather-thonged whip. Rhoades would cut off the hair of each of his female victims – it was part of his signature. Abusive fathers often force their children to have humiliatingly short haircuts, so perhaps this was done to him.

For the next few hours, the sadist felt a measure of peace. He'd used the horse bridle to show his victim that she had the lowly status of an animal and had made her scream, getting a misguided revenge on the woman or women who had failed him in his childhood. He'd ejaculated whilst witnessing her pain, and this tends to cause a temporary reduction in a sadist's rage.

But his hatred later built again, and he woke the sleeping teenager and violently raped her, telling her that she was worthless. He then forced an oversized dildo into her vagina and anus, becoming aroused again by her screams. When she had to urinate, he led her out onto a deserted exit lane on a dog's collar and leash. The abused child was exacting a terrible revenge.

That night, he made Shana kneel on a chair with her back to him whilst he whipped her. The pain was terrible – but he told her that when he tired of administering it, he'd murder her and abduct another girl.

January ended and, rarely fed, Shana grew weaker. But on 1 February Robert Rhoades took her to his apartment where he allowed her to have a bath, fed her, then sodomised her again.

Afterwards she was cuffed, taken back to his truck and driven to a car park where he stopped to pick up a work consignment. Luckily he'd forgotten to close one of the cuffs, and Shana seized her chance. The silver chain still dangling from her throat, she fled to a nearby work yard where a horrified workman phoned the police.

Moments later the police stopped Robert Rhoades and asked Shana if this was the man who had abducted her. She risked a sideways glance at his cold stare and remembered the endless days and nights when he'd chosen if she should eat, sleep or even urinate. He still seemed all-powerful, and she was too afraid to identify him so muttered that this wasn't the man. The police were suspicious but they reluctantly let Rhoades go after noting his name and address.

That evening they documented the girl's many injuries – livid whip marks across her breasts and buttocks plus cuts on her mouth where the bridle had bitten into the corners. Her wrists and ankles were also bruised from the handcuffs and chains, and they found further bruises when they cut the padlocked choke chain from her neck.

Now that she felt safe, Shana shamefacedly told the police that Robert Rhoades was the man who had abducted and tortured her. They sympathised with her reactions, knowing that there had been instances of torture victims too terrified of even an absent attacker to risk making an escape.

Regina's abduction and murder

Meanwhile, Rhoades drove on to Texas in search of another torture victim to replace Shana. On 3 February, he got talking to 14-year-old Regina Walters, who planned to hitch-hike to Mexico with her new boyfriend Ricky Lee Jones. It's likely that Rhoades shot the young boy in order to have Regina to himself – Rhoades had written 'Ricky is a dead man' in Regina's notebook and had drawn a gun and drops of blood. And Ricky was never seen again.

For the next few weeks, the 14-year-old girl suffered horribly at her captor's hands. He whipped her, pierced her intimately, hurt her with an oversized dildo and raped her repeatedly. He photographed her out of doors dressed in sexually provocative clothing and shoes, and also photographed her shackled to the inside of the truck. There was a fetishistic element to many of these assaults, with him bringing her shoes, which had an especial significance for him. They most likely belonged to earlier victims whose abuse had given him the strongest erotic charge. Now he was experiencing a diminishing return, and, desperate for gratification, wound a wire around her neck and tightened it 14 times until she died.

Six weeks after abducting Regina, Robert Rhoades phoned her father and told him 'I cut her hair' and 'She's in a loft in a barn'. When the man asked if she was alive or dead, the killer ended the call. That night, Rhoades phoned Regina's mother and suggested that she meet him, but he didn't show up. He made several other similar calls to both parents, yet another sign of his sadism.

Another victim

By March, the sadist had found himself yet another victim, 27-year-old Katie Ford. He started talking to the mentally ill young woman at an Arizona truck stop and offered her a lift part of the way to Texas. Once isolated in his truck, her victimisation began.

He attacked her but she managed to bite him and scratch his face before he stripped her, put a collar around her neck, handcuffed her and chained her to the wall. He also whipped her breasts and legs numerous times, leaving long red welts. Determined to make her suffer further, the sadist used nipple and labial clamps on her, saying matter of factly, 'I've been doing this for 15 years.'

Rhoades parked his lorry in order to have a break at Casa Grande, Arizona. As he slept in his cab, a patrolman approached, intending to ask him to move to a safer area. But he heard a commotion in the back and hoisted himself up to look through the window. Horrified at the sight of a naked, screaming woman chained to the inside of the vehicle, he ordered the driver out of the truck.

Rhoades was completely calm as he was arrested, and he remained calm in custody – sociopaths often appear indifferent during such pivotal moments. He told officers that Katie wasn't 'playing with a full deck', and tried to pass the incident off as a misunderstanding, but they could see that her nipples and labia had been punctured and that her breasts and back were brutally criss-crossed with the marks of a whip. And when they opened his briefcase they found a wide assortment of leashes, handcuffs, riding crops and clamps.

The police searched his apartment, finding women's clothes, soiled underwear and jewellery, standard souvenirs kept by serial killers. There were Polaroid pictures of naked girls, one taken with the girl chained inside his truck. Even more alarmingly, a once white towel was scarlet with blood.

Later, the police identified some of the photos as being of 14-year-old Regina Walters. In one, Rhoades had shaved off her pubic hair. In others, he'd used sex toys on her and in yet others, he'd made her dress up in clothing that was too big for her. She looked terrified in many of the photographs and there were fading bruises on her breasts.

Body found

On 29 September 1990, a farmer found Regina Walters' remains in his barn. Her skeletonised frame was naked and there was a wire garrotte twisted cruelly around her neck. Her hair had been cropped humiliatingly short.

Sentenced

That December, Rhoades was sentenced to six years in prison for Katie Ford's abduction and assault. He was soon beaten up by other inmates and had to be moved to solitary confinement. The police then charged him with Regina Walters murder, as a witness had come forward. The man, who was working on a loading dock eight feet above the ground, had seen Rhoades with a young girl with closely cropped hair. The girl had indicated with her eyes that she was frightened, but the foreman had decided not to get involved. Now his eyewitness testimony, alongside the photos of Regina found in Rhoades' flat, were enough to convict.

Other murders

The police were convinced that Regina Walters wasn't Robert Rhoades' first murder victim and believed that towards the end of his torture spree, he was abducting three girls every month. They've noted that he was in the vicinity of 50 other unsolved murders where skeletonised remains were found.

Quietly spoken and charismatic, he was able to lure vulnerable young girls – hitch-hikers, runaways and prostitutes – from quiet highway cafés. But as soon as he got them to a remote area, he showed his true sadistic desires. The sheer size and complexity of his torture kit, and of the bondage devices in his truck and home, showed how long he'd been perfecting the act of controlling and harming unfortunate girls.

The roots of sadism

The defence were convinced that Robert Rhoades had been sexually abused as a child by his paedophile father, but he refused to discuss his formative experiences. He pleaded guilty to Regina's murder and was given life imprisonment.

One of the special agents sent to take Rhoades to prison told him, 'You're the one that's going to get fucked,' referring to the rape that is rife in many prisons. And when Rhoades was rumoured to have contracted cancer of the colon, his third wife said that she hoped he'd die in agony.

Rhoades didn't die, but his incarceration photograph, taken at Pontiac Correctional Center, reflects his suffering. One of his eyes is almost closed, possibly due to a recent beating, and the other eye holds a manic expression. His head is shaved, his skin unhealthy and his always-lopsided mouth looks even more twisted than before. His right arm, right shoulder and abdomen are all deeply scarred and he looks older than his actual years. The beaten child became a merciless sadist and is probably a victim again.

And still the Rhoades story is ongoing, for, in 2003, he fought to avoid being extradited to Utah to face charges for the kidnap and murder of 24-year-old Patricia Candice Walsh. It's alleged that the sadist encountered the 24-year-old and her 28-year-old husband Douglas Scott in 1990, as the couple travelled between Georgia and Seattle. He may have offered them a lift.

The sadist allegedly shot Mr Scott dead then tortured Ms Walsh for a week, keeping her chained inside his truck's sleeper-compartment-turned-torture-chamber. He is then said to have shot her several times in the head and dumped her in central Utah, where her decomposing naked body was found by horrified deer hunters. For well over a decade, she remained just another Jane Doe and it was 2003 before her remains were identified, by which time new forensic tools allowed investigators to detect Rhoades' DNA.

The charges against him have been sealed and the case has been postponed so details remain sketchy, but, if eventually convicted, he will face the death penalty.

CHAPTER EIGHT

REX ALLAN KREBS

A sex offender from age 13, Krebs attempted to bind and rape two women in separate incidents, crimes which earned him a 20-year sentence. Paroled ten years early, he abducted and murdered a woman in 1998 and another in 1999.

Formative experiences

Rex was born on 28 January 1966 to Connie and Allan Krebs. He had a three-year-old half-sister whom his mother had given birth to when only 16, during her first marriage which only lasted three months. The family lived with Connie's mother for a while then relocated to Allan's father's dairy farm in Idaho. The following year they moved again, this time to Washington.

Toddlers need stability, but little Rex was moved across the country at least annually as his labourer father couldn't find a job which he could tolerate. Meanwhile, his parents' relationship became increasingly violent and the children often saw their father beat their mother and once overheard a particularly vicious marital rape. Rex and his sister were hit, kicked and thrown across the room by their short-tempered father and would eventually fantasise about killing him.

In 1970, Rex was presented with a new baby sister and yet another baby sister joined the household in 1971. Sadly, the latter ended up with severe brain damage due to a virus.

In 1971, Rex's parents separated and Connie and the children began a new life with her boyfriend in Nevada. The six of them lived in one room above a pub, and the adults took refuge in the bar virtually every night. Soon the domestic violence started up again, and Rex had to listen to his mother being beaten and humiliated. He too was regularly beaten by his stepfather and lived in constant fear. There were also allegations that a close male relative sexually abused at least one of his sisters – and given his later obsession with anal sex, Rex himself may have been sexually abused.

Like many mistreated children, Rex began to soil himself. His stepfather would then chastise him further. The man also made him sit on a potty and wear his excrement-encrusted underpants on his head.

At night, Rex and his siblings would sit, frozen, in the family car whilst their parents partied in the bar. The seven-year-old's life was decidedly joyless. Social services investigated allegations of abuse but didn't take the children away. Incredibly, the couple were even allowed to foster four girls, something which boosted the family budget considerably.

When Rex was ten, his biological father took him back and put him to work on his farm. The unkempt young boy had to get used to a new school where he was laughed at for his ill-fitting clothes and nervousness. He often came to school sporting bruises and even black eyes. He soon ran away and lived in the woods, but the authorities brought him back.

Feeling that his mother had let him down – both by failing to protect him from his abusive stepfather and for abandoning him to his violent father – Rex began to hate the female of the species, to fantasise about demeaning and torturing them.

Early sex crimes

At 13 it became obvious how disturbed Rex really was. He broke into a schoolgirl's house, put his knife at his feet and masturbated in her closet. The girl and her mother caught him in the act and were frightened and upset. But they were also understanding, telling police that they wouldn't press charges if Rex would go into therapy. Unfortunately his father only took him for one counselling session, felt that he himself was being psychoanalysed and refused to go back. The following year, Rex began making obscene phone calls to women. His father found out and beat him again.

A few days after his fifteenth birthday, the troubled teenager upped the ante, breaking into a neighbour's house and stealing a pistol. In the same time period, he dragged a piece of metal onto the railway track, derailing a train car, injuring the railway worker and badly frightening him. There have been similar cases throughout the years of sadists destroying forms of transport – and sometimes lives – in this way. Some flee from the railway line before the train is derailed, relying on their imagination and newspaper clippings of the carnage to enrich their diseased fantasies. Others mingle with the survivors, enjoying the sight of suffering and blood.

That year the malnourished young boy was admitted to hospital for a ruptured eardrum. Corey Mitchell's impressive biography *Dead and Buried* notes that the doctor suspected Rex was being abused but decided not to file a report.

Freedom from fear

Thankfully, Rex's dad now took him to a mental hospital, telling them that he was out of control. The staff believed that he could do well if removed from his current environment so he was sent to an Idaho children's home. Often such homes are soulless, indifferent places, but this one offered a therapy-centred caring environment.

At first, Rex remained as disturbed as he'd been at home, throwing tantrums and lying constantly. But, over the next few months, he responded to the care he was given and eventually became their model resident. He also won a certificate for his baseball skills, improved at school and got an after-school job. For the first time ever he looked and acted relaxed and was at peace with himself and his surroundings, and the staff at the children's home thought that he would go on to have an enjoyable and productive life.

Unfortunately, he improved so much that he no longer required a supportive environment, and, despite the fact that he'd talked about the violence at home, he was returned to his father, a man who had never visited him during the past 21 months.

Rex reluctantly went back to the dilapidated farm with no running water. Almost immediately, the abuse started up again, with his father regularly punching him in the face, telling him he was a 'worthless bastard' and referring to his sisters as 'whores'. He also watched the man kick his sisters and beat them with a switch. Desperate to block out the horror, the teenager began to drink heavily and soon progressed to using amphetamines.

Sexual assault

In February 1984, he was drinking with a group of other youngsters when he encouraged a 12-year-old girl to imbibe vodka. Separating her from the group, he lay on top of her and ripped off her jeans. He failed to penetrate her and, increasingly frustrated, began to strangle her instead. He then punched her repeatedly in the face, the exact same act of violence that had so often been carried out on him. Belatedly coming to his senses, he apologised and begged her not to tell anyone. Thankfully she told a passing couple who phoned the police.

The teenager was arrested the following day and charged with attempted rape but he entered a not guilty plea. The charge was subsequently plea-bargained down to an assault, for which he served only 90 days. This type of situation is all too common in both the USA and Britain, where the authorities don't take early sexual offences sufficiently seriously. This is also true outside of the legal system, with teachers and parents often taking a punitive stance towards normal adolescent sexual explorations with a girlfriend/boyfriend or with erotica, yet downplaying an assault as boys being boys.

Prison

Freed from juvenile detention, Rex continued his downward spiral. Six weeks after his release he stole a car and broke into a second car. This time he received a three-year sentence and was sent to a minimum security prison in Idaho. Corrections officers found the 18-year-old to be immature but polite and non-confrontational. This shouldn't have surprised them – teenagers from chaotic homes often improve in a structured environment. At the end of Rex's three-year sentence he was released to the custody of his mother, who was living with her fourth husband near San Luis Obispo in California.

Bondage and attempted rapes

Rex now turned the family garage into an apartment for himself and soon started dating. But his girlfriend noticed that he was obsessed with anal sex. Most young boys who are obsessed with trying out this particular sexual act have previously been the recipient and now feel the need to take the active role again and again. He also wanted to bind her wrists and ankles before they had intercourse but she refused.

The boy who had overheard his own mother being raped all those years ago now had increasingly dominant sexual fantasies. He also found it impossible to be faithful to just one woman and went out again and again in search of variety. When his girlfriend left him on 17 May 1987 he was frightened, lost and very, very angry. Another woman was about to pay…

A week after being deserted, he went on the prowl carrying a large coil of rope, his head full of revenge fantasies. He followed an attractive woman home and broke into her apartment, waking her in the darkness and threatening her with a knife. Rolling her onto her stomach, he tied her wrists together then he slowly and ritualistically cut off all of her clothes. He tried to rape her for the next half hour but couldn't maintain an erection, a common reaction in men who are using sex to meet non-sexual requirements. Eventually he hog-tied her, forcing her bound hands back towards her bound ankles and tying them together so that her body was completely helpless and cruelly stretched. Luckily, at that moment the woman's flatmate returned – doubtless saving her life – and Krebs fled.

For the next three weeks the agitation built up, then Krebs sought to subdue it by attacking again. This time he targeted a young mother whom he had previously spoken to whilst installing a garage door for her neighbour. Breaking into her house in the middle of the night, he threatened her with a knife and a screwdriver and said that he wanted her body, but she fought hard to avoid being raped. Krebs became increasingly enraged as she scratched and hit him, but after a lengthy struggle he fled.

The woman told the police that her attacker resembled the man who'd worked on her neighbour's property and they identified him as the recently released criminal Rex Allan Krebs. The police picked him up and discovered a scratch on his face and other scratches on his body. And he'd lost his cord hat and his knife at the scene.

Eventually Krebs admitted the attempted rape and also confessed to the previous attempted rape. He was sentenced to 20 years in jail.

Imprisonment and parole

For the next ten years, Rex was housed at Soledad State Prison. There, he worked hard and caused no trouble. After all, in a woman-free and heavily structured environment he was relatively at peace. Unfortunately, he didn't participate in the sexual offenders programme as to do so would have marked him as a nonce (sex offender), and he preferred to tell other prisoners that he was in jail on a murder charge.

Krebs worked out in the prison gym during these years, turning from a slender sensitive looking man into a bulky and intimidating looking one with a shaven head and luxurious handlebar moustache. He was reasonably articulate and a good listener so he became increasingly popular with the other inmates. The parole board didn't realise how sadistic he was because he hadn't had a chance to enact his cruel fantasies and, halfway through his sentence, they released him back into the community. On 2 September 1997 he was free.

But the community knew that he was a dangerous sex offender and he was hounded by the locals and forced to move to a less populated area. He rented a remote cabin in the Davis Canyon Woods, south of San Luis Obispo, and soon found himself a labouring job and a new girlfriend.

The 31-year-old now had a second chance at life and for a few months he made the most of his opportunities. He romanced his girlfriend, taking her out for meals and showering her with attention. He also did well at work, putting in long hours and impressing his boss.

But as soon as he had the upper hand in his new relationship, he began to show his true colours, becoming excessively jealous. No doubt reacting to childhood conditioning, he also tried to control his girlfriend and everything else in his environment. Soon the lovers were squabbling frequently and storming out on each other. Meanwhile his father was arrested on a drugs offence and got back in touch for the first time in years.

Increasingly unhappy and still plagued with sadistic sexual fantasies, Rex Allan Krebs began to drown his sorrows and to take recreational drugs, despite the fact that these violated his parole conditions. His mood darkened further by August 1998 after he attempted to break up a bar fight and received head injuries which left him disoriented for several days.

The first murder

On 12 November 1998, he drank heavily in a San Luis Obispo bar and was inebriated when he left the premises in the middle of the evening. He saw student Rachel Newhouse walking across the Jennifer Street Bridge in the winter darkness, just half a mile away from her home. Krebs took a skull mask from his truck (its very presence proof of premeditation) and put it on, then jumped on the girl and battered her unconscious. Throwing her into his truck, he drove carefully towards his out-of-the-way neighbourhood. Meanwhile, other pedestrians on the bridge noticed the large pool of blood and phoned the police.

At last, the sadist had a victim all to himself. He briefly parked his truck and tied her feet and hands, tore off her panties and used them as a gag, then drove to an abandoned house near his home. There, he ungagged and untied her then raped her before turning her onto her stomach and cruelly hog-tying her – as he'd done this to a previous victim, it's likely that this particular form of bondage was his favourite sexual fantasy.

We'll probably never know exactly what happened next. Krebs' own self-serving account was that he went home for 15 minutes to drink some whisky and that when he returned

Rachel had strangled to death. In reality, a sadist simply wouldn't leave a victim of his own volition after just one rape.

At midnight the following day, he wrapped her corpse in garbage bags then buried it on a grassy hill. He also removed the bloodstained carpet from his truck.

Impending fatherhood

Two months later, in January 1999, Rex's girlfriend told him that she was pregnant. At first he was delighted but then he reflected on his violent urges and told her that he wasn't a suitable father as he didn't have a conscience.

Rex again went out drinking heavily and began to stalk 20-year-old college student Aundria Crawford. He followed her home and parked outside her house, then peeked under the window blind. For the next few nights he followed her around, on two occasions climbing up the side of her house to peer in her window. His urges began to escalate.

The second murder

On 11 March 1999, he entered Aundria's apartment by squeezing himself through her tiny bathroom window, bruising his ribs badly in the process. When she encountered him, he battered her unconscious, hog-tied her and put duct tape across her mouth. He also put a pillowcase over her head and bound it in place.

After carrying the young woman to his truck, he returned to her apartment and wiped up the blood. He also stole her VCR, some of her clothes and an unusual key ring which he wanted as a souvenir.

He drove the student up to an abandoned cabin near his home, but saw a neighbour there so drove on to his own house, his cruel lust stronger than his need to avoid leaving a forensic trail. Putting her on the bed, he freed her from the hog-tied position but kept her hands bound together.

Throughout the day he raped and sodomised her multiple times. He also tied her spreadeagled to his bed, then reverted to his favourite position of hog-tying. It was classic sadistic behaviour, with the sadist trying out various forms of abuse but inevitably returning to his long-held masturbatory fantasies: in this case, hog-tying a young girl. Finally he strangled his unfortunate victim with a rope whilst kneeling on her back. Within hours of her death he'd buried her in his backyard.

The net closes

The next time that Rex's parole officer visited, he noticed that the former felon was walking slowly and holding his ribs. Rex said that he'd fallen over in the woods – but the officer knew that a man had forced his way through Aundria's tiny window and would have severe bruising. He contacted the police and told them of his concerns. They, in turn, visited Krebs' home and found airgun pellets and a BB gun, a violation of his parole.

Arrested, he broke down in tears. Aware that several of Aundria Crawford's possessions were hidden in his house, he now said he'd been in the area at the time of her disappearance, and after a little more questioning he took them to Rachel Newhouse's burial site. Detectives uncovered the decomposed remains of the once-beautiful and vibrant student: now she could only be recognised by the silver identity bracelet on her wrist.

Krebs then directed them to Aundria Crawford's corpse, buried close to his house in the Davis woods, her wrists and ankles still wrapped in the bindings which had held them in place.

An active choice

For the next two years, Krebs' lawyers filed motions to delay his trial. They then succeeded in getting the trial relocated to

Monterey. It finally started on 19 March 2001 and the charges included the kidnap of Aundria Crawford plus multiple counts of rape and sodomy.

Krebs' story to the police had been that Rachel had strangled to death by mistake and that he'd 'had' to kill Aundria as her blindfold had come off and she'd recognised him. He'd probably hoped for a double manslaughter charge – but when someone dies during a kidnapping or sexual assault, the assailant is guilty under Californian law of murder in the first degree. Oddly, Krebs' defence team now countered that his statement shouldn't be enough to convict him of homicide. They reminded the jury that he had once been a 'small boy, neglected and abandoned by his mother, the child abused by his father'. The subtext seemed to be that he might falsely admit guilt due to disordered thought processes.

In turn, the prosecution played the jury tapes of the sadist's detailed confessions, and a video in which he took them to the lonely murder sites.

The jury retired for the weekend and returned on Monday 2 April 2001 with a guilty on all counts verdict. A fortnight later the penalty phase began. This time the jury heard from one psychiatrist that the defendant was a sexual sadist and an alcoholic. The psychiatrist explained that having a sadomasochistic sexuality was not a voluntary decision, that 'one of the factors which contribute to the development of this pathological sexual make-up is early childhood abuse'. A second psychiatrist noted that sexual sadism wasn't a disease, that people with sadistic sexual fantasies were the same as people with more mainstream sexual fantasies. In other words, giving in to the urge to sadistically kill was an active choice.

The defence then argued for a life sentence, stating somewhat disingenuously that they could eliminate the evil side of Rex whilst retaining the good side. But the jury were taking no chances and voted for the death penalty.

Rex Allan Krebs is currently on Death Row in California. An appeal in 2003 by his legal team was turned down.

CHAPTER NINE

DAYTON LEROY ROGERS

Many people find any sexuality other than their own to be a source of humour or derision, but Rogers' lethal foot fetish marked him out as a particularly unusual predator. He murdered at least eight women in Oregon in 1987.

Early beatings

Dayton was born on 30 September 1953 to Jasparelle and Ortis Rogers in Idaho. Ortis was a house painter and Jasparelle a housewife. Both were Seventh Day Adventists who believed in the maxim of spare the rod and spoil the child. Ortis didn't like or want children but was apparently overruled by his wife who gave birth to Dayton and two baby girls, then adopted three girls and a boy.

From the age of three, Dayton and his adopted brother were beaten approximately three times a week by their father. He would immobilise their ankles with their undergarments, and make them kneel on the bed awaiting the belt. If they flinched or cried out they'd receive additional lashes on their buttocks, thighs and the soles of their feet. Their mother also beat them on the bare buttocks and feet with her hand or with a fly swat, though she sometimes intervened when the beatings from their father were particularly prolonged. This foot-beating ritual would eventually become part of the adult Dayton's murder signature as he strove to be on the administering side of these hellish acts.

Dayton also saw his father regularly beat his sisters from the time they were three or four until they were 12. One of them would understandably admit that she often prayed her father would be killed in a car crash. But Dayton was punished the most often, possibly because he was exceptionally bright.

Sadly, he rarely had a friend to confide in, for as soon as the family settled in one place, they'd decide it was unsuitable and move again – psychologists would later speculate that this was the insecure parents' way of maintaining almost total control over their brood. As a result, Dayton was moved from school to school in the Seventh Day Adventist faith, an average of three schools per year, where the teachers noted that he was hyperactive and found it hard to concentrate. His father also taught religious instruction in some of those schools, but his employment brought in so little money that the children were ragged and sometimes had to live in an abandoned car or chicken shed.

Further trauma

Dayton soon learned never to refuse his parents' demands, no matter how inappropriate, for to do so would earn him further censure. So when his mother demanded that he massage her feet, he reluctantly complied. She would gasp and squirm as he did so, and it was a deeply unpleasant experience for a young boy.

Little Dayton's life was increasingly inappropriately sexualised. His religion forbade onanism, yet one of his sisters saw a religious adult male relative masturbating. And psychiatrists were later convinced that Dayton had been sexually abused. His biographer, Gary C. King, was told that Dayton had watched a relative push a pin into the head of his own penis, an image which had left the boy traumatised.

Early bisexuality

By 11, Dayton apparently had sexual knowledge beyond his years, and he found comfort in the arms of another 11-year-old boy. He would continue this homosexual relationship on and off into his twenties, though it caused him endless guilt. His foot fetish had now fully established itself and he began to masturbate whilst holding his sister's shoes. These items of footwear seemed like safe choices as his father had told him that women who had sex before marriage should be stoned. By making love to an inanimate object rather than a girl, the sensitive boy believed that he was saving young girls from pain.

Dayton's childhood experiences began to take their toll and he chewed his fingernails until they bled. His IQ of 145 put him in the top one per cent of the population, yet, like many desperately disturbed children, he performed badly at school.

Early criminality

At 16, he and a friend were so angry at the world that they broke the windows of several cars and were put on probation. As usual, Dayton was brutally beaten by his father – and this time he was sent away to a religious boarding school in Spangle, a small town in Spokane County, Washington. He hated it and soon dropped out of the educational system, moving to Oregon where he became a house painter, one of the many jobs his father had had in the past.

First marriage

Dayton worked in this capacity for the next two years, then met and married a girl two years his junior. His wife was a Lutheran who'd previously been in rehab fighting an addiction to both drink and drugs.

Unsurprisingly, the marriage wasn't a success and within a month Dayton was going mad with the pressure. He simply hadn't been shown how to treat other people, especially women, in a loving and balanced way. Smarting at this latest failure, he left the marital home and drove around until he saw a 15-year-old girl whom he'd previously had sex with. Now he drove her to the same wooded area where they'd had intercourse and encouraged her to lie down on the grass with him.

A near-fatal stabbing

Dayton looked down at the girl, who had her eyes closed, her lips parted. To a normal man she was a desirable if underage partner, but to Dayton she was a whore whose actions would send him to a supposed Hell. Taking his hunting knife from its holster, he stabbed her in the stomach, telling her that he could no longer trust her. Shocked, she pulled the knife out and he seemed to come to his senses, gasping 'What did I do?' The terrified girl begged him to take her to the nearest hospital, something he eventually did – but he made her promise to tell everyone that she'd stabbed herself.

The traumatised victim did as she was told, only telling the truth the following day when sceptical police questioned her further. Dayton was taken into custody where he told detectives that the devil had made him do it. He admitted that he was finding it difficult to adjust to marriage and had turned to extra-marital sex for comfort, but his victim hadn't put her arms around him or shown much affection and he'd just snapped.

Sent to see a police psychiatrist, Rogers was tense but lucid. The doctor concluded that he was a depressive neurotic, possibly with an underlying schizoid personality disorder. Incredibly, he was only given four months' probation for the stabbing, having plea-bargained the charge down to second degree assault. And his growing sexual sadism had yet to be recognised.

Further assaults

Dayton returned to his still-troubled marriage and tried to lighten the atmosphere by taking in two teenage female lodgers. But after six months he again gave in to his violent urges, battering both girls on the head with a beer bottle before jumping in his car and crashing it. Realising that he was never going to be the perfect husband, his wife quickly arranged a divorce.

He was sent to see another psychiatrist who diagnosed him as a sexually dangerous sociopath. This time he was found not guilty of the assaults by reason of insanity and sent to a mental hospital in Salem. The date of his incarceration was 6 March 1974.

Initially clinicians thought that Rogers would spend the rest of his life in the hospital, but he seemed to respond to a sex offenders programme and was soon relocated from a maximum security unit to a minimum security ward. In reality, he'd simply pretended to change his ways.

That said, Dayton doubtless told the truth when he said that he fantasised about binding and raping women but that his fantasies sometimes took a terrifying turn when the women got the upper hand and attacked him back. Sadists have invariably been the victims of cruelty before they become the aggressors, and they fear being beaten and tortured again. As such, they sometimes project their sadism onto innocent people then hurt them in a twisted parody of self-defence. With his history of stabbing a lover and bludgeoning his lodgers, Dayton clearly fell into this confused category and was a danger to everyone he met.

Frighteningly, the hospital let him out on day release to do painting work and to attend church services. And a mere nine months after his incarceration they freed him permanently, letting him go and live with a local minister.

Second marriage

Within weeks he'd met the daughter of another minister and had started courting her, though he still picked up girls in bars to have sex with. As ever, he concentrated his attention on their feet.

On 25 October 1975, he married for the second time, taking care to hide his history from his deeply religious young wife and her family. They helped him set up a garage where he could use his mechanical skills.

Rapes

Two months after his wedding, he chatted up an 18-year-old girl and she agreed to go for a drink with him, but he drove her to a secluded location where he bound her and raped her brutally. After a short recovery period he raped her again, then let her out of the vehicle to urinate, whereupon she escaped.

Dayton Rogers attempted to drive off at speed – but his tyres stuck in the mud and he was still trying to leave the area when the police arrived. He was subsequently charged with first degree rape, though he told his wife that it was a trumped-up charge. Whilst awaiting trial, he raped another young woman – tying her up, biting her feet and threatening her with death – but was found not guilty. He then raped two schoolgirls and was found guilty of coercion and given a five-year prison term.

The District Attorney noted that he was one of the most dangerous sexual predators that he'd ever met, but once again, Dayton Leroy Rogers proved to be a model prisoner. Settled in the Oregon State Correctional Institution, he began to have homosexual affairs with a number of other prisoners. He was paroled in January 1982.

Torture victims

Back home with his second wife, Dayton continued to live the life his parents desired – married to a very devout woman and running his own garage. Yet he remained deeply troubled, suffered from frequent migraines and continued to go out three to four times a week picking up prostitutes.

His routine rarely varied. He would pick up a girl in his truck telling her that he was Steve (the kind of normal name he'd longed for when he was teased at school) and that he was a gambler. It was a fun-sounding occupation, a far cry from the responsible and demanding job he actually held. Dayton was good-looking and unthreatening in appearance, so the girl would happily agree to a price for sex and get into his truck.

For their first two or three encounters he would simply ask them to take their shoes and socks off so that he could rub himself to orgasm between their toes. Or he'd ask them to simulate being bound and he'd then masturbate. But after several dates, when he was sure that the prostitute trusted him, he'd drive her to a more remote location and torture her for hours.

Dayton Rogers hog-tied a 34-year-old call girl then began to bite her feet and calves. The more she screamed, the harder he bit down. Then he turned his attention to her breasts, biting them until she became hysterical, after which he cut the soles of her feet with a knife. Eventually she went into mild shock and became limp, whereupon he untied her. He drove her back to her chosen location and kissed her on the cheek.

Later, he tied another prostitute so tightly that he almost cut her circulation off. Again, he bit cruelly at her breasts, and the more she screamed and begged, the more he hurt her. This is unusual – sadists are usually so turned on by a victim's screams that they ejaculate and the sadism stops for a while. But Dayton had been told as a child that he mustn't move or cry whilst he was being punished, an impossible task that he was now setting his innocent victims. Indeed, he told one victim, 'Stop crying or I'll really give you something to cry about,' the kind of comment a cruel parent makes to a distressed child. She, too, went into a fugue state, whereupon he untied her and took her home.

He tied up a third prostitute then hit her in the face, telling her that she was evil. He also slashed one of her feet, threatening that he was going to cut it off. She got free of her bindings and jumped naked from the truck, after which he returned to his senses and gave her back her clothes.

By November 1986 he was getting closer to his first kill, binding a 23-year-old prostitute and biting her breasts, buttocks, shoulders, back and feet for three or four hours until she was incoherent with pain and terror. Eventually he carried her, naked, from his truck and dumped her in the street, saying that he hoped she would die. Over the next few years, he would bind and torture dozens of prostitutes in similarly fetishistic ways. Some went to the police and told them about the man who called himself Steve the gambler, but most settled for hobbling about on crutches for a few days, warning other call girls of how dangerous Steve was.

Countdown to murder

By the mid 1980s Dayton's business was prospering but it wasn't enough to make the deeply damaged young man believe in himself. He'd been told all his life that he was evil and he continued to feel self-loathing. His migraines intensified and only the prospect of sex with a prostitute gave him something to look forward to, an outlet for all of his hate. Even then, he had to have three or four vodkas during a session in order to relax. His wife gave birth to his son in 1985, giving him additional pressure, and he escaped to the bars and sidewalks several nights a week in search of extra-marital, foot-and-bondage-based sex.

By spring 1987, he'd begun to disintegrate, finding it impossible to sleep at nights. He spent less and less time at his garage, so numerous work orders remained unfulfilled. He also lost two and a half stone in weight.

A victim escapes

On 7 July 1987, Dayton picked up a prostitute and began to drive her to a remote location, telling her that he was going to tie her up and rape her. Realising from his manner that he intended to kill her, she jumped out of his moving truck, sustaining a concussion. A passing driver picked her up and drove her to the nearest hospital. Sadly, Dayton's next targeted victim wouldn't survive.

The first murder

On 8 July, he picked up Maureen Ann Hodges, a young heroin addict who supported her habit by shoplifting and through prostitution. She'd had an argument with her boyfriend and was pleased to see Dayton's friendly looking face. He offered her a generous amount of money to get into his truck, took her into the woods, bound her and stabbed her, concentrating the eventually lethal mutilations on her feet.

The second murder

Three days later he picked up Cynthia Diane DeVore. Like most of his victims, she'd had an unhappy childhood as she'd been born to an alcoholic mother and spent much of her life in foster care. Now the end of her life was as painful as the beginning, as Dayton Rogers took her to a secluded location, tied her up and stabbed her five times in the back.

The third murder

On 21 July, he espied 16-year-old Reatha Marie Gyles who had many friends who were prostitutes. She herself had been arrested for prostitution just a fortnight before. Dayton drove her to the forest, bound her and tortured her for an unknown period with his sharpened knife. He also sawed at her left foot until he was 80 per cent of the way through the bone, then manually snapped the limb off. At some stage during this prolonged abuse, Reatha died.

The fourth murder

Two days later, at 2am, he picked up Lisa Mock, a heroin addict. He bound the girl, tortured her with his knife and hacked off both of her feet. Her corpse was eventually identified by a tattoo which said Biker Harley Davidson Bitch.

The fifth murder

Later that same month, Dayton picked up 26-year-old Nondace Cervantes, known as Noni to her friends. She had a drug and drink addiction, so was glad of the proffered cash. The serial killer took her into the forest, tied her up and cut her left nipple. Experimenting further, he stuck his machete in her vagina before ripping it all the way up to her chest, effectively disembowelling her.

The sixth murder

Christine Adams, a prostitute whose three children had been taken into foster care, was also picked up in the same time frame by the killer and taken to the Mollala Forest where she was tied up, tortured and eventually murdered. (Christina's 15-year-old daughter would later give evidence at Rogers' trial, testifying in tears that studs found in the killer's woodburning stove had once decorated her mother's jeans.)

The seventh murder

Dayton Leroy Rogers took at least one other young woman to his killing ground where he stabbed and cut her. But, due to the advanced decomposition of her body when it was found, she has never been identified. What's certain is that the sadist hurt and demeaned each victim as much as possible – several of the women had been bound with wire coat hangers and had then had dog collars fastened around their necks. They were also extensively and repeatedly bitten and stabbed.

The last murder

Just after midnight on 6 August 1987, he left his workplace and drove around until he found a prostitute. It was 1.30 a.m. when 25-year-old Jennifer Lisa Smith stepped into his van. Dayton promptly drove the mother of two to a dark car park near a Denny's restaurant, where Jennifer took off her clothes. The 34-year-old serial killer swiftly bound her hands with laces, then made her kneel, the way he'd been forced to kneel during his childhood beatings many years before.

He cut her back, enjoying her screams and writhings. When she twisted around, he turned his attention to her breasts, slashing both and cutting one of the nipples. His sadism increasing, he tortured her with the knife again and again. But, unknown to him, her screams hadn't been sufficiently muffled by the van's closed windows and a man sleeping in a nearby apartment had heard.

Meanwhile Jennifer was struggling so hard that she broke her bonds and grabbed for the knife, which cut both of her palms. Still fighting she fell, naked, from the vehicle. But the killer was close behind her and he stabbed her multiple times. Her cries were heard by several Denny's diners and, as they rushed towards the bloody scene, Dayton cut her throat and slipped away.

Luckily a sharp-eyed passerby saw him getting into his truck and followed in his own vehicle, reaching speeds of 100 miles an hour before being able to make out Rogers' number plate. He then gave the licence number to the police.

Arrest

Though one of the customers from Denny's tried to resuscitate Jennifer Smith, she died before the ambulance arrived so Rogers was facing a murder charge. The police went to his compulsively neat workshop and interviewed him there. They noticed that his hand had been cut – murderers often accidentally cut themselves with the murder weapon – but he said that he'd hurt it on a hacksaw earlier that day. He added that he'd been working all night, but police were able to disprove that when they found that his truck engine was still warm.

They also noticed that he had miniature bottles of vodka on the premises, the type that many of the prostitutes had seen their torturer – the supposed gambler Steve – drinking. Dayton explained that by saying his wife didn't approve of alcohol so he could only drink at work.

Arrested and read his Miranda rights, he refused to make further comments, but the evidence soon stacked up against him when one of Jennifer's tennis shoes was found burning in his stove. Buttons and zips from numerous other articles of women's clothing were found and the detectives suddenly realised that they were dealing with a serial killer.

The body farm

No one knew who Dayton had killed or where he'd stashed the bodies until August of that year when a deer hunter made a grim discovery, finding a naked body in the Molalla Forest. The woman's left foot had been cut off at the ankle. Within minutes of being called to the scene, investigative detectives had found a second nude female who'd had both feet chopped off. A third naked corpse was found 15 feet away and had been disembowelled. By the end of the first day's search they'd found five naked corpses, all of which had been extensively mutilated. The following day they found two more.

One woman still had her hands bound in front of her, whilst another bore cut marks to her ankle, as if the killer had been disturbed whilst sawing through the bone.

The first trial

Indicted on 4 February 1988 for Jennifer Smith's murder, Dayton Leroy Rogers made the incredible claim of self-defence. It was a gift for the prosecution, who noted that, whilst supposedly defending himself, he'd pursued the naked and bleeding woman from his truck, thrown himself on top of her and cut her throat.

They called prostitute after prostitute who described being bound by the sadistic serial killer and having a knife used on their breasts, buttocks and particularly their feet. He'd had to carry several of them from his truck as they were too wounded to walk. Others spoke of limping from the vehicle with their shoes filled with blood.

Surprisingly, Dayton Leroy Rogers took the stand, saying that Jennifer Smith had lunged at him with a knife and that he'd fought her off, killing her by accident. Less surprisingly, the jury returned a verdict of guilty of aggravated murder.

Prior to the sentencing phrase, they heard about Dayton's horrendous childhood. A psychiatrist for the defence noted that the killer had frontal lobe dysfunction and that this, coupled with intense depression following an abusive childhood, had fuelled his desire to kill. He noted that the sadist bore scars from long-ago beatings on his back, buttocks and behind his knees. He was subsequently sentenced to life imprisonment.

The second trial

On 4 May 1988, he was indicted for the murders of Maureen Hodges, Cynthia DeVore, Reatha Gyles, Lisa Mock, Nondace Cervantes and Christine Adams. Though he wasn't charged with the murder of the unidentified prostitute found beside the other bodies, his attorney admitted in court that Dayton was responsible.

Almost a year later – on 30 March 1989 – the trial began in Clackamas County, with the defendant still protesting his innocence. Again, prostitute after prostitute testified to how he'd tortured and terrorised them and the jury heard that remnants of clothes and shoes from the murdered women had been found in Dayton's stove.

Within hours the jury had found him guilty on all counts, and the trial moved into the penalty phase. The defence pleaded for his life to be spared, noting that he was running church services in prison for the other prisoners. In turn, the prosecution noted that he was a violent time bomb which could explode again. The jury believed the latter, and he was sentenced to die by lethal injection.

Legal madness

Dayton Leroy Rogers remained on Death Row until 1992, whereupon the death sentence was thrown out as the US Supreme Court ruled that all juries should consider additional factors in such cases. Rogers then attended a second sentencing hearing, after which the jury reimposed the death penalty.

But in 2000, Oregon's state supreme court overturned the death sentence again, insisting that the jury must consider the option of sentencing him to life without the possibility of parole. Meanwhile the sadist refused to talk about his crimes, admit the identity of his Jane Doe or show any remorse.

In March 2006, he was returned to court for a third time so that the court could again decide his fate. By now the formerly slender sadist had gained weight and was sporting a pot belly. This enraged the relatives of the victims as he was clearly thriving in prison whilst their loved ones had long since turned to dust. The court heard how Rogers considered that he was now a different person, having spent 18 years in prison. But the jury suspected otherwise and reimposed the death penalty for a third time.

Many Oregonians fear that Oregon's State Supreme Court will again overturn this decision, at an untold cost to the taxpayers – but whether he dies by lethal injection or natural causes, Dayton Leroy Rogers is destined to die in jail.

CHAPTER TEN

ROBERT CHRISTIAN HANSEN

Hansen is the worst known serial killer in Alaskan history as he murdered at least 17 young women and raped numerous others over a 12-year period spanning the 1970s and early 1980s. A classic sadist, he would torture victims in his remote cabin then set them free in the Alaskan wilderness, only to track them down like animals and shoot them dead.

Firstborn

Robert was born on 15 February 1939 to Edna and Christian Hansen in Esterville, Iowa. Christian, who had a Dutch father, stuttered badly and his grasp of spoken English was poor. He was also an extremely critical parent. Both he and his wife were deeply religious and the family ethos was based on hard work and strict discipline.

When Robert was three the Hansens moved to California, and when he was eight they gave him a baby sister. Two years later the family moved back to Iowa, this time settling in Pocahontas, and started a bakery there. By now Robert – who had always had to perform numerous chores to please his house-proud mother – was expected to help his father for hours on end in the family bakery. As a result, he often fell asleep at school.

His IQ tested at 91, which is slightly below average. He was further hampered by his parents' insistence that he become right-handed, despite the fact that he'd been born left-handed. (They thought that left-handed children had been tainted by the devil.) Constantly overworked and under praised, he began to stutter like his father and he rarely played with the other children at his Catholic school. Instead he attended church, sang in the choir and studied his Bible every night. His father frequently criticised his schoolwork and his work in the bakery, and supposed infringements resulted in harsh corporal punishment. He was frequently victimised – and men who feel victimised often go on to rape.

He was also very slim and small in stature, so found it hard to be taken seriously. In his fantasies he was king, but to the outside world he was a wimp.

Miserable, he began to eat sweets in vast quantities, a diet which played havoc with his already poor complexion. Awareness of his chronic acne made him stammer even more fiercely when he talked to girls. On the few occasions that he asked a girl to go out with him she always refused and he stored up more and more resentment. He also had panic attacks when asked a question in class by the teacher, and would break into a heavy sweat.

It's a safe bet that the youthful Robert often cried himself to sleep, his mind filled with thoughts of the other school kids' taunts, his body bruised from heavy blows by his father. He would later recall these incredibly painful years and admit that everyone regarded him as a freak. Criticised for his voice, his left-handedness, his facial appearance, his height and his schoolwork, he believed his father's frequent comments that he could do nothing right.

By high school he found that he excelled at particular solo pursuits such as hunting and fishing. Some boys would have been able to increase their self-esteem by nurturing this talent but for Robert Hansen it was too little too late. His fantasies now revolved around demeaning and hurting women, just as he himself had been demeaned and hurt all his life.

Photos of him taken at age 18 show a smartly dressed boy with very short hair, sticking out ears and a smile which doesn't reach his eyes. His invariably downcast expression would become more and more unhappy over the years.

Cheated by a prostitute

For a while after leaving school he continued to work in his father's bakery then joined the Army Reserves and did his basic training in New Jersey. Moved to New York, he and another soldier hired two prostitutes but as soon as Hansen ejaculated, the prostitute left with the cash. He felt angry, cheated and deeply unsatisfied – after all, this wasn't the control-based sex which dominated his increasingly cruel fantasies.

When his army training ended, Robert returned to working in his father's bakery, though he found himself an apartment. He also began to date a girl he'd met in church and he became a volunteer fireman in a desperate bid to gain the authority he craved. The 20-year-old was living the life his parents had mapped out for him, and he was overworked and constantly angry. Something had to give.

Arson and two marriages

He set fire to a barn which was used by his former school, this being a way to get back at the school superintendent who had disciplined him. Referring to the incident years later, he spoke of 'that monster that did Bob Hansen a personal wrong'. Superficially, it looked like an act of revenge but arson is often a tool of the sadist, who takes sexual pleasure from destroying property and thinking about the suffering this destruction will cause. Sadists often masturbate whilst watching the flames devour a building, and masturbate again later to the memory.

In March 1961, he was jailed for this destructive act but his mother paid his bail so that he could marry his girlfriend, after which he was sentenced to three years at the state reformatory. There, the young outsider spent his time preaching the gospel to other inmates, glad of a captive audience. He was paroled a year early in May 1963, but by then his first wife had been granted a divorce.

Ashamed of his arsonist son, Christian Hansen now relocated the family to Minnesota. There Robert met and married his second wife Gloria, who was also deeply religious. He found work in a bakery whilst she went to university. He loved oral sex but felt that he couldn't ask a good, religious woman to perform this act so he began to pay prostitutes for fellatio.

Soon desperate for other thrills, Hansen began to steal radios, athletic goods and clothes. Once the family's pastor spoke up for him and persuaded a store owner not to press charges. He was eventually arrested for stealing a sports ball, an item he could easily afford. These were clear signs of an anti-social personality, but his community continued to view him as a decent family man who had made one or two mistakes.

When Robert was 24, Gloria graduated from university and the couple decided to move to Alaska. There she became a teacher and he found work in yet another bakery. They again became active in the church and in 1971 had their first child, a girl. Meanwhile he revived his favourite hobby of hunting and began to win records for bagging the biggest Dall sheep and caribou.

Attempted rape

On 15 November 1971, Hansen was in his car at the traffic lights when he noticed that the girl in the adjacent vehicle was an attractive teenager. He followed her home and pretended that he was looking for someone else in her apartment block. They talked for a few minutes then he asked her out but she explained that she already had a fiancé. For the next few days Hansen fantasised about what he would like to do to the 18-year-old if he could get her completely alone.

Then he acted, ambushing her one night as she walked towards her apartment, holding a gun to her head and pushing her towards his car. Thankfully her screams alerted nearby residents who immediately called the police. They arrived quickly and found Hansen acting suspiciously in the vicinity. The traumatised victim identified him and he was taken into custody.

Back at police headquarters, Hansen reluctantly admitted that he might have held the young woman at gunpoint, adding that he'd had a blackout and still felt dizzy. He was charged with the crime of assault with a deadly weapon and given bail. A few days later the court ordered him to see a psychiatrist and return for sentencing in January.

Rape

Freed on bail, Robert Hansen committed his first known rape. On 19 December 1971, he intercepted an 18-year-old dancer as she got into her vehicle late at night in a cafeteria car park. He forced her into his car at gunpoint, hit her and tied her up, binding her wrists tightly behind her back. He hit her again then drove to a secluded location and ordered her to strip, which she did. After that he kissed and caressed her, before driving on to a highway inn. Leaving her tied to the inside door of the car, he booked accommodation. Unfortunately the nature of the building meant that he didn't have to walk past a reception desk, so was able to smuggle the victim directly to his room.

Inside the room, he raped her, often using the line, 'Try harder or I'll put you in the hospital.' It's telling that this is the kind of phrase an abusive parent will say to a child.

After the rape, Hansen ordered the dancer to dress then said that he was taking her to his cabin in the mountains. Fortunately for the teenager, they found the mountain road blocked with snow and, after driving around for a while, he got out his gun and told her to run. Aware that he was about to shoot her in the back, she begged for her life, explaining that she didn't want her baby to be left motherless. In turn, he said that he couldn't let her live because she'd go to the cops. Thinking fast, she gave him her identification, saying that now she couldn't report him because he knew where she lived. Satisfied, he drove her back to the area where he'd abducted her.

Many years later, Hansen would tell the authorities that he'd raped over 30 such women and let them go. He claimed that most were prostitutes and that he told them he had connections and could have them arrested for soliciting. He said that if they gave him free sex he'd let them go without harming them, but that if they still demanded money he took their lives. This is unlikely – he only let the 18-year-old dancer (who wasn't a prostitute) go because he found the road to his cabin impassable and because he'd terrorised her into keeping quiet.

A local murder

The teenager initially kept her word and didn't report the kidnapping and rape to the police – but three days later she read that a young woman named Celia VanZamen had been abducted, partially stripped and had her hands tied behind her back. Her assailant had thrown her into a ravine where she'd died of exposure. (Hansen was never formally linked to this death.)

The girl now reported the rape, and Hansen was arrested with her name and address still in his wallet. In court, the defence tried to suggest that she wasn't a reliable witness because she was a dancer who'd had a child out of wedlock. In contrast, they painted Robert Hansen as a devoted family man – and his pastor said that he was a peaceable man with a good reputation and that he wouldn't feel threatened if Hansen was released. He said that he was convinced his parishioner was innocent.

The jury were unconvinced and on 26 January 1972 they indicted Hansen for kidnapping, rape and assault with a deadly weapon. He was remanded in custody at the South Central Regional Correctional Facility in Anchorage.

At the plea-bargaining stage, the case involving the teenage dancer was dismissed but Hansen pleaded guilty to holding a gun to his previous teenage victim's head in November. His defence team pointed out that he'd now been diagnosed as schizophrenic but was considered treatable. He was sentenced to five years in jail, with the recommendation that he soon be given work release. Three months later he was transferred to a halfway house and began working in the community, with his wife driving him to work and back.

But he was such a model prisoner that he was soon allowed to drive himself every morning and would park on Fourth Avenue to watch the prostitutes. He knew that one day he'd have the chance to abduct and rape another of these girls.

By the end of 1972 his cruel dream was closer to becoming a reality since he was now allowed to live at home, though he still had to have psychiatric treatment twice a week. He bought a boat, took his wife fishing and learned to scuba dive. But his need for sadistic and control-based sex built and built, so he was delighted at the start of July 1973 when his wife said that she was taking their baby daughter to see her grandparents, and that she'd be out of town for several days.

It's probably no coincidence that three days later – on 7 July 1973 – 17-year-old Megan Emerick went into town and was never seen again.

Forced fellatio

The following year, Hansen offered a 16-year-old girl a lift. He seemed unthreatening so she got into his car, but he was soon questioning her about her sex drive. When she tried to get out of the vehicle, he produced his gun and ordered her to strip. She obeyed him, after which he demanded fellatio and humiliated her further by making her flash her breasts at a passing motorist. He sexually assaulted her again and again over the next few hours then handed her his gun and said that she could shoot him or make him drive to the police station at gunpoint. Thankfully she refused his offer – it's most likely that the gun wasn't loaded and he wanted an excuse to commit further sadistic acts on her or even take her life. He warned her not to tell the police and she kept her word for many years.

Another woman goes missing

Many months passed and it was July 1975 before Hansen committed a murder that he would later admit to. 23-year-old Mary Thill got a lift from friends to Seward, then promptly disappeared. Her distraught husband put up a $1,000 reward asking for clues to her whereabouts but no one – except the predatory Robert Christian Hansen – knew where she was. Hansen later brought detectives to an area along Resurrection Bay where he'd buried her body, but it was never found.

Another rape

In late summer 1975, Hansen travelled to Oregon for a few weeks to play the dutiful son. But by October his need for control had resurfaced so he returned to Alaska and propositioned a dancer. She agreed to party in his car, but when she entered the vehicle he grabbed her by the hair, pulled it brutally backwards and put his gun to her head. When she was acquiescent, he drove to a secluded location and raped her, making it clear with his body language, voice tone and pistol that he was in charge. She was able to identify Hansen from police photographs but chose not to press charges as she was a respected schoolteacher moonlighting as a dancer. And when Hansen was confronted by his parole officer, he said it was a date and that when he refused to give her money she cried rape. He would later tell detectives he felt prostitutes were 'even lower than he was' and he believed that no one cared about their fate.

A second child

That year Robert's wife gave him a second child, a son, and he took on a second job in order to fund his growing family. But he felt bored and began to steal frequently for thrills – he would later tell a psychologist that he got an erection whenever he stole. (British serial killer Archibald Thompson Hall, who killed with accomplice Michael Kitto, had the same sexual response to stealing expensive jewellery.) When Hansen was caught stealing a chainsaw, he was indicted for larceny.

Deciding to pursue a psychological defence, Hansen returned to a psychologist he'd seen earlier, Dr Allen Parker, but he didn't like Dr Parker's perceptive evaluation of him. The doctor wrote that Hansen was 'markedly disturbed, somewhat antisocial, paranoid by nature and with a relatively weak ego. There are indications of severe heterosexual conflict, both with a desire for women and a fear that he will not be able to relate to them. He is capable of acting out impulses. He has a great deal of free-floating anxiety.'

Meanwhile another doctor diagnosed him as bipolar, suggesting that the kleptomania formed part of his illness. He was prescribed the tranquilliser Thorazine, but this affected his ability to work so it was changed to lithium. This doctor thought that Hansen might stabilise if he remained on the drug, but added that he'd be capable of committing crimes when in the manic phase of his illness. And his probation officer noted that he'd often seen his client hanging around dance clubs and that he'd urged him to return to counselling, but Robert Hansen had replied that he didn't need help.

Hansen now made a statement to the court, saying that the lithium had rid him of his stutter and that as a result his self-esteem had rocketed. He added that his family needed his financial support, and cast himself as a victim rather than a criminal.

In turn, the judge sentenced him to five years and ordered that he have psychiatric treatment. Unfortunately this length of sentence had to be served at the Juneau Correctional Institute which had no psychiatric facilities. So the judge added that after two years Hansen could be transferred to the Eagle River Correctional Facility which did have a rehabilitation suite.

Hansen's family must have had mixed feelings about his arrest. On the plus side, he never hit his children but he was sometimes emotionally abusive towards them and towards his wife.

An abducted victim escapes

In 1978, Hansen was released early from prison and returned to his wife and children. He immediately resumed his shooting hobby, killing foxes, coyotes and wolves, with other hunters noticing how deeply he loved the thrill of the chase. He bought himself a Ruger, a semi-automatic which could fire off several shots in quick succession and which he'd eventually use to shoot his human prey.

Hansen chartered a small plane (though he would never hold a pilot's licence) and began to shoot at animals whilst airborne. For a year, this form of killing seemed enough to sustain him, then he went on the hunt for a girl to sadistically rape.

In October 1979, he went to a dancing club and asked one of the dancers to meet him outside for oral sex. When she got into his camper, he grabbed her hair and pulled it tightly, momentarily disconcerted when her wig came off in his hands. Then he stripped her naked and cruelly bound her wrists with wire before throwing her into the back of the van. Realising that further torture was sure to follow, she managed to free herself moments after he began to drive into the wilderness. Promptly locking the camper's back door, she began to scream hysterically.

Afraid that someone would hear, Hansen parked the van and broke the window to get to her. She then jumped through the broken glass and raced, naked, down the street with Hansen in hot pursuit. Fortunately he couldn't keep up and she escaped. The traumatised woman went to the police and gave them full details of her ordeal but she was unable to identify her assailant from photographs. (Years later, when he decided to tell the FBI everything, Hansen would admit to this crime.)

Eklutna Annie's murder

Later that autumn the increasingly sadistic Hansen picked up a young girl in downtown Anchorage, who agreed to have sex with him for money. He was on his way to Eklutna Road to hunt bear. At some stage Hansen offered to drive the girl home, then took off in a different direction. When the woman protested, he pulled his gun on her. He drove towards Eklutna Lake but became stuck in the mud and she had to help him winch his vehicle. After the truck was freed, she started to head off at speed into the woods. Hansen raced after her and grabbed her by the hair and she began to plead for her life, then produced a large knife to defend herself with. Hansen grabbed the knife and forced her to the ground. When she was lying on her stomach he stabbed her in the back then buried her in a shallow grave. She was never identified so the authorities named her Eklutna Annie after the area in which she'd been killed.

Shortly after this, Hansen was drinking beer in a club when the girl whom he'd previously abducted in his camper van recognised him and called the police. But the police decided that he was a respectable family man who'd had a momentary weakness with a prostitute so he wasn't charged.

Joanne's murder

Hansen liked to see a girl struggle in her bonds – but he was enraged when she fought back, and for any girl who did her death was almost assured. This allegedly happened in May 1980 when he took unemployed Joanne Messina out for a meal. He'd later state that the attractive brunette offered sex for money and that this triggered his rage – but sadists are experts at blaming other people for their cruel acts.

Hansen drove her along Seward Highway towards Snow River, but she realised that he was taking her into the wilderness so jumped out of the camper van. He told detectives that he pursued and battered her, whereupon she fought back and he shot her twice in the head with his .22 Magnum revolver then shot dead her German Shepherd dog. In reality, it's more likely that he shot the dog first to make sure that it couldn't defend its owner. He would also have enjoyed seeing Joanne's terror at the demise of her pet. We'll never know exactly what Robert Hansen did to the unfortunate young woman, but he eventually buried her in a shallow grave and threw the dog's body into the woods and when Joanne's corpse was found two months later it had been half eaten by bears.

Hansen often gave the impression that his victims had escaped – and had to be shot dead – before he had a chance to torture them, but bandages found in some of the graves suggested otherwise. They had either been used to tether the victim's wrists and ankles, or else had stemmed the blood after the girl had been tortured, perhaps by being nicked numerous times with a knife. It's likely that some of the girls were also violated with implements, as sadists enjoy causing such vaginal and anal trauma – and we know that Hansen's last victim, who eventually escaped, had a hammer thrust into her.

Roxanne's murder

The following month, the baker was ready to kill again. This time he made a date with 24-year-old Roxanne Easland, who sometimes used the name Karen Baunsgarden. Hansen took the small dancer to his favourite bear-hunting location deep in the Alaskan woods. The authorities would later surmise that he bound and tortured the girl (and many of his other victims) in his cabin for several days, until his rage-fuelled lust was sated or he had to return to his family and his job. Hansen lost his stutter once he had control of a girl and he enjoyed telling her that he was going to kill her, making her beg for her life.

Lisa's murder

He struck again in September of that year, this time targeting a petite long-haired brunette called Lisa Furrell. She was a dancer who looked much younger than her 42 years. Lisa was very maternal towards younger dancers who arrived in Alaska and was respected and well liked. Hansen bought Lisa a drink then stayed to watch her dance. After her shift ended, he met her outside.

Like most of the other victims, she was abducted at knifepoint, handcuffed and gagged then flown by Hansen into the Alaskan wilderness. Once she was safely trussed up in his cabin, he would have carried out his favourite atrocities – the police would later find that his possessions included laces to bind victims as well as gags made from bandages, metal cuffs and chains. He eventually shot the woman dead and buried her close to Knik Bridge, one of his preferred burial sites.

Missing

The following year, in February 1981, three more dancers were reported missing, all of whom worked at bars which Hansen frequented. By now he was sometimes wearing false beards and moustaches to avoid being recognised by dancers whom he'd tied up and raped. But no one paid much attention to the small, slim acne-scarred man with the hang dog expression. They only noticed him when he introduced himself as a doctor or photographer and offered them several hundred dollars for a date or photo session…

Malai's murder

In June 1981, he probably offered money to 28-year-old dancer Malai Larsen who didn't enjoy working in the Alaskan bars and was homesick for her native Thailand. She'd found, as other dancers had, that the dance bars kept a large percentage of her earnings so it was hard to save enough for her passage home. Hansen arranged to meet her, flew her to his cabin and repeatedly carried out his depraved fantasies before burying her alongside the Knik River.

Sherry's murder

Five months later, on 17 November 1981, the hunter claimed another victim. This time Hansen told his prey, 23-year-old

Sherry Morrow, that he was a photographer. The shy blonde dancer agreed to meet him at a café and go on to a studio where she'd pose for him for 300 dollars. Hansen met her in the car park, invited her into his vehicle then held her at gunpoint. He blindfolded her with a bandage, stripped her, handcuffed her hands behind her back then drove to an isolated stretch of the riverbank. We'll never know exactly what happened next, but, according to Hansen, she went mad, kicking him so hard on the legs that she left bruises. He said that he then shot her twice with his Ruger then buried her naked body in a sandy grave.

But would a naked, gagged and blindfolded victim have been able to kick effectively at her assailant? And, even if she did, why would he immediately shoot her dead given that his fantasies involved torture and rape?

Stories like this suit the sadist, who is usually desperate to hide the worst of his excesses from the authorities. According to predators like Hansen, the victim invariably dies quickly before any form of torture can be carried out. In reality, he would have worked hard to keep her quiet and tied up whilst he escorted her to his safe place.

In September 1982, Sherry's remains were found by two off-duty policemen who were out hunting moose. A bandage appeared to have been wrapped all around her head so it's possible that Hansen was using it as a blindfold as well as a gag.

The police later discovered her necklace amongst the souvenirs he'd taken from his murder victims, a trophy he'd have masturbated over again and again.

Andrea's murder

A fortnight later he was ready to carry out another torture-murder. This time he promised to take dancer Andrea Altiery on a shopping spree. The 23-year-old got into Hansen's car, only to be handcuffed, blindfolded and warned to do exactly what she was told. He drove her to an isolated area alongside Knik River (probably tying her up in the meat shack which he often used as a safe house) and forced her to fellate him whilst he held a Browning automatic pistol to her head. Again, we will never know what torments followed but, according to Hansen's sanitised account, she grabbed the gun and tried to shoot him so he immediately killed her in self-defence. In truth, she may have been one of the victims who were stripped naked, tortured and then told to run, sadistically hunted and eventually shot dead. Some criminologists believe that Hansen hunted several of the girls in this way, some on the ground and some from his plane – he had even been seen practising by shooting at ice floats from his aerial vantage point. But other crime writers think he only killed one in this way, shooting the others at much closer range.

Self-employment

Throughout his murder spree Hansen had been working for a supermarket bakery but now he opened his own store, financing it from a fraudulent insurance claim. The business was hugely successful from the start, allowing Hansen to stop renting other people's aeroplanes and buy his own, a Super Cub. He lovingly customised it, just as other serial killers have customised their torture vans. Hansen put tundra tires on his plane so that he could land in remote swampy locations and took out the rear seat so that he could tie up his handcuffed victims in the back.

Sue's murder

For the first few months of 1982, Hansen was possibly busy with his new business and aeroplane but he was definitely back at the dancing bars by May 1982. There he saw 23-year-old Sue Luna, a dancer, and introduced himself as a photographer who wanted to take pictures of her. Like most dancers, Sue needed the money so arranged to meet him at a café for breakfast the following day. The café owner saw Sue eat part of her breakfast then go out to meet a man wearing glasses. He gave her the money for her meal and she handed it in to the staff then walked out to his car.

Sue was taken to Knik River, stripped, abused and eventually hunted before being shot dead. Hansen would later identify her from photographs.

Sue's sister was so concerned that she placed an advert in the paper asking for information of her whereabouts – and when Hansen saw this, he was deeply perturbed. He'd assumed that no one cared about the victims but now someone was asking questions and the café staff might identify him. Determined to regain control, he phoned Sue's sister and stutteringly said that Sue had gone off with a black man. He asked her to meet him but she sensibly refused, a move which doubtless saved her life.

Sue's best friend Reva later left a tribute to her on a memorial website for murder victims, describing her as someone with 'a zest for life and a deep love of people' who loved to laugh.

Tami's murder

Three months after Sue Luna's murder, Hansen offered pretty Tamara Pederson $300 for a photo session. The talented dancer, known as Tami, lived with her boyfriend and was in love with him. Her wages were low so she was understandably keen to make legitimate cash.

Robert Hansen took her in his plane to his safe house and satisfied his cruel urges before burying her one and a half miles from the old Knik Bridge.

When Tami's divorced parents were told that she was missing, they searched tirelessly for her to no avail, even talking to some intimidating dance bar owners who were allegedly connected to organised crime.

Burglary

Meanwhile Hansen's need for thrills continued unabated, and he began to burglarise the cabins on Hawk Lake, loading radios and cassette players into his aeroplane and transporting them to his bakery. But soon he reverted to his preferred type of thrill…

Angela's murder

In February 1983, he approached 24-year-old brunette Angela Feddern on Fourth Avenue. Angela was a dancer who occasionally supplemented her income by prostituting herself. She got chatting to Hansen and agreed to meet him for one of his infamous $300 lunches. She told a colleague that he was ugly but rich. Angela doubtless also received the bondage and gagging treatment before Hansen carried out his brutal sexual fantasies. But no amount of bondage, torture or rape could make him feel important in the long term, so he had to repeat these controlling acts before shooting her and burying her naked body at Figure Eight Lake.

Tereasa's murder

The following month – on 25 March 1983 – he struck up a conversation with Tereasa Watson (known as Nicolle, her middle name) and offered her $300 to have lunch and spend some time with him. She told her flatmate that he seemed nice and took off for the restaurant.

She, too, was flown to the wilderness and abused repeatedly before being shot. But the ground was frozen solid and Robert Hansen found it impossible to dig even a shallow grave. Defeated, he left her body outdoors on the Kenai Peninsula where it was half eaten by animals.

DeLynn's murder

In early April he murdered again, abducting 20-year-old DeLynn Frey and flying her into the Alaskan woods where she was presumably raped and tortured before being buried at Horseshoe Lake. Again, the cruelty only satisfied him for a few days before he had the urge to kill again.

Paula's murder

Later that same month – on 24 April 1983 – Hansen visited a bar where the women danced naked. He approached the newest dancer, Paula Goulding, and asked her for a date. Paula had found it difficult to make ends meet whilst working as a secretary and had been lured to Alaska's tenderloin district by the talk of good wages and large tips. Hansen's stammer and cleancut look made him seem a safe bet and she tentatively accepted, so just before midnight they went for a drive in his car.

She relaxed in the vehicle as he drove into a quiet car park, and was taken completely by surprise when he grabbed hold of her hair and held a gun to her head. He warned her to do exactly as she was told, then handcuffed her arms behind her back, driving her to the airport where he kept his plane.

He flew Paula to a wooded area beside Knik River and pulled her into a meat shack used by hunters. There, he handcuffed her hands behind her back around a long post. From what we know of sadists, she would have been extensively tortured in this safe house – but according to Hansen he now uncuffed her and she slapped him and fled. He said that he immediately picked up his rifle, took aim at the fleeing woman, and shot her through the heart. But the authorities believe that he abused each woman repeatedly until he eventually tired of them.

During this particular abduction, Hansen didn't have a spade with him, so he dug a shallow grave with a ragged piece of wood and dumped Paula in it. Her skeleton wasn't discovered until 2 September that year.

The suitor

Finding victims through the dancing bars was becoming more difficult. For one thing, many bars were closing down as the area was becoming less prosperous. Second, he was using them so often that he was afraid of being recognised, even though he was still in disguise. So now – less than a fortnight after murdering Paula Goulding – Hansen placed a singles ad, describing himself as a lover of the outdoors who yearned for a sincere relationship. He conveniently forgot to mention that he had a wife, a 12-year-old daughter and an eight-year-old son...

Keen to temporarily free himself of his incumbents, Hansen arranged for his family to enjoy a European vacation. They left to visit friends in Austria and he now had the house to himself. He began to meet the respondents to his advertisement, taking them for coffee or for dinner. Some of those relationships progressed as far as several dates, and one woman even took flying lessons in his plane.

All of these women had ex-husbands, grown children or friends who had an interest in their welfare so Hansen didn't sexually assault them and the relationships just naturally drifted to an end. Realising that these weren't suitable victims, Hansen returned to the streets for likely prey.

A torture victim escapes

On 13 June 1983, he went cruising and eventually saw 17-year-old prostitute Cindy Paulson. He negotiated the price of fellatio, and she got into the car and began to pleasure him, but suddenly he produced his gun and cuffed her then drove swiftly to his house. There, Hansen handcuffed her to a sturdy pillar. He also chained her to it around her neck before sodomising and raping her, clearly turned on by her screams. But for sadists like Hansen, the real pleasure comes in inflicting maximum pain and sexual mutilation so he bit viciously at her nipples, forced a hammer deep into her vagina, raped her again and left her chained to the support.

When she told him that she had to urinate, he fetched a towel and told her to empty her bladder onto it, enjoying her evident humiliation. He left her chained up in a standing position overnight – a stance which can lead to a victim dying of exhaustion – and raped her again in the early hours. Then he unshackled her, leaving her wrists handcuffed, and took her out to his car, explaining that he was going to fly her to his cabin for a week.

Realising that his sadism would increase when he had her in a remote setting, Cindy waited until they reached the airfield then fled. Barefoot and bleeding with her hands still cuffed in front of her, she ran in front of a car and begged the driver for help. It was 5 a.m.

Noting that his victim had found help, Robert Hansen raced back to his house and cleaned away the traces of Cindy's captivity. Then he phoned a business acquaintance and said that he'd picked up a prostitute who was now claiming she'd been raped. Would his friend give him an alibi for the night in question? The acquaintance unthinkingly agreed.

Meanwhile, the police interviewed Cindy Paulson and she was able to give a clear description of the man who had abducted and raped her. She also gave the name of the street where he lived and described the moose heads and other animal trophies mounted on the walls. She even gave them the colours of his plane, a blue and white Super Cub.

A search of Hansen's home revealed a hidden cache of weapons in the basement but it didn't include the rifle that Cindy claimed she'd been threatened with. Some of the police believed her, but others thought she'd simply had an argument with a punter over how much she was to be paid.

She was taken to hospital, where medics found a tampon pushed high into her vagina which was saturated with semen. There were also marks on her neck and abrasions on her wrists where she'd pulled desperately at the metal cuffs.

The following day she quickly picked Hansen out of a photo line-up. The police interviewed him, but he'd now persuaded a second business acquaintance to back up his false alibi. These alibis, combined with the fact that there was no forensic proof that Cindy Paulson had been in his house, made the authorities decide not to arrest the man. Yet they could have charged him with unlawfully keeping weapons, as it's a felony for a criminal to possess a handgun, and Hansen had convictions for assault with a deadly weapon, felony theft and arson in his distant past.

The officer concluded that Hansen was a family man and successful businessman whereas the complainant was a prostitute. The case was closed.

The net closes in

Later that summer, Robert Hansen's wife and children returned from Europe and he again played the role of the happy family man. That August, his father died of a heart attack and he inherited his gun collection, adding it to his already sizeable collection of hidden weaponry.

But by now the police had found the bodies of many of the murdered dancers and knew that others were missing. Several of them remembered Robert Hansen's abduction of Cindy Paulson and recalled that he'd previously held a gun to an 18-

year-old's head and attempted to abduct her. They knew that he also had a record for arson and theft.

A profile

Keen for confirmation that they were on the right track, they asked the FBI for a profile of the murderer. Profiler John Douglas told them that the man was a sadistic thrill killer who probably had a stutter. He'd be around 40, have suffered rejection in childhood and would have a record for arson and/ or shoplifting.

The police were amazed that Douglas had identified that the man had a stutter, but the FBI agent was simply working on the basis of statistics. Numerous murderers have had speech defects. Christopher Wilder, profiled in this book, had a slight lisp as did the Son of Sam killer. David Carpenter aka The Trailside Killer had a stutter as did prostitute-killer Joel Rifkin. And serial killer Charles Starkweather, who was terrified of his father, frequently stammered as a child.

The police told John Douglas that they had a suspect who fitted the profile perfectly but that he had an alibi for the abduction of Cindy Paulson. Douglas suggested that the police tell Hansen's acquaintances that they'd be in serious legal trouble if they were lying and continued to lie. Both men now shamefacedly admitted that they hadn't been with him on the night in question. It was time to bring the suspect in.

Arrest

Early on the morning of 27 October 1983, the police staked out Hansen's bakery and arrested him. Still maintaining his good guy act, he surrendered without a fight – he didn't even ask what crime they were charging him with.

They read him his rights and started the five-hour interview. Meanwhile officers with a warrant searched his home. Hidden behind the headboard of his bed they found an aviation map with over 24 marks on it, each believed to represent a spot where Hansen had murdered. The FBI were convinced that he'd masturbated frequently whilst looking at the map and thinking about what he'd done to the bondaged girls. They also found a Ruger, a Magnum and evidence that Hansen owned another three guns. More damningly, the business card of the murdered DeLynn Frey was found alongside other women's ID hidden in his garage and some of the victims' jewellery was found concealed in the attic insulation.

Asked about the abduction attempt of the 18-year-old in 1971, he admitted that he'd pulled a gun on her, stating that his desperately unhappy childhood had left him with an uncontrollable rage. He also admitted paying for the services of numerous prostitutes, but denied forcing anyone to commit sexual acts. Shown photos of the murdered dancers Sherry Morrow and Paula Goulding, he denied knowing them.

The interviewer pretended to empathise with the sadistic killer, telling him that he understood what it was like to be rejected by girls – and that Robert probably felt he was merely turning the tables around when he got out the wires, handcuffs, laces and chains. But Hansen continued to deny any wrongdoing and eventually asked for an attorney. The police had been hoping for a full confession and were dismayed that he'd chosen to lawyer up.

Kidnapping charges

On 3 November 1983, he was indicted for assault and kidnapping, five counts of illegal possession of a handgun, theft and insurance fraud. He entered a not guilty plea and was remanded in custody. Recognising that she was a completely innocent victim, the Anchorage community pledged their support for Hansen's shellshocked wife. As further details of her husband's crimes emerged, she took the children to Arizona to protect them from the truth.

Meanwhile the authorities were finding that the marks on Hansen's aviation map identified the known grave sites of Joanne Messina, Eklutna Annie, Sherry Morrow and Paula Goulding. The extractor marks on the bullets used to kill Paula and Sherry matched those produced by Hansen's Ruger – and a witness identified Hansen as the man she'd seen with Sherry on the day she went missing after meeting someone at a café, and a necklace found in his attic was identified as belonging to the murdered Andrea Altiery.

Seventeen of the marks indicated further potential graves – but the harshness of the winter made digging impossible till the following spring.

Confession

As the weeks passed, the prosecution built their case against Hansen, locating further witnesses who'd seen him with the dancers just before they disappeared and finding more of the victim's possessions hidden in his attic. He recognised that he was going to be found guilty and sent to the notorious maximum security prison at Marion, Illinois, so did a deal with the District Attorney – he'd confess if he could be sent to a less violent prison.

On 23 February 1984, he admitted killing Sherry Morrow, Paula Goulding, Eklutna Annie, Joanne Messina and a woman who the DA suspected was Andrea Altiery. He'd kept her fish necklace in his extensive trophy collection, a one-off design which her friends immediately recognised. He also recognised a photograph of Sue Luna, and one of Tami Pederson and pointed out the latter's grave site. And he told them about a black woman he'd murdered at Summit Lake in 1978. Shown his aviation map, he identified a total of 11 grave sites, admitting that the passage of time had dimmed his memory of which victims inhabited the other graves.

Taken out in a police helicopter, Hansen identified some of the burial sites from the air. When the helicopter landed, the handcuffed man took them to the sites where he actually tore at the snow with his hands in an effort to unearth the bodies. He was flushed and smiling, and it was clear to the troopers that he was aroused. He also admitted to more than 30 rapes spanning 12 years.

Trial

Brought before Superior Court Judge Ralph E. Moody, Hansen pleaded guilty to four homicides – Goulding, Morrow, Annie and Messina – and acknowledged his commission of 13 other homicides. (It's common for serial killers to only be charged with a few of their murders; the ones which are simplest for the prosecution to prove.) The Assistant District Attorney told the court that Robert Hansen had enjoyed terrorising and repeatedly raping the women then setting them free naked in the woods and hunting them down as if they were deer. The authorities also suspected that he'd shot some of them from his plane as they ran through the Alaskan wilderness in a desperate search for sanctuary. The defence didn't give a statement, as Hansen wished them to remain silent and when asked if he wanted to make a statement he replied that he did not. As a result, the entire trial lasted a mere two and a half hours.

The judge noted, 'This gentleman has been known to us for several years, yet we've turned him loose several times knowing that he had the potential to kill.' He sentenced the serial killer to 460 years plus life without the possibility of parole, whereupon Hansen was transferred to the maximum security prison at Lewisburn, Pennsylvania.

Body search

That spring, Alaskan State Troopers began the search for the remaining bodies. On the first day they found the remains of Sue Luna and Malai Larsen beside Knik River. On the second day they found a Jane Doe by Horseshoe Lake. Day three yielded the jawbone of Angela Feddern by Figure Eight Lake: animals had eaten the rest of her corpse. Day six resulted in the recovery of Tami Pederson's body on an island in the middle of Knik River, and a week later Lisa Furrell's remains were found in a shallow grave south of Knik Bridge. A week after that, the body of Tereasa Watson was recovered at South Lake, partially eaten by animals. Added to the four bodies that had previously been located before Hansen was sentenced, this brought the total to 11.

In 1985 a pilot landed on a sandbar on Knik River and found the body of DeLynn Frey, the last of Hansen's victims to be reported missing. But detectives believed he'd bound and killed at least 18 girls, one more than he admitted to. That estimate was later revised to more than 30 sexually motivated kills. John Douglas of the FBI commented that Hansen might have started killing in his twenties and that 'there were probably victims he wasn't proud of… ones who weren't prostitutes or perhaps very young'. The other bodies had doubtless been eaten by animals and the bones scattered far and wide.

Divorce

Robert Hansen's wife now divorced him. Hansen himself had urged her to do this, afraid that some of the murder victims' boyfriends would seek vengeance on his family. He told detectives that his wife didn't deserve to have any problems, but seemed to repress the fact that the victims and their families had also done nothing wrong yet received a wealth of pain.

The great escape

Robert Hansen served the first two years of his life sentence at Lewisburn, Pennsylvania but he was threatened numerous times by other prisoners so in 1986 was moved to Oak Park Heights prison in Minnesota where he could spend less time with the rest of the prison populace. When that prison became overcrowded in 1988 he was transferred to Lemon Creek prison at Juneau, spending the first year under special protective custody. Thereafter he was given work as a prison clerk.

The prison perceived him as a model prisoner until they found his escape plan, consisting of aeronautical charts, letters to a boat salesman and features about plastic explosives and airline safety. The authorities feared that he intended to escape by private plane then transfer to a boat. They also wondered if he meant to blow up a commercial aircraft as a way of getting back at the world, a common sadistic fantasy.

Hansen was immediately moved to Cook Inlet prison in Anchorage then transferred to Seward's new maximum security prison, the Spring Creek Correctional Center, where he was initially only let out of his cell for three hours a day.

In July 2003, a Las Vegas video company told a local TV station that they were organising hunts where paying customers could stalk and shoot paintballs at naked women. Perhaps remembering Hansen's homicidal hunting, numerous members of the public phoned in to complain. But the company had apparently invented the hunts in order to play a prank on the TV station – only to find themselves inundated with calls from men, and a few women, eager to pay up to $10,000 to hunt naked female prey.

That same year, Alaskan State Troopers appealed to the public to help them find the identity of Hansen's Jane Doe, the victim given the moniker Eklutna Annie. They described her as a white brunette in her twenties dressed in jeans, a brown leather jacket, a sleeveless knitted top and reddish-brown high-heeled boots.

Now in his late sixties, Robert Christian Hansen is still incarcerated at Spring Creek which is heavily guarded, the 500 inmates watched over by more than 200 corrections officers. He writes humorous short stories and it's rumoured that he's also written his autobiography. He will eventually die in jail.

CHAPTER ELEVEN

JOHN JOSEPH JOUBERT

John Joubert was only 20 when he killed three boys and tried to abduct a woman. The young scoutmaster's boyish face hid his cruel sexual fantasies.

Formative experiences

John was born on 2 July 1963 to Beverly and Jack Joubert, who went on three years later to have a daughter. The family lived in Lawrence, Massachusetts, and ran a diner there for many years. When it failed, Jack found other work in the catering world and Beverly became a bookkeeper. The children were often left with a pretty young babysitter whose mother was Beverly's friend.

The three women would constantly criticise Jack Joubert in his absence, as they saw him as a weak man and a low achiever. And when they were together, the couple argued all the time. John would become very upset at witnessing these shouting matches and begged his parents to be nice to one another. But the discord escalated and by the time he was six years old, his mother had demoted his father to sleeping on the settee.

John began to fantasise about finding the babysitter dead and cannibalising her body because he thought that if she disappeared his parents would stop their endless arguing. Later these fantasies crystallised so that he was the one killing her.

Though he had an IQ of 123, which is university entrance level, he didn't do particularly well at school because he was so unhappy. He didn't go to any of the extracurricular activities, keeping more and more to himself.

Divorce

When John was eight his mother left his father and moved him and his sister into a dilapidated apartment. She forbade him to see his father, whom he loved and who lived just across the street. It was one of many rules in the Joubert house – John wasn't allowed to watch the same television programmes as his fellow pupils and this, coupled with his shyness, ensured that he quickly became an outsider figure at school.

In 1974, his mother moved the family to Portland, Maine. He begged to live with his father, who'd now remarried, but his deeply religious mother declined: she eventually wanted him to go to an exclusive boy's Catholic secondary school in the area so that he'd have an even stronger grounding in her beliefs.

At 11 he saw detective magazines in the local grocers which showed frightened women in bondage and he began to fantasise about tying women up and hurting them. Later John began to feel attracted to other boys, but his upbringing forbade this so he quickly repressed his desires. Many of society's most vicious sadists are in conflict over their sexuality.

One day a schoolmate asked John if he was gay, and thinking that this meant happy, he answered yes. He consequently became the laughing stock of the playground. It also made it harder for him to approach the one girl he would later claim that he was attracted to.

Realising that he'd never fit in at school, John joined the Boy Scouts and began to earn merit badges. Outwardly he looked like a pleasant – if unhealthily conservative – youth, but inwardly he fantasised about tying people up and torturing them. He masturbated several times a day to these fantasies, eventually working up the nerve to act them out.

Teenage cruelty

On a cold afternoon in October 1979, the 16-year-old grabbed hold of an eight-year-old boy in nearby Oakdale and attempted to strangle him. Thankfully the child struggled so hard that he managed to break free.

The following month Joubert approached a girl of a similar age. She was friendly and her lack of apprehension disturbed him. After all, he wanted victims who were visibly in awe of him and whom he could immediately dominate. Shaken, he failed to carry out his planned attack, instead returning to the comfort of his sadistic fantasies.

In December he struck again, cycling past a ten-year-old girl and stabbing her in the back with a pencil, breaking the lead and leaving some of it embedded in her flesh. He cycled home and masturbated compulsively to the memory of her screams.

But it was in the following January that he upped the ante, stabbing a young student on her way to an evening class. Though seriously injured, she survived.

Later that week Joubert was briefly questioned by officers who were talking to everyone in the vicinity, but his innocent expression and slender build doubtless helped them decide that he wasn't a sadistic fiend.

Two months later he stabbed a nine-year-old boy in the throat, leaving him with a wound which required 12 stitches. By now police had stepped up the hunt for the Oakdale Slasher and Joubert decided to keep a low profile for a while.

College

He started college and for the first time in his life had a little fun, tasting his first alcoholic drink and sampling marijuana.

He also began to play Dungeons and Dragons (a role-playing game where players become powerful characters) and became very good at it. Unfortunately he failed to devote a similar number of hours to his studies and dropped out at the end of his first year, soon spending hours hanging about the house and becoming increasingly melancholy. His mother understandably wasn't prepared to support him forever and demanded that he find work. Such altercations are often pivotal in a sadist's life: unable to cope and angry at key authority figures, he decides to make someone else feel even worse…

The first murder

Determined to hurt and demean another human being, he cycled along a path called Back Cove, near central Portland, an area of the city he often frequented. It was early in the evening of 22 August 1982. Espying 11-year-old Ricky Stetson out jogging, he began to follow him. Several people saw the teenager cycling behind the 11-year-old boy, but they thought nothing of it. They had no way of knowing that Joubert was a 19-year-old sadist with repressed homosexual desires.

His excitement mounting, Joubert overpowered the child in a quiet area of the cove and strangled him manually and with a ligature before stabbing him several times in the chest. He also bit the boy on his calf, probably chewing and swallowing the flesh just as he'd done in his fantasies when cannibalising his babysitter. Finally, he interfered with Ricky's clothing so that his underpants were visible. Then, remembering that the bite-marks on the child's flesh could be traced back to him, he gouged the marks out with his knife. But some traces of his toothmarks remained, which would later link him to the child's torture-death.

SADISTIC KILLERS

Air force

Perhaps Joubert wanted to escape the area of the murder, or maybe he just wanted to get away from home. Whatever his motivation, he now joined the air force and was soon sent 1,500 miles across country to Nebraska. It was the new start he craved.

He quickly made friends with another cadet and for his first few weeks he was very happy, but there were rumours that Joubert was gay and his best friend backed off, afraid of being seen as homosexual too.

Lonely again, John applied for the job of assistant master with the Boy Scouts and was accepted. He now had access to dozens of young boys. He became close friends with one boy and often played Dungeons and Dragons with him, though Joubert insisted on always taking the Dungeon Master role.

The second murder

But fantasising about being dominant wasn't enough and on Sunday 18 September 1983 he stalked 13-year-old Danny Joe Eberle who was beginning his usual early morning paper round. Joubert threatened the boy with a knife, then bound his hands behind his back and gagged him with surgical tape. Dumping him in the boot of his car, he drove to a quiet field where he laid the boy in a ditch.

The young airman now untied the boy and ordered him to undress down to his underwear. When he'd done so, the sadist retied him again. He then tortured the boy with his knife, stabbing him five times in the back and four times in the front. He also sliced into his neck. His victim was probably dead or in shock by the time the teenage sadist began biting at his legs and shoulder. He then carved a chunk out of the boy's left leg to remove the indentation left by his teeth.

Within days police found Danny's butchered and bondaged corpse, the crucifix he always wore still wrapped around his wounded neck. The FBI would later comment that the boy had been hog-tied and that this doubtless formed part of the sadist's fantasy. (In fact it figures in many criminal and recreational sexual fantasies and there is at least one American bondage magazine that's entirely devoted to it.)

They found that the rope used to bind the 13-year-old was incredibly unusual, having 106 differently coloured textile fibres inside it. Though they searched throughout America and abroad, they couldn't find a comparable rope.

The third murder

For the next few weeks, the young airman masturbated frequently to the memory of torturing Danny Joe Eberle, then the pressure built up again. He stalked various boys and girls but was always frustrated by potential witnesses before he could force them into his car. Then, on 2 December 1983 at 7.45 a.m., he saw 12-year-old Chris Walden walking to school and forced him into his vehicle at knifepoint. Driving to a nearby wood, he ordered his weeping victim to undress down to his underpants.

The sadist then manually strangled the boy until he lay on the ground, helpless. Taking out his knife he stabbed his victim twice in the back before slitting his throat. He also carved an emblem, resembling the Boy Scouts badge, on Chris's chest, presumably to hide his trademark bite-marks. Then he fled the area, replete, for now, with sexual images of being in charge.

Three days later the 12-year-old's body was discovered by horrified pheasant hunters, his school jotter with his name written on it lying nearby.

SADISTIC KILLERS

A failed abduction

Overhearing people comment that the slasher killer must be gay, Joubert determined that his next victim would be female. In truth, he'd attempted to abduct female children in the past. He wanted to see his victims squirming in pain and begging for mercy so their gender was secondary. That said, he clearly had a fetish about young boys stripped to their underpants.

On 11 January 1984, he drove to a school, thinking that it was a church, and shakily ordered the female teacher he found there to get into his car. Instead she raced past him and summoned help. The police were given a good description of the kidnapper's vehicle and found that it was rented to a John Joseph Joubert who was working as a radar technician in a nearby air force camp.

When they searched his room, they found the distinctive rope which had been used to bind Danny Joe Eberle. Further searches of the 20-year-old's locker and car revealed the tape used to gag his victims and the knife which had inflicted the tortuous and fatal blows. Even more damning, one of Danny Joe Eberle's hairs was found in Joubert's car boot. The detectives knew that they had their man, though he still looked like an innocent boy.

Arrest and trial

For several hours, Joubert continued to protest his innocence, then he broke down and confessed to both Nebraska murders and also to being the Oakdale Slasher. (He was not yet linked to the Portland murder of Ricky Stetson.) He asked to be allowed to tell his young friend from the Boy Scouts, and afterwards the two boys shared a brotherly hug.

The young airman pleaded guilty to murdering Danny Joe Eberle and Christopher Walden, the defence noting that he was a sexual sadist with a schizoid personality disorder. In October

1984 the Nebraskan court sentenced him to die in the electric chair.

Two years later, as he languished on Death Row, John Joubert was found guilty of the Ricky Stetson murder, his teeth matching the bite indentations on the child's body. This time he was given a life sentence.

Though he sometimes attempted to withdraw his confessions, at other times the troubled young killer was more honest about his motivation. He said that 'it was the power and domination and seeing the fear' in his victim's eyes which turned him on. He didn't add that their physical suffering had also aroused him – but sadists often keep quiet about this aspect of their crimes.

For the next ten years, John Joseph Joubert remained on Death Row in Nebraska's Lincoln Correctional Facility, filing appeals declaring that society would benefit if they let him live and studied him. During these years he aged markedly and becoming increasingly bloated until all that remained of his earlier self was his sadistic fantasies. Realists knew that if he was ever released he'd put these fantasies into practice again, something Joubert himself had hinted to a journalist who befriended him. On 7 July 1996 at 12.25 a.m., the 32-year-old child-killer walked from his cell to the death chamber where he was executed in the electric chair.

CHAPTER TWELVE
JESSE JAMES CUMMINGS

A lifelong sadistic wife-beater, Cummings finally persuaded one of his bigamous spouses to murder his half-sister. He then raped and murdered his 11-year-old niece before committing further paedophiliac crimes.

Early hell

Jesse was born on the 19 November 1955 to Marie and Jesse Cummings in Modesta, California. His parents were migrant workers so they moved around constantly, harvesting fruit, picking cotton or chopping wood. They went on to have a daughter together but their itinerant lifestyle meant that neither of the children enjoyed any stability.

Marie was a violent woman, possibly schizophrenic, who beat both children with a bullwhip from the time they were small. She particularly picked on Jesse, who would often arrive at school with a bloodied and lacerated back. A kindly boy, he tried to shield his little sister from similar punishments, but eventually passed on the cruelty and began to catch and torture small animals.

At 12, barely able to read and write, Jesse left school to help his father support the impoverished family. But by 14 he could no longer stand the abuse from his mother and ran away from home. He lived by stealing and also went joyriding, taking some vehicles to nearby towns. Eventually he was caught and sent to a California detention facility.

In the same time frame, the Manson family were put on trial and Jesse became fascinated by Charles Manson as their lives were somewhat similar. Manson, too, had been ill-treated by his mother before spending time in juvenile detention halls. Manson was also as poorly educated and impoverished as Jesse – but he'd made himself irresistible to girls who had low self-esteem then had persuaded them to prostitute themselves, bringing him both kudos and cash. Damaged men are often drawn to even more damaged women whom they can control and demean.

By the time he emerged from youth custody, Jesse Cummings knew just how to become top dog. Like Manson, he would find women with desperately low self-esteem and persuade them to fall in love with him – then he'd treat them the way he wanted to treat his cruel mum.

The first marriage

At 18, whilst living with his parents in Oklahoma, he began dating a small, heavyset 15-year-old girl called Margaret. She'd had polio as a child and required a leg brace and crutches to get around. Jesse pretended to adore her – sadists are initially very loving – and she gladly ran off to Mexico to become his bride.

But as soon as Jesse got his new wife back to Oklahoma, everything changed. She found out that they were to live in a dilapidated bus in his parents' backyard and she realised that Jesse's mother was a violent and terrifying neighbour who sometimes fetched a gun and took pot shots at her son. It doubtless made Jesse even more keen to victimise Margaret, who closely resembled his mother, and he'd hide her crutches so that she had to crawl around. Eventually she realised that having no man was better than marriage to a mad man. Fearing for her life, she fled whilst he was out at work.

The second marriage

Early-stage sadists like Jesse Cummings in this period hate to be alone – after all, they can only feel good about themselves when they are torturing other people. So Jesse moved to Arkansas and soon found himself a new girlfriend, Janet, whom he married bigamously when he was 23. By now he was living from stealing and conning people, using some of the money for painkilling drugs. Like many people haunted by an unhappy childhood, he used these drugs to excess, once remaining in a semi-conscious drugged state for five days.

The third marriage

Whilst still living with his second wife, Jesse began courting his third. Sherry was only 16 and already had a failed violent marriage behind her and a recent miscarriage. She had desperately low self-esteem which she tried to bolster with drink.

By age 17 she was pregnant by 28-year-old Jesse and she moved with him and his wife Janet back to Oklahoma. Again they lived in the old bus in his parents' yard, with Janet sleeping at the back, and Jesse and Sherry at the front. Janet was understandably humiliated by this arrangement, which was just what Jesse wanted. He now had two women at his beck and call. But he pushed his luck too far, beating Janet mercilessly during one argument and attacking her with scissors, just as his mother had often attacked him with knives.

Janet fled back to her parents, ending eight years of hell. In the same time period, Jesse's mother died so he was even more desperate than usual to exert control. He now bigamously married the teenage Sherry, four months after she gave birth to a baby girl.

Like many violent men (and women), Jesse originally seemed to adore his new daughter, showing her off to his many relatives. Sherry had no idea that he'd become cruel to his children when they were old enough to walk.

Meanwhile his abuse towards Sherry increased. At first it was verbal and he criticised her so relentlessly for not losing her post-pregnancy weight that she stopped eating. Then he told her to prostitute herself to other men for money, and when she refused he broke her jaw.

The fourth marriage

Cummings still wanted to create a mini Manson family, so searched for a fourth wife he could control and realised he'd struck gold when he met single parent Juanita, always known as Anita. She'd been beaten by a previous boyfriend and had a very poor self-image. She was short and well built, just like Jesse Cummings' mother. In other words, she was the kind of woman he loved to hurt.

On 14 June 1989, he bigamously married her, insisting that his third wife Sherry watch the ceremony. Within three weeks he persuaded both women to make up a *ménage à trois* – and when Anita threatened to leave him, he broke her jaw and knocked out one of her teeth.

The family moved to a run-down house in Oklahoma, where Jesse's cruelty deepened. He persuaded Anita to let him handcuff and tie her to the bed then he left her there for several hours. When he came home he had sex with the distraught woman, reminding her that his father (who often visited unannounced) could have walked in and found her in her naked and bondaged state. On another occasion he sat on her chest for three hours, slapping her repeatedly in the face and laughing at her increasing distress.

The cruelty took its toll and Anita stopped eating. Jesse then acquired a bullwhip and beat her until she agreed to eat.

Cruelty to children

By now he was regularly beating his own little daughter and handcuffing her to the bed, sometimes sending her to relatives when he knew that Child Protective Services were due to visit. But when Anita's son was only one year old, he beat him too, whipping him with a belt until he went into convulsions and lost consciousness.

As the children grew older, he beat them with a paddle and with sticks and encouraged the women to spank the children, warning them to spank hard or they'd have to repeat the entire punishment. Both women chose to stay in this environment rather than free their offspring from such daily pain and fear.

Cummings' sadism towards his wives also increased. He tied Sherry to the bed and punched her repeatedly in the ribs whilst having sex with her. On other occasions he would handcuff Anita and pinch her nipples until she screamed. He also bought a stun gun and used it on them, once applying it to Anita's genitals and causing serious burns.

Cruelty to animals

Jesse Cummings had enjoyed hurting animals when he was a teenager, but now his cruelty reached new depths and he began to capture heavily pregnant dogs and cut them open to remove the puppies. Sherry and Anita held the struggling animals down. Most died from shock and subsequent infection, and those which lived were hugely traumatised. He also enjoyed tying up nearby woodland ponies so that they couldn't bend their necks to graze and slowly starved to death.

Paedophilia

Jesse's parents had had several children with other people, and Jesse kept in touch with one of his half-sisters, Judy Moody. He often taunted her about the fact that she weighed 26 stone. Judy's eight children had been taken into care by social services because they were being sexually and physically abused by their father, but Judy had moved to Arkansas then given birth to a ninth baby, Melissa. The latter had been spared from molestation because her father had contracted TB and died.

Melissa was now 11 years old, and, to a psychopath like Jesse Cummings she was infinitely desirable. It's likely that he began to molest her as she kept telling her best friend and her mother that she didn't want to be left at Jesse's house. She also complained of stomach pains – one of the many symptoms of child abuse – every time she had to go to her uncle Jesse's. But Judy found him a convenient babysitter and said that Melissa had to go.

Judy's murder

Jesse wanted Judy permanently out of the way so that he could enjoy Melissa – and he may also have wanted to see how much control he could exert over his remaining two wives. As a test, he allegedly told Sherry to kill Judy but the shocked woman refused. So he allegedly asked Anita, then left the house at 7 a.m. to drive his father all the way to Oklahoma City where the older man was seeing an oncologist.

Later that day – 16 October 1991 – Anita fetched the family gun and crept up behind Judy as she sat on the settee in Jesse's house, shooting her until there were no more bullets left in the .38.

She told Sherry what she'd done, and the two women dragged Judy's corpse to the cellar. That evening Sherry spoke to Jesse on the phone and he told her he'd be home soon and to handcuff 11-year-old Melissa to the bed. Appallingly, the woman did so. Later, Anita glanced into the bedroom and saw the child handcuffed, but did nothing to help her escape.

Jesse came home and disposed of his half-sister's body in a nearby lake, pulling her bra and underwear off so that it would look as though she'd been sexually assaulted. When he returned to the house, Anita and Sherry stripped Melissa and watched as he raped the child and ordered her to give him a blow job, an order she didn't understand.

Jesse and Sherry then drove the sobbing child to the woods north of Boswell. Exactly what happened next may never be known. Sherry later claimed that she remained in the car and that Jesse led the trembling girl into the woods where he raped her, knifed her several times in the body and slit her throat. Jesse's later take on events was that Sherry and Anita had murdered Melissa whilst he was still in Oklahoma City with his father.

The following day one of Judy's friends asked where she was and Jesse said that he didn't know and reported her and Melissa missing. When her body and Melissa's skeleton were eventually found, the police strongly suspected him as he and his father had once being arrested on suspicion of murder, the case eventually being dropped due to lack of evidence.

Meanwhile, according to Anita, he liked handcuffing her to the bed and telling her what he'd done to Melissa, allegedly climaxing when he talked about slitting the 11-year-old's throat.

Further victims

Horrifyingly, Anita allowed herself to get pregnant by her sadistic husband and in July 1993 she gave birth to a baby girl. By now her son was so traumatised by the cruelty he'd suffered that he wet the bed, had an increasingly blank expression and had been diagnosed with Attention Deficit Disorder. Yet social services failed to remove the child, and the new baby, from this dangerous environment.

Jesse Cummings was being given the message by the authorities that he could do what he liked and get away with it. In autumn 1993 he spanked and fingered a three-year-old girl – a distant relative – leaving her hurt and bewildered. On one occasion Sherry walked in on him molesting the naked child in the barn, but her response was to warn the child not to tell anyone.

Self-defence

Eventually, Anita began to crack up and she feared that her husband was about to kill her. Only then did she alert the authorities that he'd killed Melissa three years before, admitting that she feared he'd kill her children that very day if she didn't get them out of the house. In telling her story she had to admit to Judy's homicide and was immediately arrested. Sherry was also arrested as she'd helped move Judy's body, covered up her murder and handcuffed Melissa to the bed for her husband to sexually assault her. She'd also gone on that last car journey with the child, knowing that Melissa wasn't going to return.

Dividing the blame

The authorities now took Jesse Cummings into custody, where he passed the part of the polygraph test where he was asked if he'd killed Judy. But he failed it when asked if he had *caused* her death. He also failed, according to the police, when he said he hadn't killed Melissa. Somewhat surprisingly, he was charged with his half-sister's murder as well as that of her child.

Meanwhile, Sherry was given 35 years for her part in the various atrocities and Anita was given life. Women's groups immediately said that the sentences should have been more lenient – but an innocent woman and an 11-year-old child had died because of their failure to act appropriately and they'd also done nothing when a three-year-old girl was sexually abused. Both said that Jesse Cummings constantly threatened their children – but on the day that Anita killed Judy and Sherry handcuffed Melissa to the bed, he was in another state. They could have taken their children from the house just after 7 a.m. and been many miles away by the time he returned at midnight, an escape window of 17 hours. Child Protection Services, already deeply concerned at the physical abuse the youngsters were subjected to, would have helped, as would have battered women's groups, the court heard.

Trial

Jesse James Cummings' trial began on 6 May 1996 in Coalgate, Oklahoma. Sherry testified to hearing Judy being shot and to helping dispose of her body. She also talked about Melissa's rape and the final car journey which had culminated in her death.

Anita took the stand and talked of her lifelong abuse at Jesse Cummings' hands, but the defence produced a love letter she'd written to her husband shortly after their marriage which expressed her devotion to him.

The prosecution noted that Anita could have left Jesse if she hated everything that he did – she had parents she could have returned to. Or why didn't she shoot Jesse rather than Judy if she felt that her only option was to take a life? They also noted that Jesse must have ordered Judy's murder. After all, he beat his wives for tiny so-called misdemeanours so would surely have battered them mercilessly if they'd killed his half-sister of their own volition.

Sherry's teenage sister Sarah also took the stand and recounted being raped by Jesse Cummings when she was only 14 whilst Sherry watched.

Cummings' minister testified in his defence and said that he'd never seen Jesse hit his children. The minister said that Jesse was worth saving, but, when questioned further, he admitted believing that *everyone* was worth saving.

On 9 May, after several hours of deliberation, the jury returned two death sentences. Cummings blanched. He paled further when the judge told him that he was to die by lethal injection, though the effects of this drug cocktail are much less painful than the tortures he put his many human and animal victims through.

Appeals

Jesse Cummings continued to appeal and in 1998 his conviction and death sentence for the murder of his half-sister Judy (who Anita shot dead) was overturned. Anita turned to religion and started studying theology in prison and Sherry took a general certificate in education.

Death Row

Jesse Cummings is currently on Death Row at the Oklahoma State Penitentiary for the murder of his niece Melissa Moody. There, he continues to protest his innocence, stating that he was convicted solely on the uncorroborated evidence of two of his wives. He states on a website dedicated to Death Row inmates that 'There is biological evidence in my case that could be tested for DNA and yet no one will test it or allow it to be tested.'

It's a case where there are many shades of grey. On the one hand, Cummings wanted to be like Charles Manson – and Manson didn't commit a single murder, getting his girlfriends to do it. So Jesse persuaded Anita to kill Judy, but did he persuade someone else to murder Melissa? Both wives said that he'd raped the child twice but when she was found her body was skeletonised and all that could be determined was that she'd been stabbed in the ribs. On the other hand, Cummings had an insatiable appetite for sexual cruelty – and, according to the authorities, his polygraph suggested that he'd played a part in Melissa's death.

His incarceration assures that he will no longer be a danger to women, children and animals. His offspring have all been taken into care or fostered, but Anita's son, who he abused relentlessly, remains deeply distraught.

This sexual sadist now has a web page, courtesy of the Canadian Coalition Against The Death Penalty, on which he protests his innocence. He is currently held in an Oklahoma jail.

CHAPTER THIRTEEN
RICHARD FRANCIS COTTINGHAM

Cottingham abused several teenage girls before committing five horrific murders in the late 1970s and in 1980. Because two of his dismembered victims were found near Times Square, he became known as the Times Square Torso Ripper but he was much more sustainedly cruel than Jack the Ripper or the Yorkshire Ripper ever were.

Formative years

Richard was born on 25 November 1946 to Anna and William Cottingham. His father was an executive in an insurance firm, his mother a housewife. The couple also had two daughters and the family lived in the Bronx. Very little is known about the family – Richard Cottingham's biographer would later describe William Cottingham as 'a quiet almost brooding career man' and Anna as 'taciturn' and 'prim'. But young Richard spent most of his time in her company as he found it difficult to make friends.

He was desperately shy, a shyness which increased when he was sent to a school run by nuns who were strict disciplinarians.

He soon began to fantasise about hurting girls and would later admit that he'd 'always had a problem with women'.

Because the school was a long journey from his home, he couldn't play with the other schoolchildren after class so had endless hours to hone his cruel fantasies.

Richard had such poor eyesight that he had to wear glasses from the age of nine. He hated his glasses, hated his name and was generally seen as a slightly unhappy underachiever by his contemporaries.

Work

The boy with the bad eyesight and equally bad haircut left school at the earliest opportunity, uncertain what he wanted to do next. But his father found him a job in an insurance firm and he took courses to become a computer operator, a job which he was more than competent at. In 1966 he transferred to another firm which offered slightly more money: he would stay there for the next 13 years. Originally he worked during the day, but he proved to be such a valuable employee that he was given the option of three shifts to choose from. He chose the shift which ended at 11pm, knowing he could go on to the bars and clubs and pick up women for casual sex before going home.

Endangering lives

His religion had taught him that sex outside of marriage was wrong, yet he craved release and excitement. The dichotomy apparently took its toll and, shortly before his twenty-third birthday, he got behind the wheel of his car whilst heavily inebriated. Driving through Manhattan he mounted the pavement, narrowly missing several pedestrians. The police hastily arrested him but, because he had no previous criminal record, he was merely given a ten day jail sentence and a $50 fine.

Marriage and masturbatory aids

On 2 May 1970, he married his quiet girlfriend Janet at Our Lady of Lourdes Church in New York. At first he was able to satisfy himself with vanilla sex, but his main sex drive was focused on sadomasochism and obviously that urge would never go away. Richard now did what most recreational sadists do and built himself a vast library of domination and bondage novels. His wife seems to have been aware of his interest, yet he kept his books in a locked room to which only he had the key.

His mother chose to relocate to Florida at this time and asked Richard and Janet to go with her but they decided to remain in New Jersey, causing a family row.

Theft

Richard soon came to the notice of the authorities again, this time for shoplifting from a department store. Like many sexual sadists he got some of his kicks from stealing and from the possibility of being caught. Such acts gave him an adrenalin surge, made him feel more alive. He felt invincible up until the moment when the store detective detained him. On 30 August 1972 he appeared in court and was given a $50 fine.

Fatherhood

The following year – in October 1973 – his first son was born. Richard at first appeared delighted and called the boy Blair, a name he would later use to introduce himself to prostitutes. He continued to have ordinary sex with Janet but his fantasies grew increasingly dark...

Alleged sodomy

Shortly before Blair's first birthday, on 4 September 1974, the 27-year-old allegedly tortured a teenager. A 17-year-old prostitute was extensively bitten, sodomised and sexually assaulted in a hotel room by a man answering Richard Cottingham's description. He also robbed her of her inexpensive jewellery. He was arrested and taken to court, but the teenager failed to show up so the charges were dismissed.

Another alleged assault

Six months later – on 12 February 1975 – a man again strongly matching Richard Cottingham's description took a 19-year-old prostitute to a west side hotel in New York, where he handcuffed and sexually assaulted her. He also robbed her of her costume jewellery, something Cottingham would do fetishistically again and again. A chambermaid testified that she'd found the distressed prostitute in handcuffs, but there wasn't enough proof of sexual assault to make a watertight case and again the charges against the supposedly respectable family man were dismissed.

Further children

Richard and Janet continued to procreate, producing a second son in March 1975 and a daughter in October 1976. The family settled in a modest three-bedroom house in Lodi, half an hour's drive from New York.

After the birth of their daughter, Richard refused to resume sexual relations with his wife, telling her that she was fat and ugly. In this, he resembled many criminal sadists who endlessly criticise a woman once they know she's in love with them.

Retreating into his extremely rich fantasy life, Richard put a lock on the basement door and turned it into his den where he'd stay for hours, masturbating over his large collection of sadomasochistic novels. But he wanted to put a real woman into non-consensual bondage and make her scream.

Maryann Carr's murder

On 15 December 1977, 26-year-old radiologist Maryann Carr was heard talking with a man in her flat at a time when her husband was out of town. A neighbour heard Maryann scream 'I will, I will', then all went silent. The beautiful young woman was abducted from her apartment, handcuffed at her wrists and ankles and had her mouth taped shut.

Taken to an unknown location, she was beaten with a blunt instrument and extensively bitten and possibly suffocated during the assault: whatever the abuse, her lungs collapsed. Her body was dumped near the car park of a New Jersey motel (a motel to which Richard Cottingham would take future victims) – and a man matching his description had been seen talking to Maryann in the car park shortly before she disappeared. Cottingham also had a friend who lived in Maryann's apartment complex, a friend whom he'd fallen out with. After the row, his friend's house had been ransacked and the key to the apartment complex's door had been stolen, a key which would have given the killer closer access to Maryann. Equally damning was the fact that Maryann's car was abandoned in a street where Richard Cottingham used to live.

A year passed after Maryann's murder in which there were no other known bondage murders in the area. But Richard spoke about the death to his colleagues constantly, speculating as to how the killer had managed to infiltrate the complex when it was securely locked. Again, this was classic serial killer behaviour – several of the serial sadists in this book talked in general terms to colleagues about murders they'd been responsible for, or even hinted that they'd committed some dark deeds.

Karen's ordeal

On 23 September 1978, Cottingham approached 22-year-old Karen Schilt in a bar in New York. Karen had just been to hospital to visit her estranged husband and was having a quick drink before starting her waitress job. The innocuous looking computer operator asked her if she was a working girl and she explained that she worked in a restaurant. They talked for a while and she told him that she had two children by her estranged husband and that she was pregnant with her new boyfriend's child. Cottingham insisted on buying her several drinks, drinks he'd drugged.

Beginning to feel dizzy but assuming that it was because of her pregnancy, Karen left the bar and began to walk along the sidewalk. As she stumbled along the road, Richard Cottingham drew up and asked her if she wanted a lift.

She lost consciousness in the car and revived later to find that it was dark and that they were parked behind an apartment complex. Cottingham now lit a cigarette and extensively burnt her breasts, aroused by her moaning. He also bit them repeatedly.

After removing her jewellery from her body, he threw her out of the car into a car park where she was found unconscious. (The car park was next to murder victim Maryann's apartment.) Karen remained insensible for five hours and was kept in hospital for several days.

Susan's ordeal

On 11 October 1978, Richard arranged to have sex with 19-year-old Susan Geiger for money. He bought her a drink first and slipped two heavy-duty tranquillisers into it.

In retrospect, Susan Geiger's instincts told her that Cottingham was no good. He'd parked his car so close to the car in front that she couldn't see his licence plate, insisted on buying her alcohol even when she didn't want any, and stirred her glass again and again, demanding that she drink the contents through a straw to avoid germs on the glass.

But Susan needed the money so she ignored her misgivings and drank the alcohol. As she became drowsy, Cottingham walked her to a motel room where she passed out. He stripped her and beat her with a rubber hose but she revived during the beating and was forced to fellate her captor before she lost consciousness again. When she next awoke she found that the man had raped and sodomised her and bitten her all over, concentrating especially on her nipples. He'd also taken her jewellery and her clothes.

Chillingly, she bumped into Cottingham a few days later and he tried to brazen it out, asking, 'What happened to you that night?' The traumatised teenager began screaming and two men came to her rescue, whereupon Richard Cottingham fled the scene.

Separation

The following year, Janet Cottingham filed for divorce citing mental cruelty. For the last few years she had rarely seen her husband – and when he was home he alternately mocked and ignored her. She now moved herself and her children to Poughkeepsie and supported herself through part-time work. Cottingham was enraged at her decision and tried to halt the divorce proceedings. He might not want her, but he wanted to remain in control.

Two murders

On the evening of Wednesday 29 November 1979, Cottingham booked into a downmarket hotel on West 42nd Street, a street frequented by prostitutes. He soon persuaded 23-year-old Kuwaiti beauty Deedeh Goodarzi back to his hotel. The young

Muslim prostitute had given birth to a baby four months earlier which was being cared for by friends.

He also lured a teenage girl – unidentified and so later referred to in court as Miss X – back to the same room, though no one knows if he killed one woman and then abducted another or if he tortured them both at the same time. (Sadistic co-killers such as the Hillside Stranglers and Bittaker and Norris sometimes abducted and killed pairs of girls. And Ivan Milat, profiled later in this book, killed heterosexual pairs.)

Throughout that night and for the next three days, Cottingham indulged himself in an orgy of sadistic excess. He burnt his gagged and bound victims over and over with cigarettes, beat them with a whip and bit extensively around their breasts.

After eventually murdering both women, Cottingham cut off their hands and heads and packed them with the rest of his luggage. The sadist knew that it would be very hard for police to identify bodies which had no facial features and no fingerprints – and if they couldn't identify the women, they couldn't trace the murders back to him.

Determined to rid the room of any forensic traces, he poured lighter fluid over the vaginas of both corpses and set them alight. Then, as the flames leapt from the mattress and began to burn the carpet, he calmly left the room.

Carrying a bag which probably held the prostitutes' heads and hands, he bumped into movie production assistant Peter Vronsky who noticed that the overweight guest with the bad haircut was perspiring slightly. Cottingham ignored Vronsky and seemed lost in thought.

Another girlfriend

From February to May 1980, he was busy dating yet another girlfriend, a 28-year-old nurse. He'd told his colleagues that nurses were often promiscuous so he eagerly sought them out. It was a gross generalisation but no one picked him up on it.

Several of Richard's workmates used prostitutes and he would brag about having sex with these girls then departing the motel without paying them. He showed them how to leave via the fire exits of cheap motels.

He also made loans of several thousand dollars to some of his colleagues on the understanding that they paid him interest. Cottingham used the money from his loan sharking to go gambling and became very good at it. But a night in a casino or in the arms of a loving girlfriend couldn't compete with the thrill of torturing a girl until she agreed to do anything that he desired.

Valorie Street's murder

On 4 May 1980, he got into conversation with Valorie Ann Street (who also used the name Shelly Dudley) and she accompanied him to a motel in Hasbrouck Heights, New Jersey. There they stripped off their clothes and he handcuffed the 19-year-old prostitute's arms behind her back and gagged her with adhesive tape. He whipped her on the shins and progressed to beating her all over her body, also viciously raping and sodomising her. He cut her stomach and breasts with a knife, biting the latter so savagely that the right nipple was almost torn off.

It's likely that Valorie was unable to scream loudly enough to alert hotel staff as she'd been given strong tranquillisers and alcohol. Eventually, after at least six hours of extensive and repeated torture, he strangled her to death.

The sadist now found that he'd lost the key to the handcuffs so he left them in situ and stuffed Valorie's naked corpse under the bed where it was found the following day by an aghast chambermaid.

Pamela's ordeal

On 11 May 1980, Cottingham may have struck again. Pamela Weisenfeld, a 27-year-old prostitute, met with a man answering Cottingham's description who drugged her, beat her and ferociously bit her breasts. She regained consciousness in a New Jersey car park to find that her handbag and jewellery were missing. But the court would later find him not guilty of this particular attack due to lack of evidence.

Jean Reyner's murder

Soon Cottingham's cruel lust rebuilt, and on 15 May 1980 he approached 25-year-old Jean Mary Ann Reyner. The young prostitute accompanied him to a hotel she frequented near Madison Avenue.

There she suffered for an unknown period of time after Cottingham cuffed and gagged her. He mutilated her body with a knife and finally progressed to stabbing her again and again until she expired. Post-mortem, he severed both her breasts, putting them on top of the bed's headboard before setting fire to her vagina and leaving the hotel. Sadists carry out such acts after death has occurred as a confused way of further 'hurting' the victim and because they're aware of how shocking the scene will be to everyone who enters the room.

During this period he continued to date women who weren't prostitutes, sometimes taking them away for weekend breaks. He gave one girlfriend a novel to read which featured mutilation murders, telling her that it was great.

The final torture victim

On 22 May 1980, he picked up 18-year-old Leslie Ann O'Dell and bought her a meal at an all-night diner. She told him that she was desperate to escape from her pimp and he agreed to help. In turn, she agreed to have sex with him for $100 and was pleased that her luck was about to change.

Incredibly, Cottingham took her to the motel where he'd left Valorie's corpse under the bed 18 days before. He felt invincible. After all, he'd been torturing and killing women for years and had never gone to jail for it.

When they were naked on the bed he offered Leslie a back rub and she rolled onto her stomach, whereupon he snapped handcuffs on her wrists. Telling her that she was a whore and that she had to be punished, he added that he intended to cut her face, breasts, vagina and anus.

For the next four hours he did just that, biting her breasts until they bled and cutting them lightly. He sodomised her so brutally that her anus was torn. He also raped her and beat her all over her body with a leather belt – and when she looked as if she was going to pass out from the pain and fear, he revived her by wiping her face with a damp cloth. This is textbook sadistic behaviour, with the sadist determined that his victim isn't going to escape into unconsciousness.

Uncuffing her wrists, he put the cuffs around her ankles and ordered her to kneel at his feet, fellate him and call him master. She did so, but also felt under the bed and grabbed his pistol, knowing that she had to kill or be killed. The terrified teenager aimed at him and pulled the trigger, only then realising that the weapon was a replica. Backing away, she pleaded with him not to hurt her again.

Cottingham threw himself at her in a rage and she began screaming. Staff intervened, and after trying to explain it away as a lover's quarrel, the sadist fled. But the police had been called and they managed to intercept him in the corridor, the bag containing his torture kit held tightly in his sweating palm.

He now swore that he'd been having a consensual session with the young prostitute, but the trembling girl's cut and badly bitten body told a very different story. She explained that he'd been trying to kill her – and her injuries were so severe that Cottingham was originally charged with attempted murder as well as with sodomy and rape.

Examining the contents of his bag, police discovered a knife with a three inch blade, a leather gag, two studded slave collars and three sets of handcuffs. It could have been a consensual sadomasochistic kit but for the addition of the toy pistol which he used to terrorise his victims and the several bottles of strong drugs he kept to subdue them with.

Failed suicide

In jail awaiting trial, Cottingham knew that the odds weren't in his favour so he smashed his glasses and cut his left wrist. He was rushed to the nearest hospital for emergency care.

His only hope now lay with his mother who refused to believe that he was guilty, despite the fact that he'd been caught outside the room where prostitute Leslie Ann O'Dell had been tortured. By now his fingerprint had been found on the handcuffs binding Valorie Street's wrists together so he was also facing charges for her murder. It was equally clear to the authorities that he was most likely the Torso Ripper who had tortured and decapitated the two victims near Times Square. Cottingham's signature torture marks had also been found on Jean Reyner's body, and a man answering to his description had been seen talking to Maryann Carr shortly before she was abducted, put into bondage and killed.

Determined to clear her only son's name, Richard Cottingham's mother spent her life savings getting him the best defence possible. In her efforts to defend him she would even have to sell her retirement home.

Happy families

Meanwhile, the press described Cottingham as a devoted family man, something they invariably do with any married man who hasn't taken an axe to his offspring. In reality, he'd mocked his wife so relentlessly that she was divorcing him for cruelty. And he hardly saw his children when they lived together as he was asleep when they had breakfast and he had left for his 4 p.m.–11 p.m. shift by the time they returned from school. Many of his weekends were also child-free, being spent with various mistresses or with prostitutes.

But newspapers find that those closest to the defendant clam up so they are forced to speak to those who only casually knew the family. Neighbours said that Richard took his children trick or treating at Halloween, and this was enough for journalists to describe him as the father of the year.

Later, when the press became aware of his collection of sadomasochistic novels, they hinted that these were to blame – but in reality many more killers have the Bible or the Koran at their bedsides. And religious beliefs have been at the core of numerous torture murders throughout the centuries.

One man, Donald Fearn, began fantasising about hurting women after reading how a sect called the Penitentes had religious ceremonies which included torture. Fearn waited until 1942 when his wife was in hospital giving birth to their first child, then he abducted a 17-year-old nurse and drove her to a hut in a remote part of the desert. For the next six hours he tortured her with wire which he'd heated, also mutilating her with pliers and raping her multiple times before eventually killing her.

The trials

Now it was Richard Francis Cottingham's turn to go on trial for torture and rape. He firstly appeared at Bergen County

Court a year after his prolonged abuse of Leslie Ann O'Dell. He was tried for her attempted murder, for the murder of Valorie Street and for the torture of Karen Schilt, Susan Geiger and Pamela Weisenfeld. The jury heard from the traumatised women about the agonies which he'd inflicted on them.

Surprisingly, he insisted on taking the stand. (Lawyers usually advise their clients not to testify if they believe that they are guilty.) Unfortunately for him, his arrogance and his hatred of women shone through. Shown photos of one of his bite-marks, he dismissed it as 'only a scratch'.

He said that Leslie had agreed to his fantasy, that he'd told her it would involve 'tying her up, possibly spanking her with my hand'. He smiled coldly as he was cross-examined, only his body language betraying his nervousness, his legs tapping endlessly as he refused to make eye contact with his questioners.

He admitted that he'd been fascinated with sadomasochism from an early age and that he frequented massage parlours where such practices were on offer. He also admitted that his wife had been partway through divorcing him on the grounds of mental cruelty – but she'd put the divorce on hold after his arrest and was standing by him. (The police considered her to be a good woman who didn't want to kick a dog when it was down.)

The defence wanted to produce an expert who would explain to the jury that sadomasochism wasn't unusual but the judge disallowed this, saying that if the practice was widespread then the jury would already be familiar with it.

The forensic evidence against Cottingham was damning. He denied knowing any of the four women but their fingerprints had been found in his car and fibres from his car rug had been found on their bodies. They'd identified him in court, their flesh still bearing scars from his assaults.

He paled as he was found guilty of Valorie Street's murder, three kidnappings and several assaults (but not guilty of Pamela Weisenfeld's kidnapping) and sentenced to 197 years in jail.

Richard Cottingham's father was dead by the time of his trial but his mother and one of his two sisters attended the first trial throughout and refused to believe the guilty verdict. They had concluded that Richard had angered the Mafia by making loans to his colleagues and that the underworld had framed him for the prostitutes' torture and deaths.

Cottingham's subsequent trial was held up after he collapsed with a bleeding ulcer and had to be hospitalised. He again tried to take his own life and would later make a third suicide bid. But he finally faced the charge of murdering the medical technician Maryann Carr. In some respects her murder bore his signature – she'd been bound and strangled. However, she'd had no alcohol or drugs in her system, unlike his later victims. Moreover, the only mark of torture on her body was a small bruise on her breast.

She was also a respectable married woman – Cottingham's future murder victims were prostitutes. But she worked as a medical technician and the prosecution speculated that Cottingham might have mistaken her for a nurse, a profession he wrongly believed to be universally promiscuous and deserving of punishment. In October 1982 he was found guilty of Carr's murder and given 25 years to life, to run concurrently with his other sentences.

On 30 March 1983 – under tight security as he'd made an escape bid, fleeing from the gents toilets in the court to the street outside before being recaptured – he was taken from Trenton's maximum security prison and transferred to Manhattan to answer the charges of murdering Deedeh Goodarzi, Miss X and Jean Reyner.

The court heard that Deedeh's jewellery had been found in Cottingham's safe, as had jewellery and other souvenirs from several of the torture victims. His handwriting matched that of the man who had signed the hotel registers, though he'd used a false name. Equally damning, the bodies had all been tortured in similar ways to that of his murder victim Valorie Street. His guilt was virtually a foregone conclusion and on 28 August 1984 he received an additional 75 years to life for the three hotel-based homicides.

An ostensibly contrite Cottingham shakily told the judge that he would never again break society's laws if he was released, but given the appalling savagery of his five murders, he's likely to die in prison.

PART THREE

THE WILDERNESS YEARS: AUSTRALIAN SADISTS

CHAPTER FOURTEEN

CHRISTOPHER BERNARD WILDER

Australia-born Wilder started his raping spree close to home, and may also have murdered two young women there when he was 20. Emigrating to America, he abducted and sadistically murdered at least eight young women and teenage girls, returning to Australia briefly and committing further sexual crimes. At one time he was on the FBI's Most Wanted list. Today, the authorities believe that the total body count may be as high as 17.

A nomadic childhood

Christopher was born on 13 March 1945 in Sydney, Australia, the first son of a comparatively wealthy family. He almost died at birth and was given the last rites. Two years later, he apparently fell into the family swimming pool and was found unconscious, and a year after that he had convulsions and briefly lapsed into a coma whilst in the back of his parents' car. Some criminologists would later imply that this suggested brain damage, but in truth small children are prone to convulsions when they get seriously overheated or ill.

The Wilders went on to have three more boys and the family moved constantly between Australia and America as Christopher's father worked for the American navy. They lived in Alabama, Albuquerque and New Mexico and this obviously involved the children having numerous changes of friends and school.

Christopher's father was the family disciplinarian so he was much closer to his mother. As he grew, he felt increasingly ambivalent about becoming a man.

Sexual abuse

Christopher would later tell a friend that he had numerous sexual experiences from the age of nine. As a child doesn't normally become overtly sexual at this age, it's clear that these experiences must have been abusive. The frequently uprooted boy with the slight speech impediment would have been an easy target for a seductive paedophile. His abuser would have told him that 'sex is good and healthy', a message that was in sharp contrast to the 'sex is dirty' message that his family's religion peddled, and he found it impossible to reconcile the two. By age 11 he had begun to peep at young girls and by age 12 he had begun to bite his nails until they bled. Other children noted that he was a lonely and nervous youth who kept very much to himself.

At home, he wasn't told any of the facts of life and was outwardly so repressed that he'd blush if other boys made sexual references. But in his dreams he was all powerful – and as he moved into his teens his sexual fantasies became equally omnipotent and he masturbated to images of turning girls into slaves.

By 15 he was frequently afflicted by a nervous stomach and later admitted to a therapist that he felt depressed and anxious throughout his teenage years.

At 16 he graduated from high school and became a carpenter, undertaking an apprenticeship that would last for the next five years. He was good at his job, was fit and attractive, yet his formative experiences had left him with no self-esteem, and his dreams were filled with hate.

Teenage rape

At 17, the victim became the victimiser for the first known time when he and his friends gang-raped a girl on an Australian beach. Wilder went first and was clearly the ringleader – though he told the police that she'd had sex with him consensually and that only the other boys had forced her to comply. Rather than imprisonment, he was ordered to undergo psychoanalysis.

Bizarrely, part of his treatment for this sexual dysfunction was electroshock therapy which is more routinely used to treat depression. They thought that this would create an aversion, that Wilder would never sexually coerce a female again. But it was just one more form of pain meted out to a boy who was already hurting, so it's unsurprising that he turned it into one of his sexual fantasies and would eventually torture his female victims with electric shocks.

By age 18 his nervous digestive problems had worsened and by 22 he sometimes found it difficult to breathe – again, this seems to have been as a result of stress.

Two unsolved murders

In 1965, when Christopher was 20, a man fitting his description was seen accompanying two young women to a beach near Sydney. Afterwards both girls were found raped and strangled. Police would later state that they believed him responsible for these gruesome deaths.

A failed first marriage

Christopher kept doing his carpentry work and in his spare time he liked to surf so spent endless hours on the beach. But he remained deeply dissatisfied and when he was 24 he emigrated alone to America, arriving in the country with a suitcase and a little cash. He rented a flat in Florida and soon married – but the marriage only lasted eight days, after which his wife left him because of his sadistic desires. She'd also found a trunk in his car filled with photographs of girls wearing only bikini bottoms and she'd found women's clothes which he'd apparently been stealing from washing lines. Even at this stage there was the suggestion of transvestism, a trait which would remain with him throughout his life.

The divorced Wilder lived off his wits for the next few years, doing odd carpentry jobs in the neighbourhood and running a topless bar. It was a hand-to-mouth existence which improved markedly when he met up with a building contractor and jointly set up a construction business. The two men landed several extremely well-paid contracts to build a village, and were soon employing dozens of men.

Eventually, on paper at least, Christopher Wilder was a millionaire and he went on a spending spree. He invested some of his earnings in real estate, installed a swimming pool in his house, bought himself a speedboat and several top-of-the-range cars. He increasingly left the day-to-day running of his business to his business partner, preferring the playboy lifestyle instead.

He also became a racing driver, something which further endeared him to young women. Not that the six-foot, attractive Australian needed cars to act as an aphrodisiac, as females were already drawn to him. But lots of consensual sex doesn't make a disturbed man happy – after all, many rapists are married men with one or more mistresses.

Further sexual offences

For the next few years, the Australian behaved inappropriately with numerous American teenage girls but he avoided the attentions of the authorities, perhaps because he appeared to be so contrite afterwards and because young girls tend to blame themselves for unwanted sexual activity. (Later, police would take statements from 60 teenagers who reluctantly admitted to being sexually humiliated by the superficially charming millionaire.)

Oral rape

On 10 January 1976, he committed his second *reported* rape, though by then he'd molested dozens of young girls, often forcing them to reveal their breasts and perform oral sex on him. Carrying out some building work for a family in Boca Raton, he got to know their attractive 16-year-old daughter over several days. Wilder had been feeling depressed and anxious, but now his predatory nature had a whole new focus and he turned on the charm. He established that she was looking for secretarial work, lied and said he could drive her to a suitable job.

The excited teenager got into his pickup truck carrying a spare blouse with her as she planned to go on to her boyfriend's house to socialise. Realising he had an excuse to ask her to undress, Christopher Wilder suggested he pull over and she could change into the prettier blouse for her interview. But when he stopped the truck, he shook her hard and slapped her face. Telling her that she must do what he wanted, he tore off her clothes.

Wilder forced the terrified girl to both fellate and masturbate him, then – his sadism temporarily sated – came to his senses and asked her if she wanted him to drive them both to the police station. Fearing that he'd kill her if she said yes, she promised not to tell anyone and he cheered up markedly and dropped her off at her boyfriend's house.

The victim didn't tell the police until three months later, at which stage Wilder was arrested. Interviewed by a psychiatrist, he wept copiously and admitted that he was terrified of going to jail. The psychiatrist noted that he had severe conflict concerning his heterosexual role in society and that he had a problem with male authority figures and couldn't identify with them. He felt hostile towards people who tried to control him and acknowledged that he didn't feel love.

Wilder admitted that he fantasised about rape though he knew it was wrong and it was clear that he saw his environment as essentially hostile. He seemed unaware that he was the one with the hostility and that he was projecting it onto others, people who invariably meant him no harm. The therapist noted that Wilder was 'tense, fearful and apt to experience emotional upheavals which result in complete loss of intellectual controls'. Insightfully, he added 'he is not safe except in a structured environment and should be in a resident program geared to his needs'.

Sadly, a second psychiatrist was more of an optimist and concluded that the rapist was 'not dangerous to others'. This doubtless influenced the court.

Christopher Wilder went to trial for the oral rape of the 16-year-old, but the jury found him not guilty, possibly because she'd changed her blouse in front of him and hadn't reported the assault for several months. A typical sociopath, he made no changes to his behaviour, refusing to enter therapy and continuing to harass young girls. Sociopaths seldom learn from their mistakes and often believe that they are omnipotent. Wilder had these traits and he also had strong sadistic desires, making him doubly dangerous.

Drug rape

On 21 June 1980, he posed as a television photographer and told a young Tennessee girl that he was making a pizza advert. In fact, he'd drugged the pizza which he gave her to eat. When she began to lose consciousness he led her to his truck where he fondled her breasts and persuaded her to remove her blouse.

The confused young girl asked if this was part of the advert and Wilder said that it was, but as he stared at her naked breasts he became visibly aroused. Belatedly realising what he had in mind, she tried to resist his advances but he viciously raped her. However, she managed to note his licence number and he was arrested the next day.

Unfortunately – because the drugged girl had voluntarily removed her blouse and the drugs had left her system – the charge was lessened to sexual battery and he was only given five years probation and ordered to undergo outpatient therapy. During his probationary period, his probation officer thought that Wilder was making progress, but in reality he continued to pose as a photographer and attempted to lure young women to his truck and home. He gave some of these women, and a number of prepubescent children, a hypnotic drug then photographed them when they went into a trancelike state, photos he kept as souvenirs of his dubious power.

Years later, police would find these disturbing photos hidden in his studio and would marvel that he'd gotten away with so many crimes for so long. And Wilder himself knew that his interest wasn't healthy, telling a female friend that this photography was a sickness that he felt compelled to repeat again and again.

Transvestism

Wilder also joined a dating agency, telling the interviewer that he worked too hard and needed to socialise more. He added that he didn't like bars and wanted 'someone with depth'. But the 36-year-old said that potential partners mustn't be older than their early twenties, so it was clear he needed someone that he could control. He even gave the impression that he missed his homeland, a homeland he had fled with little more than the clothes on his back when he was 24.

In the same time frame, the building contractor had women's lingerie delivered to the house and was seen wearing women's panties, something he'd done for many years.

Wilder now began to disappear for two to three days at a time – and when he returned, acquaintances noted that he looked badly shaken. He told them that he was having blackouts and couldn't remember what he'd done. This might have been true or it could have been his attempt at establishing a mental health defence for future court appearances – after all, he was still committing sexual assaults and rapes (and possibly murders) and experience had shown him that he'd eventually be caught.

Another Australian sex offence

Two and a half years later – on 22 December 1982 – Wilder struck again whilst in Australia visiting his parents: doubtless returning to the scene of his unhappy childhood was emotionally painful. Approaching two 15-year-olds on a New South Wales beach, he introduced himself as a fashion photographer and offered them work. He photographed them on the sand, then forced them into his vehicle and drove them to a deserted park where he made them remove their clothes. Wilder angrily demanded that the naked and weeping girls pose pornographically for him whilst he snapped away with his camera. He also indecently assaulted them both. He was arrested and was only allowed to return to America when his parents posted $350,000 bail.

Back in Miami, the increasingly sadistic millionaire continued to make lots of money. Superficially his life was going well as he'd made many female acquaintances for whom he threw regular late-night parties. He also set up a photographic studio in his garage and found numerous young women willing to pose nude for fortune and fame. But he had such low self-esteem that he couldn't enjoy the proceeds of his business. He despised himself and deep down he despised everyone else.

Another oral rape

But abusing young girls temporarily made him feel better about himself, and on 15 June 1983 he approached a ten-year-old and a 12-year-old girl at Boynton Beach City Park and abducted them at gunpoint. He drove them to a forest and made both of them fellate him before he drove them back to the park. Wilder got away with this crime as it was only after he was a fugitive almost a year later that his photograph was shown to the girls, who immediately identified him.

The Collector

Wilder could have had numerous consensual girlfriends, but what he really wanted was total ownership of a young woman. His favourite book was John Fowles' classic *The Collector*, and he owned several copies and had underlined various paragraphs.

Ironically, Fowles' book is about freedom and about the importance of rising above a dysfunctional childhood. The anti-hero, Frederick Clegg, has been raised by a small-minded aunt who has coached him to see every event in terms of 'nice' and 'disgusting'. He leads a very restricted life.

But a pools win enables him to give up work and buy a house, whereupon he kidnaps an art student called Miranda whom he has admired from afar and keeps her in captivity. He doesn't touch her – his dream is that he 'kept her captive in a nice way' to inspire her love.

But Miranda cannot love him and is understandably disgusted by his hobby of collecting butterflies, explaining, 'I'm thinking of all the butterflies that would have come from these if you'd let them live.' Later she urges, 'You've got to shake off the past... You've got to be a new human being.' And finally she begs him to live seriously, to *use* his life.

Having read – not even studied – a book such as *The Collector*, the healthy response is to become more open and less judgemental, to try to be all you can be. But sociopaths like Christopher Wilder (and serial killer Leonard Lake, who also cited it as his favourite book) only see the warped satisfaction of owning another human being, and, unlike Frederick Clegg, they sexually assault and deliberately kill...

The first murder

Christopher Wilder's personality continued to disintegrate as his work, social life and consensual girlfriends gave him no pleasure. He adored his three red setter dogs and gave generous donations to Save The Whale and to a charity which rescued seals, but his love of animals wasn't enough to stop him carrying out his homicidal desires.

On 26 February 1984, he was hanging around the Miami Grand Prix track when he saw attractive 20-year-old Rosario Gonzalez giving out aspirin samples. She'd previously modelled for him after other race track meetings so had no reason to be apprehensive when he offered her further work. From Christopher Wilder's viewpoint, Rosario was everything he wasn't – happy, focused, engaged to be married. He was about to ruin that happiness and that of her caring family.

We may never know exactly what he did to the Florida beauty contestant after he abducted her, as her body has yet to be found. But Wilder had access to numerous construction sites where a girl could have been held and abused before her corpse was quickly concreted over.

SADISTIC KILLERS

The second murder

Less than a fortnight later – on 5 March 1984 – Wilder had the urge to kill again. This time he contacted a former girlfriend, 23-year-old Elizabeth Kenyon. They had dated briefly two years before and he had asked her to marry him but she had gently declined. Elizabeth was 17 years his junior and not ready to settle down, though she had remained his friend.

But privately Wilder never forgave a rejection and now he phoned the intelligent and community-spirited young teacher and arranged for them to meet. They did so – then she disappeared.

As is usual when an adult goes missing, the police refused to treat it as more than a missing persons case, but her determined father hired a team of private investigators who soon uncovered the fact that she'd been seen at a gas station with Christopher Wilder and that he'd also known the missing Rosario Gonzalez.

Hoping to put pressure on the police, the private detectives leaked a 'Racing Driver May Be Linked To Missing Girls' story to the local paper. Though it didn't mention Wilder by name, he recognised that the authorities were on to him, put his dogs into kennels, wiped his house free of every single fingerprint and prepared to flee the state.

The fugitive

First, he went to his business partner in tears, admitted that he was petrified of spending time in prison and said that he was planning to disappear for a while. Manipulative to the last, he stole the man's credit cards.

Next, Wilder put a torture kit into the boot of his car, and prepared to start an extensive sadistic kidnapping and murder spree. Having decided that he wouldn't let the police take him alive, the 39-year-old had nothing to lose.

The third murder

That same day – on the afternoon of Sunday 18 March 1984 – he approached Theresa Ferguson in a Florida shopping mall. Theresa was pretty enough to be a model so wasn't surprised when the photographer with the expensive camera introduced himself and told her a little about his work.

The 21-year-old went into the Ladies and changed into the new clothes she'd just bought before tossing her old clothes into her vehicle. Thereafter, Wilder may have persuaded her to get into his car to look at his portfolio, or may simply have hit and abducted her.

Shortly afterwards he got stuck on a dirt track road and had to be helped out by a vehicle breakdown service. Police later speculated that Theresa may have been trussed up and gagged in the boot.

Wilder kept the young woman captive for a few hours and beat her viciously with a tyre iron before strangling her. Five days later her body was found floating in a Polk County creek approximately 70 miles from the abduction site.

A torture victim escapes

Two days after abducting Theresa, Christopher Wilder was ready to terrorise another victim. On 20 March 1984, he was prowling a Tallahassee shopping mall when he espied a pretty blonde 19-year-old Florida State University student called Linda Grober and began to follow her. He approached her in the car park where he introduced himself as a photographer and suggested that she'd be ideal for fashion work, saying that they could go to a nearby park and he'd pay her $25 to pose for photographs. She politely declined, whereupon he punched her viciously in the stomach, completely winding her. He then punched her in the face, one of the signs of a woman-hater. As she fell to the ground, he grabbed her and pushed her into his car.

He drove with the unconscious woman beside him until she began to revive, then he put her in the boot and strangled her until she passed out again. The sadist drove on to a motel in nearby Bainbridge, Georgia where he paid in cash, something he would do whenever possible. The hotelier had no reason to be suspicious of him as he looked calm and collected and was exceptionally well dressed in a suit and tie.

Wilder zipped Linda into a sleeping bag and carried her into his room. When she regained consciousness, he forced her to fellate him. He also tied her to the bed where he beat her, and, taking man's inhumanity to man to new depths, superglued her eyelids shut. The sadist also raped her repeatedly, watching *Dallas* on the television as he did so and telling the traumatised young woman that he liked the programme's lead male character JR because he had so much power over women.

Eventually Wilder began to tire, but he revived his flagging libido by carrying out his favourite sexual fantasy – electrical shock torture. He used a special 15-foot cord which he'd brought with him that had a plug and a switch attached. As Linda screamed inside her gag, he administered electric shocks to her naked flesh for the next two hours.

Later, he dozed off and she managed to crawl to the bathroom and lock herself in. Pounding on the walls, she screamed loudly and repeatedly called for help.

Waking swiftly and realising that other residents could arrive at any moment, Wilder grabbed his clothes, fled naked from the motel and drove off to find another girl. Linda subsequently spent a week in hospital recovering from her injuries then was taken out of the country as police feared Wilder might attempt to track her down and kill her rather than leave a living witness. She later returned to America and excelled in her studies, earning a PhD. She now works as a marine biologist, though she admitted in a recent interview that the memories of the pain that the sadist inflicted will never leave her, and she echoes the sentiments of most of us when she says 'I still can't believe that one human being could do this to another.' But someone had done terrible things to the pre-teen and teenage Wilder and now he was taking the maximum revenge…

The fourth murder

The day after Linda's escape, he approached a beautiful 24-year-old nursing student called Terry Diane Walden and asked her to do a photo shoot for him. The young mother declined politely but remained perturbed by the encounter. Back home, she told her husband about the pushy photographer.

By sheer chance, she visited the same shopping mall as Wilder on 23 March. He'd already approached numerous girls with his offers of fashion assignments and had been turned down. By now, he was trying less hard to persuade women that he wanted them for work, telling one, 'Try me – you might even like me.' They clearly didn't, and by the time he saw Terry, his head was full of revenge fantasies. He approached her and reminded her of who he was, trying to get her to take his business card. Again she declined but this time he followed her out to her car.

Terry doubtless felt safe – after all, it was a sunlit afternoon in a busy car park. But Wilder was desperate to control *someone*, to make his rage go away. Despite the risk of capture, he knocked her out with a blow to the head and bundled her into the boot of her own car then drove quickly to an unknown location where he tied her up with nylon rope and venetian blind cord, and put duct tape over her mouth to stifle her screams.

The sadist now tortured his victim with an eight-inch knife, stabbing her 43 times in the breasts and enjoying her muffled terror and frenzied writhing. Eventually his slicing blade punctured her lungs and heart and fractured two of her ribs. It's likely that he ejaculated spontaneously during this cruelty (sadists often do) as Terry wasn't sexually assaulted. She eventually bled to death. Afterwards, he dumped her body in a nearby canal before fleeing in her car: by frequently changing vehicles he knew that it was harder for the authorities to trace him. Three days later her corpse was seen floating in the water by a passerby.

The fifth murder

Wilder took a day off to recover, then on 25 March he struck again. This time he approached Suzanne Logan at a shopping mall in Reno. Suzanne – a happily married woman from Oklahoma City – had studied modelling and fashion design so may have agreed to look at the plausible photographer's portfolio.

True to form, Wilder hit her about the face and tied her up in the boot, before driving off in his stolen vehicle. He drove to a Kansas inn and smuggled her into his room, where he cut the 20-year-old's blonde tresses into a humiliating crop. This act also helped to depersonalise her, to make her less human in his eyes – and that made it easier for him to torture her without guilt.

He subsequently raped her, shaved her pubic hair and bit both of her breasts. But his rage remained and he turned her onto her stomach and began to torment her with the tip of his knife, inflicting six cruel puncture marks.

The victim's ordeal only ended the following lunchtime when he stabbed her fatally above her left breast. Afterwards he drove her half-naked body to the riverbank and dumped it under a tree, where it was found within the hour.

The sixth murder

Increasingly rootless and lost, Christopher Wilder drove to Denver and stayed there overnight, before driving on to Rifle, with the FBI in hot pursuit. They had put him on their Ten Most Wanted list and had distributed posters to various shopping malls warning women that the photographer might approach.

By 29 March, he'd doubled back to Grand Junction in Colorado and had breakfast there. At midday he approached a young woman and gave her his business card, introducing himself as a fashion photographer and suggesting he could find work for her. The woman declined politely and he walked away.

A couple of hours later he approached 18-year-old Sheryl Lynn Bonaventura, probably attacking her as she went to her car in the mall's car park. He drove her 100 miles then took her to a roadside café for a meal. The waitress noticed that Sheryl was very nervous and that she insisted on giving the waitress a lot of information, including her name. It may be that Wilder had his gun trained on her and she felt too frightened to escape. (Victims who attempt to escape in a public setting are more likely to survive than are those who let themselves be taken to a remote location. The kidnapper may not shoot with witnesses around – and, even if he does, the victim has a greater chance of being successfully treated at the scene.)

No one knows the exact sequence of events which followed, but Sheryl was kept alive for the next two days then brutally murdered. Her nude body was found five weeks later by the foot of a tree at a beauty spot in Utah. She had been tortured with a knife and shot once in the chest.

The seventh murder

Wilder was immediately ready to strike again. On 1 April he approached teenager after teenager at a beauty contest held in a Las Vegas shopping mall. Eight of them turned down his offer of a photo shoot, but the ninth, 17-year-old schoolgirl Michelle Korfman, left the shopping mall with him, planning to look at his portfolio in the car park. Other girls had arranged to meet him at a hotel for fashion photography work but he stood them up.

He kidnapped Michelle and drove to a downtown motel where he beat, raped and tortured her with his electric shock equipment. Her body was found the following month and taken to the Los Angeles County Morgue, where it was finally identified on 15 June. The FBI later recovered a photo (taken by another photographer) in which Wilder notices Michelle as she walks on stage. He is staring predatorily at her, and the Bureau described his expression as that of a homicidal maniac.

Meanwhile, Wilder's rage seemed to be growing rather than abating, and on 3 April a motel employee had to stop him from smashing up a drinks dispenser which wouldn't give him the soda he'd paid for. Perhaps recognising that he'd make further mistakes if drunk, he continued to avoid alcohol.

A torture victim lives

The next day he found himself another teenage victim, approaching 16-year-old Tina Marie Risico in a fashion store and offering her fashion photographic work. He took some photos of her on a nearby beach – it's clear that he had a fetish about girls on beaches, as he'd raped his first known victim on the sand when she was 17 and had later sexually assaulted two other girls on a beach.

After the photo shoot, Wilder tied her up and drove her more than 200 miles to a California inn, but he left within hours and drove on to an Arizona motel. There, he spreadeagled Tina on the bed and raped and tortured her with his knife until he fell asleep.

The following day he continued to torture the 16-year-old, giving her electric shocks all over her body and sexually humiliating her. He also cut off most of her hair, telling her that he wanted all his victims to look like the short-haired actress in his favourite film, *Flashdance*. As the days passed, self-styled psychics told the police that Tina was dead, which was a comparatively safe bet as she was known to have been kidnapped by Wilder who had murdered all of his previous victims. But Tina was still alive.

For, in his own limited way, Christopher Wilder had bonded with the teenager who'd been on welfare most of her life and had often gone hungry. And he realised that he could use her to help him abduct another girl.

Attempted murder

So it was that on 10 April, Tina approached a 16-year-old schoolgirl called Dawnette Sue Wilt and offered her a shop job. She introduced Christopher Wilder as the shop manager, and he suggested that Dawnette sign some forms he had in the car. Once there, he trained his gun on her and bound her wrists and ankles. He also sexually assaulted the girl in the back seat whilst Tina drove.

That night, the trio stayed at a room near Toledo, Ohio, and Wilder gave Dawnette electric shock treatment and raped her repeatedly, gagging her with duct tape so that the other residents couldn't hear her screams.

The following morning, he hog-tied and gagged Dawnette, and put her in the boot of his car, then he and Tina drove to a motel near Rochester. Again, he tortured Dawnette with his electroshock machine and raped her throughout the night whilst Tina sat in shocked silence, threatened with death.

The next day, he saw Tina's mother on television begging for her daughter's safe return. Vowing that the police would never take him alive, Wilder forced his two victims into his vehicle and took off at speed.

He decided to kill Dawnette, driving the bound and sedated girl to a dirt road where he attempted to suffocate her by pinching her nostrils together. She managed to pull free, so he produced his knife. She begged him to shoot her rather than stab her to death – but stabbing is a more sadistic act so the merciless Wilder stabbed her twice with all of his strength. Believing that she was dead, he drove off with Tina – but Dawnette managed to free herself from her bloodsoaked bonds and stagger to the roadside, where a shocked driver took her to the nearest hospital. (Though badly hurt and deeply traumatised, the 16-year-old eventually made a complete recovery.)

Meanwhile, Wilder wondered aloud if he'd actually succeeded in killing Dawnette. He turned the car round and returned to the scene of the stabbing, planning to shoot her. But, to his horror, she had gone.

The eighth murder

Realising that Dawnette could tell police about the vehicle he was driving, Wilder decided to steal another car. Spotting a Firebird that he liked the look of in a shopping mall car park, he carjacked the owner, 33-year-old Sunday School teacher Beth Dodge. He bundled her into her own vehicle whilst Tina followed in his car, obeying his instructions to keep close behind. When they got to the woods, Wilder marched Beth behind some trees and shot her dead then he and Tina took off in her car.

Tina is freed

Wilder knew that the net was closing in – and he told Tina he didn't want her to be with him when he was killed by the authorities. On 13 April he drove her to a Boston airport and gave her money for her flight home plus generous spending money. The distressed teenager walked towards the departure lounge, half expecting him to shoot her in the back. She boarded the plane and disembarked at Los Angeles, but, unable to face the thought of police and distraught relatives in her unkempt state, took a taxi to her favourite lingerie store. The press would later suggest that this was proof of her extreme disturbance but the truth was more prosaic: the poor teenager felt unclean, having been unable to change her underwear for the past nine days. After buying several items she shakily admitted to the manageress that she was the missing girl everyone was anxious about.

Another victim escapes

Within hours of saying goodbye to Tina, Christopher Wilder was ready to abduct another victim. Driving through Massachusetts, he saw a 19-year-old female driver standing by the roadside and she explained to him that her car had broken down. Wilder offered her a lift to buy petrol, but when she got into the passenger seat he pointed his gun at her and told her to keep quiet. She obeyed him, but when he slowed for a red light, she jumped out of the car and rolled across the road before making her escape. The teenager immediately contacted the police.

Death by cop

Later that day, Wilder pulled into a service station in New Hampshire – just 12 miles from the Canadian border where he had friends – and was recognised by two state troopers. The sadist reached for his pistol, and one of the troopers threw himself on top of Wilder to push the barrel in the other direction and prevent being killed. The gun went off, the first bullet hitting Christopher Wilder then coming out of his body and lodging in the officer's ribs. The second round entered Wilder's heart, killing him instantly.

An autopsy showed that his brain was perfectly normal, and, after a Catholic ceremony in Boynton Beach, his body was cremated. Several of his victims' relatives subsequently sued his estate.

Wilder's ashes were eventually returned to his family in Australia, the country where his sexual offending had begun.

CHAPTER FIFTEEN

IVAN ROBERT MARKO MILAT

After a lifetime of criminality which included rape, Ivan Milat graduated to murder in 1989. Over the next three years he tortured and killed seven hitch-hikers in Australia's Belango State Forest and attempted to kill another who thankfully survived to identify him.

Formative influences

Ivan was born on 27 December 1944 to Margaret and Stiphan Milat. Stiphan was from Croatia but had moved to Australia with his family in his twenties. He was 34 when he married Margaret, then only 16.

Ivan already had two brothers and two sisters, and when he was two, his parents presented him with another sister. Desperately poor, the family were living in a large shed. A year later the family moved to Liverpool, near Sydney, and Margaret gave birth to her seventh child, a boy, and two years later she produced another son.

By now Stiphan was drinking heavily and had begun to beat Margaret and the children. She too sometimes beat the children, stabbing one of her sons in the arm and scarring him for life.

Unable to cope, the Milats talked about sending some of the children to a Catholic children's home. As a result, one boy began to stab his own throat glands in order to make his face swell so that he wouldn't be sent away.

From the time that he was little, Ivan joined his older siblings in fixing up his father's market garden. The man would stand behind them with a belt, beating them if they tired. He also stood on Ivan and his brothers and thrashed them with a piece of wood. The neighbours called Stiphan 'The Gestapo' and found him terrifying.

Meanwhile, Ivan's parents continued to produce more brothers and sisters till 12 children were crammed into their impoverished home, and more were pending. He was put in charge of his younger siblings and was so busy with his chores that he never had time to play with his friends after school.

Further cruelty

Not that Ivan was safe from cruelty at school – the teachers at St Mary's primary and the Patrician Brothers who ran his Liverpool secondary were strict disciplinarians. He truanted frequently and at age 13 was sent to a home for delinquents, where he became an altar boy. His ten-year-old brother Bill, by now becoming equally distressed and out of control, was also sent to the same local authority home.

Ivan drew lots of houses whilst he was in care – abused and neglected children often spend hours drawing attractive and friendly looking houses, the kind of calm environment they long for. He also read comics, not being academically inclined.

Sent home at 14, Ivan arrived back to find his mother heavily pregnant with her thirteenth child, another son. It was vital that he bring in some money, so Ivan now became a roadworker like his father. He worked alongside the older man and was an equally hard worker and increasingly strong. After a long day at work he'd come home and help his mother with the younger children and the numerous chores.

Early crimes

Like many teenagers from impoverished and brutalising homes, he eventually turned to burglary. In January 1962 the 17-year-old was arrested. By now his 41-year-old mother – grossly overweight and almost toothless from so many pregnancies – was expecting her fourteenth child. (It would be another son, her tenth.) The magistrates took his mother's condition, and the fact that it was Ivan's first known offence, into consideration and let him off on a good behaviour bond.

But Ivan was incapable of good behaviour, and within weeks he broke into a garage. This time he was sentenced to six months' hard labour in a juvenile institution, a place where violence was the norm.

Released at age 18, he found labouring work but had so much money that it was obvious he was still thieving. By 20 he'd been charged with various offences, including attempted safe cracking and motor vehicle theft, for which he served time in Grafton Maximum Security Prison, New South Wales. There he was badly beaten by the guards with rubber batons, which resulted in him passing bloody urine for days. Moved to a minimum security camp, he began to lift weights in earnest, determined not to be the underdog again.

Arson

This time when he was released he became an arsonist, a crime which often has a sexual component. He would set fire to cars for kicks and to see how wildly they'd explode. Later, along with equally lawless friends, he gravitated to making pipe bombs and blowing up trees.

Family mayhem

Unsurprisingly Ivan wasn't the only violently parented Milat to turn to crime. One brother, Mick, was arrested for beating up a soldier and would later go to prison for most of his twenties, serving time for a series of armed robberies. Another, Richard, got into trouble with the authorities for possessing drugs and would later tell astonished workmates – who feared him – that stabbing a woman was like cutting a loaf of bread. Meanwhile Boris regularly beat up his wife, though she eventually persuaded him to seek psychiatric help.

The family was further devastated when 16-year-old Margaret – Ivan's favourite sister – was killed in a car crash which also injured one of her brothers, Wally. He would eventually be charged with drug and firearm crimes. Another brother, David, was left with limited movement in one arm and shoulder after coming off his motorbike. Later this same brother sustained brain damage in another road accident.

Rape

Ivan remained troubled by the suffering he'd experienced at home, at school and in the prison system. It would also later be rumoured that he'd been sexually molested by a woman who'd babysat him during his chaotic childhood. What's certain is that his experiences had left him with an overwhelming need to be in control and he partly achieved this by working on his physique and by cleaning his car until it shone, but it wasn't enough.

Out driving one day in 1971, he picked up two teenage girls who were receiving treatment at a psychiatric hospital. Suddenly he pulled over to the side of a dirt track and told them that if they didn't meet his sexual demands he would murder them. He continued to talk, clearly building himself up to act, and eventually produced two knives and two pieces of rope. He raped one of the girls before driving them both to a garage for soft drinks, talking as if they were all best of friends and suggesting they go on holiday together. The raped girl told the garage owner what had happened and Milat fled.

He went on the run to avoid the police and faked his own death, abandoning his car at a notorious suicide spot and leaving his shoes at the top of the cliff. As a result, his mother, who'd put up her house as surety that he wouldn't skip bail, faced homelessness.

Ivan was eventually captured and stood trial. But on the stand one of the girls said that she always refused intercourse but sometimes wanted it deep down, explaining, 'My mother is very religious and she never accepts the fact that I have sex with anyone.' She added that her friend had been flirtatious and had enjoyed the sex. Unsurprisingly, given her lukewarm testimony, the jury returned in record time to proclaim Ivan Milat not guilty and he walked free.

Marriage

Still aroused by forced sex, Ivan often raped his 16-year-old girlfriend, Karen, who was pregnant when he met her. She had desperately low self-esteem so married him on 20 February 1983. Thereafter the sex included sodomy, something he'd been introduced to in prison (though it's unclear if he was on the giving or the receiving end) and was now desperate to repeat. He was also cruel to animals, taking Karen into the forest where he wounded two kangaroos by shooting them, then tied one to a tree and slit its throat. Two months later his father, already weakened through bowel cancer, died of pneumonia. Karen noticed that Ivan became even more aggressive after the old man's death.

He began to control each aspect of the teenager's life so that she had to account for every moment of her day as he was profoundly jealous. She also had to produce receipts to account for exactly how she'd spent the housekeeping money, and he regularly criticised the choices she made.

Within three years his marriage was on the rocks, his badly beaten wife close to a breakdown. When she left him, he wept copiously then sold the house for far less than its market value so that she wouldn't get any cash. Though 40, he had the emotional maturity of a little child, a syndrome explained in the last chapter of this book.

He'd often threatened to burn his in-laws' house down, and a year after Karen left him, her parents' house was torched and Ivan was questioned. But, though everyone knew he was responsible, the police couldn't prove it and had to let him go.

Cruelty to animals

At work, he became increasingly strange, always carrying a foot-long Bowie knife in his rucksack. He stabbed a snake to death and cut it into chunks in front of his surprised workmates, and at weekends he went hunting, wounding sheep, goats and birds then slowly tracking them down. His sister-in-law Marilyn, whom he was having an affair with (and whom he had a daughter with) noticed that he seemed to like causing suffering. In 1989 she left him because he wouldn't commit to a serious relationship.

27 December of that year was Ivan Milat's forty-fifth birthday, but he had little to celebrate. His wife and his lover had left him and he hadn't even attempted to deal with the horrors of his childhood. Now he was back home living with his mother and it was time to pass the horror onto someone else…

Two murders

On Saturday 30 December 1989, students Deborah Everist and James Gibson set off from Liverpool in Australia to travel to a new age festival held on the New South Wales/Victoria border.

The 19-year-olds began to hitch-hike and were never seen alive again, except by their killer.

The teenagers were doubtless picked up by Ivan Milat, possibly acting in conjunction with another male. At some stage of the journey, a vicious and sustained assault took place.

James was stabbed in the spine, a wound deliberately made to paralyse him. There may have been a sexual aspect to this assault, as when he was found, his jeans were unzipped. He was also stabbed in the back and several times in the chest, breaking one of his ribs. He may eventually have been strangled as, when his corpse was found, the hyoid bone in his throat was gone.

Deborah Everist met an equally cruel fate. She was tied up and stabbed in the chest and through the ribs, and slashed across the forehead. Blows with a heavy object to her head had led to unconsciousness and, along with a stab wound to her heart, would have caused her death.

A potential victim escapes

Just over three weeks later, Ivan's bloodlust had built up again. On 25 January 1990, he offered a lift to 24-year-old Paul Onions, a British hitch-hiker. Paul had been working his way around Australia for several weeks and was now hitching from Sydney to Melbourne.

At first Ivan chatted pleasantly, but then he began to work himself up into a rage, suggesting that foreigners like Paul were stealing work from the locals. He stopped the vehicle, produced a gun and a length of nylon rope and made it clear that he was about to tie the youth up, saying that the motive was robbery.

Paul, who'd spent years in the navy, acted instinctively, jumping from the four wheel drive. Ivan leapt after him and they grappled by the roadside. Paul managed to escape and zigzagged up the road, his attacker in close pursuit. Ignoring the passing traffic, Ivan Milat fired wildly at the fleeing man.

Flagging down a vehicle, the 24-year-old persuaded the frightened woman driver to take him to the nearest police station. Meanwhile his middle-aged attacker returned to his vehicle and sped away.

Paul lost his backpack containing all of his money and his clothes during the escapade, but felt extremely lucky to have escaped with his life. He continued to have flashbacks to the crime, reliving his attacker's enraged voice and merciless stare.

It's possible that Paul Onions escape scared Ivan Milat and that he kept a low profile for a while because a year passed before his next known murder. Meanwhile he continued to torture animals and birds.

A single murder

On 20 January 1991, Ivan was on holiday, driving through Queensland and Sydney for several days. He doubtless encountered experienced traveller Simone Schmidl, who was going to meet up with her mother in Melbourne, and forced her deep into the forest. The 21-year-old German tourist was stabbed from behind through the spine, causing paralysis.

Thereafter, her killer may have tied her up – a loop of wire and piece of material were found beside her body. Her blouse was pushed up and she was gagged. Like the other victims, she was apparently sexually assaulted, her underpants removed. Simone was also stabbed again and again in the chest and spine, one of those wounds resulting in her death.

Another double murder

In late December 1991, the backpacker murderer struck again. 21-year-old Gabor Neugebauer and 20-year-old Anja Habschied, who'd been hitchhiking in Bali and Australia, set off for Darwin. They were excited about the next part of their journey, travelling around Indonesia, but anxious in case they couldn't travel the 4,200 kilometres to Darwin airport in time to catch their flight.

Sometime between 26 and 31 December, the killer attacked the unsuspecting couple. Gabor was muffled with two gags and shot several times in the head.

Anja was partially stripped – her body would be found nude below the waist – and was tied up: cord, tape and a leather strap were found in the vicinity of her body. She was eventually made to kneel and was decapitated. Her head has never been found.

In the same time period, Ivan Milat arrived home with a bullet hole in his van which had clearly been shot from the driver's seat. He also arrived at his brother David's house with a bloody knife and told him he'd stabbed a man through the spine. The comment was overheard by one of David's friends – and Ivan offered him the passport of a German male.

A double murder

Milat's final known victims disappeared between 18 and 21 April 1992. Joanne Walters, from Wales in Britain, had travelled to Australia to become a nanny. There she met up with fellow Brit Caroline Clarke and the two young women decided to travel around the continent together. En route to a fruit-picking job, they met their deaths.

Joanne was stabbed twice in the spinal cord at the base of her neck which would have paralysed her. When she was helpless her killer may well have moved on to his other victim, Caroline, and immobilised her.

He gagged and probably sexually assaulted Joanne – when found, her body had an undone fly and no underwear and her shirt was pushed up at the front. Her killer had stabbed her again and again in the chest and rained further blows with his single-bladed knife on her spinal column. Some of the chest wounds had sliced into her internal organs and caused her death.

Caroline may also have been sexually assaulted as her bra was unfastened. She was stabbed once in the back and was probably strangled – again the hyoid bone in her throat was missing when her body was found. Her sweatshirt was wrapped around her head and face then she was shot ten times from three different angles, the killer moving her head around and essentially using it for target practice. The police were surprised at so many gunshots being used, but they hadn't yet made the acquaintance of the trigger-happy Ivan Milat who, whilst hunting, often fired hundreds of rounds.

Desolate families

Meanwhile, the families of all the missing backpackers campaigned the authorities endlessly for news, even flying out to Australia. They also hired private detectives at considerable cost. But as the months passed with no sight or sound of their loved ones and none of the backpackers' traveller's cheques being cashed, they began to fear the worst.

A new girlfriend

That summer, Ivan began to date an Indian divorcee called Chalinder Hughes, something which surprised his family as he'd previously been xenophobic. By now he was dying his greying hair black and consistently trying to act like a younger man. He worked hard all day then came home and mowed the lawn, obsessively cleaned his car or made model aeroplanes, neither his girlfriend or his neighbours suspecting his darker side. Ivan also read murder mysteries, particularly enjoying the novels of Patricia Cornwell with their emphasis on forensic detail. As long as the murders remained undiscovered, he knew that he was safe from official scrutiny.

The bodies are discovered

But in September 1992, Joanne Walters' body, half hidden by leaves and large sticks, was found by two joggers. Her T-shirt bore the rips made by numerous stab wounds and the fly of her jeans was partially undone. The following day police found Caroline Clarke's corpse nearby, her head still wrapped in the red cloth peppered with bullet holes.

Over the next few weeks the other corpses were discovered, each with bindings, gags, stab wounds and bullet holes. It was clear that a sadistic killer was at large.

Custody

The police were already suspicious of the Milat family because a witness had reported hearing Richard Milat say 'they haven't found the two German bodies yet' at a time when no one knew that Anja and Gabor were dead. Richard had also told a friend that once someone got a taste for this sort of torture-murder it was just like having a beer. And Alex Milat had told the police that he saw two vehicles, each with a frightened-looking gagged female in the back seat, but that he'd just assumed the male drivers were taking them into the forest to have a good time. Not to be outdone, Ivan had joked about stabbing a German man through the spine.

Looking into the brothers' histories, the authorities found that Ivan had been off work during every one of the seven murders. Searching his home, they found numerous items belonging to the murder victims, none of which he could explain.

Brought back to Australia and shown a line-up consisting of 13 photographs, a nervous Paul Onions picked out Ivan Milat as his attacker. Ever since the attempted abduction, the man's face had haunted his dreams.

A taciturn Milat now refused to answer any questions and was remanded in custody until his trial.

Brothers in arms

Milat's defence, suggested by his lawyers, was that two of his brothers had committed the murders. But Richard Milat's work sheet gave him an alibi for the period whilst James Gibson and Deborah Everist were being killed. The defence noted that items belonging to the backpackers were found at Wally Milat's house and at Alex Milat's house as well as at Ivan's place.

But the prosecution showed how the forensic evidence stacked up against Ivan Milat. Apart from the numerous grisly souvenirs in his attic and garage, an unused bullet consistent with the ones used to kill Caroline Clarke was found in his car. Human blood was found on rope in his possession and he was unable to explain whose it was and how it got there. Equally damningly, Paul Onions identified Ivan Milat in court.

After three months of testimony, Ivan Milat himself took the stand and denied everything. Questioned as to why he'd asked a friend who worked as a security guard to get him handcuffs, he replied 'they just seemed to be interesting'.

The prosecution agreed that it was possible Milat had committed some of the murders with another member of his family. In turn, the defence wondered if Wally Milat could have planted the backpackers' possessions on Ivan out of jealousy as his ex-wife had been close to Ivan. And they suggested that Richard Milat could have gotten off work earlier than his work records showed and attacked Paul Onions.

But Richard had apparently never grown the thick moustache that Paul Onions saw on his attacker. Ivan, too, said he'd never had such a moustache but a work photograph showed him sporting one less than a fortnight before he pulled a gun on Paul.

On 27 July 1996, 51-year-old Ivan Milat was found guilty of all seven murders and given seven life sentences. He was additionally sentenced to six years in prison for the attack on Paul Onions.

Afterwards, Bill Milat, three years younger than his brother Ivan, beat up a photographer outside court and smashed both his cameras. He was subsequently fined.

Two killers?

So were there two killers in the double backpack murders? Some criminologists believe that the very different methods of torture-murder points to two men being present, one doing the shooting and the other the paralysing and stabbing. They note that solo killers tend to favour one style of killing and repeat it. They also note that one of the bodies was covered by huge logs which probably couldn't have been lifted by one man. There again, a killer in the grip of a psychotic rage has much more energy than the average man... They suggest that one man tried to prove his dominance by doing more and more extreme things to the bodies such as decapitation in order to impress a slightly more submissive brother.

But there's equally potent evidence which points to Ivan Milat acting alone. He was working solo in his mid twenties when he tied up the two girls and raped one of them. He was also alone when he pulled a gun on Paul Onions and made moves to tie him up.

Ivan enjoyed buggery, which might have explained why so many of the victims were lying on their stomachs. He loved to fire his guns and the victims who'd been shot dead had been subjected to overkill. He also knew how to stab someone in order to paralyse them, a technique previously described to him by a Vietnamese war veteran.

What is clear is that several members of the Milat family – and possibly some of their friends – strongly suspected what was going on. One brother told a friend that Ivan was doing bad things again. Another brother suggested that the authorities look at unsolved murders in Jenolan Forest, and they found that a man there had had his shirt wrapped around his head before his skull was used for target practice, just as Caroline Clarke's had been – and that Ivan had been working in the vicinity. A third brother hinted that Ivan may have killed up to 28 men and women.

One anthropologist said that the level of violence indicated 'someone who was beaten by his father' but, sadly, this fate had befallen all of the Milat boys.

Prison

Immediately on his arrival at Maitland Maximum Security Prison, Ivan Milat was beaten up by another prisoner. Shortly afterwards, hearing rumours of an escape attempt, the authorities moved him to Goulburn Jail where he has subsequently gone on several short hunger strikes and threatened suicide.

But on other occasions he seems to enjoy life, following a fitness plan and reading legal texts in the hope of mounting an appeal. He also waves to everyone in the visitor's room when he's visited by one of his many relatives. Surprisingly, given the amount of evidence against him, he has a group of supporters who call themselves the FIRM – Friends of Ivan Robert Milat – and who are campaigning for his release.

Milat appealed against his sentence, claiming that he'd received poor legal representation, but the appeal was dismissed. In 2004 he launched another appeal, stating that the Crown had put a case to the jury unsupported by its own witnesses. But this appeal was out of time.

In 2006 the sadist had a television and a toaster installed in his cell by the authorities as a reward for good behaviour – but that summer there was outrage when the victims' relatives found out about these privileges. Both items were withdrawn but later returned. It's likely that we'll hear more about Ivan Milat, as young women remain missing from areas where he used to work...

CHAPTER SIXTEEN

PAUL CHARLES DENYER

Australia's best known sadistic killers are doubtless Catherine and David Birnie, who killed four young women and were in the throes of torturing a fifth teenage girl when she escaped. The country has also witnessed massacres by some of the worst spree killers in history, each accruing a substantial body count.

But the three murders which Paul Denyer committed during a seven-week period in 1993 were so shocking that they made headlines around the world. And his ongoing gender confusion ensures that he continues to make headlines today.

Formative experiences

Paul was born on 14 April 1972 to Maureen and Anthony Denyer who had arrived in Australia from England seven years before. They moved around, eventually settling in Campbelltown near Sydney. Paul was their third child and they went on to have three more.

When Paul was a baby he rolled off a bench and knocked his head. Thereafter, whenever he did anything unusual, his family would joke, 'That's because you were knocked on the head as a child'. Head injuries can indeed change a person's behaviour, especially if damage is done to the frontal lobe of the brain which handles aggression and impulse control.

Despite the fact that he had four brothers and a sister, Paul found it hard to mix with the other children in his kindergarten class. He was already overweight and looked stressed and awkward. Thankfully he seemed to fare better at primary school.

But when Paul was nine, the family moved to Victoria so that his father could become manager of a steak house. None of the Denyer children wanted to move but Paul found it especially difficult and was too shy to make friends with his new classmates, most of whom had known each other for four years.

Though still a young boy, he continued to grow rapidly in height so that he was much taller than his contemporaries. For this he was laughed at and bullied. He increasingly turned to food for comfort and his girth also became a reason for local jokes.

Alleged sexual abuse

Paul would later say that he was sexually abused by a relative during these years, but later still he said that he'd invented this allegation. The relative he named has protested strongly of his innocence and is considered blameless. However, it's very likely that Paul was abused by *someone*, especially in the light of his later sexual identity crisis and appalling violence.

Unable to connect with other people, he began to collect knives and catapults, fantasising about a powerfulness which he lacked in real life. He also began to cut off the heads of his sister's dolls, something that serial killer Edmund Kemper also did as an abused boy. Paul went on to stab his sister's teddy bears with a knife and slapped a classmate who mocked him so that the pencil the boy had been sucking lodged deep in his throat.

SADISTIC KILLERS

Cruelty to animals

Given his immense size, Denyer probably pubertised at age ten and began to have sexually sadistic fantasies. It is known, at least, that at this age he stabbed the family kitten, slit its throat and hung it from a tree in the yard where his family were sure to notice it.

At 12, he stole a car. It was doubtless a cry for help but the authorities released him with a warning. At 13, he phoned the fire brigade and falsely reported a fire. That same year he was discovered vandalising a nearby property. Again, nothing was done to counsel this deeply disturbed boy.

By age 14, Paul wanted to kill. As such, he sought out films where people were brutally murdered, watching them over and over. By 15, he'd gravitated to sex crime, bullying another boy until he agreed to masturbate in front of a group of children. For this he was charged with assault.

Unemployment

Denyer found work in a Safeways supermarket and it was there, at age 20, that he met his first serious girlfriend Sharon Johnson. That same year they moved into a flat in Frankston together, but Denyer lost his job after deliberately knocking down a woman and child with a convoy of shopping trolleys. Again and again he displayed the sadist's urge to destroy. He found a job at a marine workshop but spent so much time making knives to fuel his fantasies that his employer fired him.

The grossly overweight young man now lay around at home imagining what he'd like to do to women, whilst his long-suffering girlfriend Sharon held down two jobs to make ends meet.

Later that year, 1992, he broke into a flat in the same block as his own and slashed all of the owner's clothes to pieces.

He also cut up her engagement photographs, determined to destroy the symbols of another's happiness.

Deciding to up the ante, he entered the flat of another girl called Donna whom he pretended to like but secretly hated. He planned to stab her to death but she was out so he settled for dismembering her cat instead. He then dragged its entrails through the house to create a bloody trail and wrote messages in blood on the walls, including the chilling words 'Donna – You're Dead.'

Not content with this mayhem, Denyer cut the throat of two kittens which lived in the house and put their bodies into the plastic bath where Donna bathed her baby. He also slashed all of her clothes.

But, satisfying as these cruel acts were, they fell short of the sadist's fantasies about murdering women. The following year he would do just that.

The first murder

On 12 June 1993 at 7 p.m. he was loitering at a bus stop in Langwarrin, near Frankston, looking for a victim when student Elizabeth Stevens walked past him. He followed her and stuck a piece of aluminium pipe in her back, telling her that it was a gun. He then walked the terrified young woman to a nearby park.

After choking her into unconsciousness, he stabbed her again and again in the throat. She was still alive and began to move about, so he thrust his knife into her chest six times. He also cut her from her breast to her abdomen, before raking his blade across her stomach again and again. The blade broke during the stabbing so he stamped on her neck.

The young woman began to make the death rattle, whereupon the sadist stripped her above the waist. He also broke her nose and cut her face, the ultimate hate crime. When her dying convulsions had ended he dragged her body to a nearby drain.

Later, back at home, his girlfriend noticed nothing different about him, for as a sadistic psychopath in the grip of an obsession he felt absolutely no remorse for his actions. But he did have one overwhelming desire – the desire to hurt, mutilate and kill again.

A failed murder attempt

Almost a month later, on 8 July, he approached 41-year-old Roszsa Toth on a Frankston pavement, pushing a knife into her side and telling her that he had a gun. He tried to pull her into a nearby wildlife reserve but she fought back, biting his fingers. She raced into the road and tried to flag down a car but none of them would stop for the shoeless woman with the torn clothing so Denyer was able to attack her again. For the second time she fought him off, then successfully flagged down a car.

The second murder

Paul Denyer fled, but he was determined to find himself another victim. That same night he took the train to Kananook and found himself a vantage point where he could watch people entering and leaving a local store. He saw 22-year-old Debbie Fream park her car and hurry into the shop, whereupon he clambered into the back of her car. There he saw a baby seat so he knew that he was about to kill a young mother – Debbie had given birth only 12 days before.

Debbie returned to her car with groceries and cigarettes, and he held his pretend gun to the back of her head and ordered her to drive to a quiet area. After she followed his instructions and parked, he told her to get out of the vehicle. When she obeyed him, he looped a cord around her neck.

When she began to lose consciousness, he stabbed her again and again in the head, neck, breasts and arms. During the ensuing struggle he managed to pull her top off, exposing her breasts. He also stabbed her in the stomach, pleased when air began to whistle through the holes in her throat.

Eventually he took her body to a nearby paddock and covered it with branches before heading home to his empty house. Later he picked his girlfriend Sharon up at the railway station but he acted calmly and she noticed nothing untoward.

The following day he returned to Debbie Fream's car, stole the $20 note he found in her purse, and took her groceries home with him. He feasted on them as her body decomposed.

For the next four days Debbie remained listed as a missing person, then, on 12 July, a shocked farmer discovered her mutilated corpse.

The third murder

Beginning to perfect his modus operandi, Paul Denyer scouted out a local bike track, realising that he could cut a large hole in the fence and push himself and his next victim into the adjacent nature reserve. He cut three holes with pliers on the morning of 30 July, then returned in the afternoon in his car. Slumped down behind the wheel, he waited for a female victim to come along.

17-year-old college student Natalie Russell was en route for home at 3 p.m. when the overweight giant came up behind her and held his knife to her neck. She struggled until he threatened to cut her throat, whereupon she stopped fighting and offered him sex or money if he'd let her live. But the evil sadist got off on causing fear and pain so he dragged her to the ground and cut her across the face. Natalie began screaming and jumped up but he forced her down again and looped a strap around her neck.

He strangled her while forcing her head back, then made a small incision in her throat and pushed his fingers into it, pinching her vocal cords and twisting them. She began to lose consciousness and he grabbed his knife and almost decapitated her, then watched her die. Afterwards he kicked the body and slashed down the side of the dead girl's face.

Later he collected Sharon from her work and spent the evening with her at her mother's house. He'd later say that he'd never hurt his girlfriend, that she was a kindred spirit. She asked him about the cuts on his hands – obtained during the stabbing frenzy – and he said he'd sustained them whilst fixing his car.

But unknown to Denyer, a piece of skin from his finger had become attached to the bloody skin of his third victim so the police were closing in.

Clues

The police had been hunting extensively for the Frankston killer for weeks, but now they had the skin of his finger to extract DNA from. They also suspected that he was the owner of a yellow Toyota Corona which had been seen parked near the track around about the time of Natalie's homicide. A policeman had taken a note of its location and description, suspicious because the vehicle didn't have number plates. Luckily he'd written down its number from the registration label so they were able to trace it to Paul Charles Denyer. They were also fortunate in that a passerby had seen a man matching Denyer's description slouching down in the car as if he didn't want to be seen.

When the police interviewed Denyer, they noticed several cuts on his hands, the kind that criminals often sustain during the commission of a violent act. But he denied being the killer, and, taken to the police station, continued to deny culpability for several hours. Only when the police asked him for blood and hair samples to determine his DNA did he realise that it was all over and admit to murdering all three women. Asked why, he said that he'd hated women for years.

Whydunnit

Paul Charles Denyer's trial began on 15 December 1993 at Victoria's Supreme Court. He pleaded guilty to all three murders, the attempted murder of Roszsa Toth surprisingly being reduced to the lesser charge of abduction.

A clinical psychologist identified the defendant as a sadist. He said that Denyer had explained that his cruelty was due to his hard upbringing which included sexual abuse by a male relative, abuse that relative strenuously denied. But the psychologist noted that he'd known numerous people who'd had worse experiences than those which Denyer reported and they hadn't gone on to kill.

On 20 December, Justice Frank Vincent sentenced him to three life terms without the possibility of parole plus an extra eight years for the abduction of Roszsa Toth.

A lesser sentence

Denyer appealed to the Full Court against his life sentence and on 29 July 1994 it reduced his tariff to 30 years after which he has the possibility of parole. It was a chilling moment for his victims' relatives, knowing that he might be released in his middle years whilst still strong and dangerously disturbed.

Apology

After several years in prison, Paul Denyer tracked down his relative and wrote to him, apologising for accusing him of sexual abuse. The man was devastated to hear from Paul, as Paul had previously threatened to kill his wife and children and they'd emigrated to begin a new life.

Sex change

Incarcerated in Barwon prison in Victoria, Denyer became a Christian then a Muslim. But religion didn't make him content and, in 2003, he decided that he was really a woman trapped in a man's body and applied for a sex change. After due consideration, he was turned down as an unsuitable candidate. Undaunted, he began to refer to himself as Paula and applied to change his name by deed poll.

He also asked the authorities to let him wear make-up and, when they refused, he appealed citing Victoria's anti-discrimination laws. Meanwhile he has used the prison sewing machine to make his clothes look more feminine and has had photographs taken of himself wearing feminine attire.

His supporters – he's been receiving gender identity counselling in prison – say that he should be allowed to become a woman despite the fact that he admitted to police that he hates them. His detractors agree on one thing – that it would be a good idea to cut his manhood off. Interestingly, this desire to cross-dress is common amongst violent men who've been sexually abused in childhood. He will be eligible for parole in 2023 at 51 years old.

PART FOUR

EVERYTHING UNDER THE SUN: SADISM WORLDWIDE

CHAPTER SEVENTEEN
SADISTS WHO KILL MEN

43 per cent of serial killers are known to have had homosexual experiences, though not all gay serial killers are sadistic – Dennis Nilsen, for example, killed his victims as quickly and painlessly as possible in order to have access to their corpses for necrophiliac sex.

Nilsen's childhood with a disapproving stepfather was lonely and unhappy, but gay sexual sadists invariably come from much more dysfunctional backgrounds: John Wayne Gacy, who mercilessly abused over 30 boys to death on his customised torture-board, was beaten and humiliated by his father and given frequent enemas by his mother throughout his formative years. Similarly, Dean Corll and Elmer Wayne Henley endured childhoods with violent fathers, and Corll's mother married five times.

The bisexual teenager Peter Dinsdale murdered 26 people in British arson attacks, standing outside their domiciles and enjoying their screams as they burnt to death. His childhood was the most tragic of all as he was neglected, humiliated and rejected by his prostitute mother for years then targeted by paedophiles in children's homes.

The first two cases in this chapter are of Michele Lupo who was born in Italy (but killed his victims in Britain) and Andrew Cunanan who was born in America. At the time, the press concentrated on the fact that these were revenge attacks by gay males who'd been shunned by the glitterati – as such, the sadistic aspect of their crimes was largely ignored.

MICHELE LUPO

Michele was born on 19 January 1953 in Northern Italy to a religious family who arranged for him to join the church choir. Enrolled at the Leonardo Da Vinci school, he was creative, being exceptionally good at art. Virtually nothing else is known about his early years but he later told police that he had 'been used and abused in the past'.

After leaving school the attractive and charismatic young man did a correspondence course in languages then was drafted into the army for the obligatory two years' national service, ending up in an elite commando unit. Police believe that he was taught how to kill during these two intensive years.

At 21, Michele – who by now was actively bisexual – travelled to London and began work as a hairdresser, a profession he would maintain for the next three years. In his spare time he occasionally slept with women but mainly frequented gay clubs in London, Paris and Amsterdam.

Prostitution

With his dark good looks and slender body, Michele Lupo was a big attraction in these clubs and he realised that he could use this to his advantage. He placed an advert offering sadomasochistic services to gay males.

For the next three years he made a living from flogging men, building up a sizeable collection of whips, riding crops, nipple clamps and chains. He also built a torture chamber, complete with black walls and complex restraining devices, in his home. In 1977 he was fined £40 for buggering a man in a public toilet – but, fines aside, he found the work enjoyable and it could have gone on for many years if fear of the deadly disease AIDS hadn't gripped the gay community.

Gay men were the first to become aware of the dangers of promiscuous unprotected sex and began to take precautions. Perhaps because of this, Lupo's clientele dried up. It's equally likely word got around that he was too sadistic even for a masochistic client.

Whatever the circumstances, Lupo cut back on his prostitution services by the spring of 1980 and became a sales assistant at the Yves Saint Laurent fashion house in Brompton Road, London. The softly-spoken and compelling Michele was so good at his job that he eventually ended up as a manager, a post which brought him into contact with various wealthy socialites.

Lupo's mediterranean good looks again won him many admirers, and he slept with both men and women amongst the trendy crowd. He also had sex in sadomasochistic (SM) bars in Los Angeles, New York, Paris, Amsterdam, Hamburg and Berlin. The police later found that he'd separately bedded a wealthy British husband and wife, neither of whom knew of the other's infidelity. The authorities had to discreetly advise both to have HIV tests.

A less comfortable life

Something unrecorded happened in 1984 which caused Lupo to leave Yves Saint Laurent and lose touch with its fashionable clientele. Thereafter he took a badly paid job in a clothes store. But he again increased his earnings by charging men for sadomasochistic services. Sometime in the mid 1980s he found that he was HIV positive but he didn't tell his many partners and continued to have unprotected sex.

As his life went downhill, he fantasised about torturing and killing these punters as he felt like little more than a rich man's plaything. By now he'd had more than 4,000 gay lovers and was increasingly tired of consensual practices.

Attempted murder

On 10 March 1986, he made his way to the Coleherne pub in Earl's Court, London – the same gay pub where Colin Ireland would find his victims in 1993. He got talking to 31-year-old Kevin Pius MacDonagh, a science graduate who worked as an osteopath. Michele had hung a black leather glove from his jeans back pocket, the sign that he was a dominant male, and Kevin enjoyed being the passive partner, so the two men agreed to a liaison and went to a nearby derelict building and entered the darkened basement. But before the sexual encounter had even started, Lupo wound a scarf around Kevin's neck and strangled him until he appeared to be dead, then he slipped soundlessly away.

An hour later his victim regained consciousness and staggered home, deciding not to report the incident to the then homophobic police.

The first murder

Five nights later Lupo re-experienced the urge to kill. He returned to the Coleherne and went to the toilets where he masturbated openly. Shortly afterwards he got into conversation with James George Burns, a 36-year-old British Rail guard. James, a gentle depressive, was eager for company.

Back at the derelict basement with Lupo, he either willingly indulged in or was coerced into a comparatively rare form of sadomasochism known as pet shop sex. This involves a tube being put into the passive partner's rectum, into which the dominant party introduces a small animal such as a mouse. The tube is then withdrawn and the terrified creature bites and claws inside the recipient's rectum as it tries to fight its way out.

Before or after this agonising practice, Lupo bit James Burns three times in the chest, hit him about the face and head and strangled him with a scarf. He also attempted to pull his eyes out. Burns lost control of his bowels as he died, and Lupo smeared this excrement over the victim's face and body. He also bit off part of James Burns tongue and threw it across the room.

Police awareness

When Kevin MacDonagh, who had been strangled into unconsciousness in the same basement, read about James Burns' murder, he bravely went to the police and gave them a good description of Michele Lupo. They now knew that they were dealing with a potential serial killer who was targeting gay men.

The second murder

On 4 April 1986, Lupo killed again. This time the victim was 26-year-old Anthony Connolly who had an arts degree but had recently been made redundant from his chef's job. Anthony loved attention and on that particular Friday night was wearing ripped jeans which showed off the pink tights he wore underneath.

Michele arrived at the Prince of Wales pub in Brixton with a platonic female friend but eventually left her with her colleagues and struck up a conversation with the extroverted Anthony. Shortly after 1 a.m., the men walked to the local railway line and entered a disused worker's hut. There they partially undressed and caressed – when Anthony's body was found, his trousers were around his ankles. Michele Lupo bit him on the chest, neck and penis during the attack. He may have used, or forced his victim to use, amyl nitrate – when inhaled, it causes the heart to speed up and gives the user a rush, but in susceptible people it can bring on a heart attack.

In the moments which followed, Lupo hit Anthony in the face, blackening one of his eyes. He then strangled him with a stocking. Afterwards he went on to a nightclub and socialised for an hour, completely indifferent to having caused another violent death.

The third murder

His next victim, in mid April, was a vagrant whom he walked past at a part of Charing Cross railway station known as Cardboard City. There, destitute men and the occasional alcoholic woman lived in boxes, enduring a cold and dangerous existence. Michele Lupo strangled the passing vagrant with a pair of tights. An unemployed man found the corpse and reported it, only to be regarded with great suspicion by the police. Already suicidal due to his reduced circumstances, he was interrogated in custody for the next two days.

Attempted murder

Later that same month, Lupo approached 22-year-old Mark Leyland who was hanging about beside the underground near Hungerford Bridge. The two men decided to have sex in a nearby derelict toilet and, when they got there, Mark began to give Lupo oral sex. Suddenly the younger man had an instinct that he was in danger and he moved away from Lupo, who immediately began to batter him viciously about the head with his fists. Lupo then left the building, grabbed a piece of wood and began to hit his victim through the broken window. He eventually collapsed to the ground and Lupo left.

When Mark regained consciousness he went to the police, but understandably gave the impression that he'd been mugged rather than admit that he'd gone with a stranger to an outbuilding for casual sex. It would be many months before the truth was revealed.

The fourth murder

In the early hours of 25 April, Lupo struck again – and this time he succeeded in killing his hapless victim. After an evening clubbing in the Copacabana in Earl's Court Road, he picked up 24-year-old Damien McClusky and steered him towards a basement in a derelict building. There both men pulled down their trousers and embraced. A beating probably followed – the younger man's corpse was bruised when it was found.

At some stage Damien began to fellate Michele Lupo, whereupon Lupo wound a ligature around his neck and strangled him to death. It was three weeks before his decomposing body was found.

Another attempted murder

On 8 May, the sadist arranged a sex session with another gay man on Wandsworth Road – but at the last moment the other man's instincts told him not to go through with it. He left the scene and Michele approached David Nigel Cole who had been looking for a tryst. The two men went to a lorry park and indulged in mutual masturbation. They also fellated each other but Lupo soon lost his erection – this is commonplace for a sadist as they often become impotent when not causing suffering or fear.

The killer looped a black stocking around David's neck and began to strangle him. The victim struggled violently and Lupo retaliated by biting his thumb. He then got him down on the ground and knelt on his chest, punching him in the face.

David continued to struggle and finally managed to pull the ligature from his neck, whereupon Lupo casually got up and loped off into the night.

It must have taken courage for David Cole to report this encounter to the police, especially as he'd left his gay partner back in their flat after telling him that he was just going out for a burger. But he described the would-be murderer perfectly and was even able to hand them the stocking which Michele Lupo had used as a ligature.

The police asked David Cole to tour Brixton's gay pubs with them in the hope that he would see his attacker – and on 15 May he successfully identified Michele Lupo in the Prince of Wales pub.

Arrest and trial

Michele Lupo was arrested and immediately admitted murdering Anthony Connolly and Damien McClusky. The following day he admitted James Burns' murder. He eventually also admitted the vagrant's murder plus the three attempted murders, though police wondered if he'd killed other men during his European jaunts. Appearing at the Old Bailey in the autumn of 1986, he was sentenced to life imprisonment.

The motive

The press (which anglicised his name to Michael) naturally assumed that Lupo wanted revenge on the gay community which had given him AIDS, but he told police that this wasn't his motivation. He said that he'd been badly treated in the past and was angry at society, but refused to give further details about the abuse.

Death

For the next nine years Lupo remained in jail but his HIV eventually metamorphosed into full-blown AIDS and he died in Durham Prison in February 1995, a month after his forty-second birthday. He died without showing any remorse for his crimes.

ANDREW PHILIP CUNANAN

Cunanan is interesting because only his third victim was repeatedly tortured – yet his sadism was evident from his teenage years.

Born on 31 August 1969 to a wealthy retired navy officer and his housewife spouse in California, Andrew was the youngest of four children. His Catholic family encouraged him to become an altar boy, and it's likely that he was sexually abused by his priest. (The cleric was later charged with abusing several of Andrew's contemporaries and Andrew himself phoned a sexual abuse hotline to report the man.)

By his teens he had become sexually interested in other boys and began to lead a double life, for at school he was openly gay, bringing a male date to a school function when he was 18, but at home he continued to conform.

Deserted

When Andrew was 19, his father was accused of embezzling at least $500,000 from his employer. Facing jail, he left his family and fled to the Philippines where he'd been born. Devastated,

Andrew dropped out of college and joined him there, but couldn't stand the impoverished conditions in which his father now lived. He returned to his mother's house in San Diego but she too had had to settle for very reduced circumstances. By now he was using violence as a means to an end and he threw her into a wall during one fight, dislocating her shoulder. Determined to recover his life of luxury, he began to prostitute himself to wealthy middle-aged gay men.

Losing control

For the next few years, Cunanan lived life to the full, partying several nights a week with the jet set and smoking the finest cigars. Some of his lovers let him live with them for several months, lending him expensive cars and giving him a generous allowance. But as he reached his mid twenties his energy began to fade and he started to take drugs in order to revive his *joie de vivre* and his libido. Two of his lovers finished with him as they were tired of his mood swings and Andrew failed to find another meal ticket – wealthy homosexuals could afford to buy slender boyish men rather than prematurely ageing and overweight ones.

By his twenty-seventh year, Cunanan was alone, bitter and in increasing debt. He even had to sell his car in order to pay his rent.

Animal abuse

He began to smoke crack to get through the day, and, as his life continued to disintegrate, he took to torturing animals, picking up crabs on the beach and burning out their eyes with cigarettes. But his main fantasies revolved around hurting men and he often bought gay bondage magazines to fuel his lust.

That spring, he had an argument with his best friend Jeffrey Trail and stopped speaking to him. The supposed slights that he'd suffered echoed around and around in his head. At the end of April or 1 May 1997, he phoned Jeffrey, asking the 28-year-old to meet him at David Madson's house – David had been Andrew's lover but they'd now split up at David's instigation.

The first murder

Jeffrey told his boyfriend that he'd be back soon to go dancing. He entered Madson's flat and within 15 minutes Cunanan had attacked him, battering his head 30 times with a claw hammer until he collapsed.

The unfortunate David Madson came back to find a corpse on his floor and blood everywhere. It's possible that Andrew Cunanan now held him hostage. In any case, the men spent the next two days in the apartment with the corpse.

The second murder

When more and more people – concerned at Jeffrey Trail's disappearance and David Madson's uncharacteristic unsociability – began to knock on the door, Cunanan knew that it was time to leave. He drove 33-year-old Madson, a world-renowned architect, to a lake outside Minneapolis and shot him once through the back of the head and once through the eye, a third shot grazing his face. He dumped the body on the shoreline where it was found by fishermen on 3 May.

The third murder

Cunanan now travelled to Chicago and committed his only torture-murder of the series, that of 75-year-old Lee Miglin. The older man was a wealthy businessman who had been happily married for many years. He had no links to the gay community so it's still unclear why Cunanan targeted him. The killer had told friends that he knew Lee's son Duke and that the two were going into business together, but Duke denied knowing Cunanan – and Cunanan had lied numerous times in the past to make himself look more exciting, claiming to be everything from a pilot to a naval officer. It's even possible that Andrew Cunanan simply saw Lee parking in his garage as he drove past and hated the fact that the man had obvious wealth and status, things he himself had irrevocably lost.

What's certain is that he made the older man suffer for untold hours, binding him to a chair in the garage and wrapping a plastic bag around his face. Cunanan made a little hole in the bag, a hole which he would pinch closed repeatedly whilst watching his victim fight for breath. During the beatings which followed, Cunanan broke every single rib in his victim's body and hit him 15 times about the head.

The sadist eventually stabbed Mr Miglin in the chest with a pair of gardening shears and almost severed his head from his body with a saw. He also backed over the man's torso with his car four or five times. Finally he left the corpse in the garage, where it was discovered by Mrs Miglin when she returned from a trip.

The fourth murder

The killer drove on to New Jersey in one of Lee Miglin's cars but knew he'd have to exchange it for a less traceable vehicle. He determined to steal the first suitable transport he found.

Driving past a cemetery on 9 May, he saw a pickup truck parked outside the cemetery keeper's lodge. Shooting dead the owner, 45-year-old William Reese, he stole the vehicle and drove on to Miami in it.

Cunanan now moved into an inexpensive motel near Gianni Versace's upmarket home. He was known to have met the fashion designer at an exhibition where they'd exchanged a few words but friends were adamant that they hadn't had a relationship. Whatever his motivation, he'd spent the last month fantasising about killing the older man.

The fifth murder

On 15 July 1997, he waited outside Versace's apartment with his handgun at his side. When Gianni approached the gates of his house, the 27-year-old killer shot him in the face. Versace collapsed and Cunanan walked up to him and shot him execution-style through the head.

Suicide

Aware that he was now on the FBI's Ten Most Wanted list, Cunanan phoned a friend and endeavoured to secure a false passport. Meanwhile, he lived in various houseboats which he'd broken into – but his cover was blown on 23 July when a caretaker boarded one of the boats. Knowing that the police were closing in on him, and realising that to kill the caretaker would only buy him a few more hours of freedom, he shot himself in the head.

CHAPTER EIGHTEEN
SADISTS WHO KILL WOMEN

Sadists kill women far more often than they kill men – hardly surprising given that sadists prefer to torture the gender they are sexually attracted to and only three to ten per cent of the population is gay.

As the following cases from Austria, Germany and Canada show, many of these heterosexual sadists kill serially, the period between murders diminishing with time.

JOHANN JACK UNTERWEGER

Unterweger served 15 years for a 1974 murder, was paroled early due to media pressure and went on to torture and kill at least 11 more women.

In a way, Unterweger went to jail before he was even born, as his prostitute mother Theresia was behind bars in Austria during much of her pregnancy. He came into the world on 16 August 1952 and she swiftly abandoned him. The little boy never knew his father, rumoured to be an American soldier, and was initially raised by his violent alcoholic grandfather.

After seven years of horrendous neglect and abuse, Jack – for he preferred to be known by his middle name – was sent to various foster homes which were equally abusive. His guardians were so disinterested in his welfare that he didn't even learn how to read and write.

Women had failed him utterly and now he was going to make them pay, so at 16 he attacked a prostitute. He served jail time for this sentence but came out ready to harm other prostitutes. He would hurt such representations of his neglectful mother over and over again.

Jack Unterweger became a violent pimp, abducting a female and forcing her into prostitution. He went to jail for this offence and served further jail time for burglary and for receiving stolen goods and stealing cars.

The early murders

In 1974 he teamed up with a prostitute to rob her friend Margaret Schefer's house. The pair then lured 18-year-old Margaret into Unterweger's car. Unterweger drove her to the woods, bound her hands behind her back, stripped her and mercilessly beat her. He also battered her about the head then strangled her to death with her own bra. Covering his trail as best he could, he pulled her naked body into the bushes and covered it with leaves.

That same year he sadistically killed prostitute Marcia Horveth, gagging her with adhesive tape, restraining her and eventually strangling her with her own stockings and a necktie. His accomplice was questioned by the police about Margaret Schefer's murder and soon implicated Unterweger, who was arrested and charged with this crime. He was given a life sentence, so the authorities saw no point in having an expensive trial to try him for Marcia Horveth's equally cruel death.

Yet the authorities were aware of how dangerous the young man was as, talking of the Schefer homicide, he'd told the

Salzburg court: 'I envisioned my mother in front of me and I killed her.' The court psychologist labelled him a sexually sadistic psychopath who would kill again if released.

A second chance

At the start of his life sentence, Jack behaved like most of the other prisoners, building up his body at the gym and adorning it with numerous intricate tattoos. But eventually he learned to read and write and became so adept with language that he produced widely praised poetry, short stories and plays – a cruel background often generates an exceptional writer or artist as the child has to create a rich inner life in order to survive. After ten years in jail he wrote his autobiography *Purgatory* which became a bestseller and was later made into an equally lauded film. The prison guards were impressed by his talent and won over by his personal charm, running errands for him and encouraging him to edit the prison newspaper.

Meanwhile, the public and the press clamoured for his release, seeing the man of letters rather than the underlying psychopath. Fifteen years into his sentence, on 23 May 1990, he was given parole.

For the next few months, he was the darling of the media and regularly appeared on radio and television to discuss literature and to promote his plays. Enjoying the attention, he bought himself a car with a personalised number plate, a wardrobe of designer suits and lots of men's jewellery. He also frequented the best nightclubs, buying champagne for the numerous women who shared his bed.

But Unterweger wanted much more than a consensual lover. He ached to cuff a woman, to brandish his knife or whip and hear her plead for mercy. His cruel lust built and, four months after his release from prison, he killed again.

SADISTIC KILLERS

The first post-prison murder

On Tuesday 14 September 1990, during a trip to Czechoslovakia, he went to the red-light district in Prague where he encountered Blanka Bockova, a butcher's assistant. Jack struck up a conversation with the pretty brunette in an upmarket bar, and the two were still drinking as midnight approached and Blanka's friends left.

The sadist probably persuaded Blanka to go with him for sex – she was known to have had many lovers and sometimes swapped sex for favours. She had no reason to fear the well-dressed and ostensibly charming journalist.

But when he got her to a quiet location, he handcuffed her hands behind her back, stripped her, beat her and stabbed her. She fought back as best she could but was no match for the angry, lustful man.

Like most sadists, Unterweger probably orgasmed whilst causing his victim's suffering. Eventually he strangled her with her own stockings and dumped her in the forest, pulling her legs wide apart and finding that she had a tampon inside her. After covering her corpse with leaves, he threw her clothes and her ID in the nearby Vlitava River and left the scene.

The second murder

Jack Unterweger returned to Austria and committed his next known murder. On 26 October 1990 he picked up Brunhilde Masser, a street walker, and took her to a forest north of Graz. He stripped her, tortured her with a knife and possibly beat her – her buttocks had been eaten by animals by the time her body was found so the pathologist couldn't be sure. She had been violently strangled with her own stockings and left naked in a stream.

The third murder

On 5 December 1990, he propositioned prostitute Heidemarie Hammerer and took her to an unknown location. There he cuffed her hands, stripped her naked and gagged her with a strip cut from her own underskirt. He beat her buttocks and she struggled so hard that the handcuffs cut into her wrists, leaving them badly bruised.

Finally he strangled her with her own stockings, re-dressed the body and drove it to a remote part of the woods where it was discovered on New Year's Eve by young hikers enjoying a winter walk.

The fourth murder

On 7 March 1991, he approached street prostitute Elfriede Schrempf and persuaded her to accompany him. We'll never know what he did to her pre-mortem as her body was skeletonised by the time it was recovered seven months later. She was naked apart from a pair of socks.

On 9 March, Unterweger phoned one of the unlisted numbers in her notebook and threatened the person who answered the phone, making obscene comments about the profession of prostitution, his mother's profession. He made a series of such calls, mentioning Elfriede's name. It's not unusual for sadists to contact their victims' families with such taunts and they often use such phone calls as a masturbatory aid.

The fifth murder

Sylvia Zagler also died in March after Unterweger approached her in Vienna. The prostitute had large eyes and a soulful look, but the sadist was indifferent to her appealing expression. He stripped, cuffed and tortured her and eventually strangled her with her own lingerie, leaving her body in the woods.

The sixth murder

That same month he approached Sabine Moitzi in Vienna and took her to a forested area outside the city. He stripped her of all her clothes except for her jersey, restrained her wrists and arms and strangled her with her own clothing. Again, the body was obscenely displayed in this, his third murder of the month.

The seventh murder

Regina Prem was the next woman to die, murdered in Vienna by the sadist in April 1991. Months later, whilst under stress after being interviewed by the police, Unterweger would phone her husband and tell her that he'd murdered Regina, that God had ordered him to punish and execute her. He made several such phone calls, aware that at the time Regina was still only listed as a missing person, that her family desperately hoped she'd be found alive.

The eighth murder

In the same time period he lured Karin Ergolo into his vehicle and hit her about the face with a blunt instrument. He cuffed her, stripped her of all her clothing except for her shoes and stuffed her underwear down her throat as a gag. Finally sated, he strangled her with her own clothing and took her to the forest in Vienna where he left her corpse in a naked and splayed state. Previously he had covered his dead victims with leaves, but now he was displaying the cadaver for others to find – causing shock like this is yet another form of sadism. It's in direct contrast to most killers who want the body to remain hidden as long as possible so that their crime remains unknown and forensic clues can be washed away.

The Los Angeles murders

The Austrian police now began to suspect Jack Unterweger because the crimes were so similar to his 1974 murders. They ascertained that he'd been in the vicinity of the homicides and that a man answering his description had been seen talking to several of the prostitutes. But Unterweger had said in interviews that he liked such call girls so police considered that he might simply have been paying for their services.

Aware that they'd put him under local surveillance, Jack outsmarted them by flying to Los Angeles in June 1991. He told the LA police that he was a journalist and asked them to show him the red-light district to help with his crime research. They obligingly drove him around and pointed out the best places to find prostitutes. He also posed with several female police officers and kept one of the photos as a souvenir.

The ninth murder

Unterweger could now start torturing and murdering women in America, where no one suspected that he was a sadistic serial killer. On 20 June he picked up prostitute Shannon Exley. Unusually, he had intercourse with her – his semen was later found in her vagina, alongside that of her six previous clients.

Shannon was wearing a bra, and the sadist particularly got off on the idea of strangling women with their own bras. Unfortunately for him the Czechoslovakian and Austrian prostitutes hadn't worn any and he'd had to strangle them with their slips and stockings. Now he removed Shannon's bra and began to fashion it into an elaborate noose. The attractive young prostitute probably had to watch this bizarre ritual as she lay handcuffed on the ground, concealed from others by a row of garages. Eventually he strangled her with the customised bra and left her lying naked on her back.

SADISTIC KILLERS

The tenth murder

Another attractive young prostitute, Irene Rodriguez, met the same fate. She was soliciting near Jack's hotel when he persuaded her to accompany him to a quiet location. She too was strangled with her bra which had part of the elastic removed.

The eleventh murder

That summer, Sherri Long was the third Los Angeles prostitute to die at Unterweger's hands. She was handcuffed, stripped, beaten and strangled with her specially refashioned bra.

On 17 July 1991, the sadist returned to Austria, convinced that no one would link him with these brutal murders. He had killed at least three women in six weeks.

The new girlfriend

Like many sadists, Jack found it easier to attract and manipulate much younger women so, now approaching 40, he started a relationship with an 18-year-old waitress called Bianca. Meanwhile the police were closing in, and Unterweger knew he had to leave Austria before he ended up behind bars.

Bianca was happy to go with him and they travelled to Miami together and rented a house, but Jack found it difficult to be satisfied by one woman alone and he found it equally difficult to stay out of the limelight. As a result, he phoned various Austrian journalists and told them that he was innocent, that he was being picked on by fate and by those who were jealous of his success.

Short of cash, he persuaded his girlfriend to start dancing topless and hand over all her money to him. In other words, he was reverting to his early role as a pimp rather than as a loving boyfriend. Bianca told everyone that they were having a wonderful time – but his diary would later show that he was plotting her death.

Eventually the happy couple decided to relocate to Florida and asked Bianca's mother to wire money. She promised to do so but in reality tipped off Interpol who were waiting for them at the Western Union office on 27 February.

Unterweger had sworn that he would never go back to prison so now he behaved like a trapped animal, dodging into an adjacent restaurant and racing through its kitchen sending food and crockery flying. He made it to a nearby car park before officers drew their guns. He began to sob when they said that he was wanted for murder in Austria and that they were going to extradite him.

Trial

In June 1994, his trial began in Graz, Austria. He was tried for all 11 known murders – the one in Prague, seven in Austria and three in Los Angeles. The defence said that a man as popular with women and with the literati had no need to resort to murder and that this alone suggested that he was innocent.

There would have been some truth in this statement if Jack had been a normal man with a normal ego – but he was a cold-blooded psychopath and extreme sexual sadist who hated prostitutes. Having vanilla sex with a 'good' woman was never going to satisfy him.

Unterweger himself said in court that he was being wrongly judged for cavorting with such call girls. He shrugged away his lack of alibi, suggested that he didn't understand the DNA evidence against him and told the jury 'I'm counting on your acquittal.'

But the prosecution built a strong case. They noted that part of one of Blanka Bockova's hairs was found in Unterweger's BMW and fibres from his scarlet scarf were found on Heidemarie Hammerer's corpse – he'd probably used it to bind her legs whilst he tortured her. Other prostitutes testified that Jack Unterweger always handcuffed them before sex, and several of the corpses had handcuff marks on their wrists caused as they struggled violently to escape his cruel ligature and knife. He'd been in Prague, Austria and Los Angeles when the respective murders took place and they bore marked similarities to his 1974 homicides. A psychiatric report judged him sadistic but sane.

On 28 June 1994, the jury found him guilty of nine out of the 11 murders – two of the Austrian victims had been too decomposed for them to still bear Unterweger's trademark signature. He looked genuinely shocked as he was sentenced to life imprisonment.

Suicide

But Unterweger had sworn that he'd never be caged again and he was true to his word. A mere six hours into his sentence, he took the cord from his prison uniform and tied one end around his neck and the other end to the bedstead then he leaned forward, strangling himself to death.

JANUSZ KOMAR

A known criminal in his native country of Czechoslovakia, Janusz Komar made his way into Germany on 2 September 1980 and asked for political asylum. Whilst awaiting a decision he joined the French Foreign Legion but he was so inept that they threw him out.

In early June 1981, he was charged with two violent assaults but Germany still chose to officially grant him asylum status. As he was only 18, he was given a suspended sentence for the two attacks. Unfortunately nothing else has been reported about his formative years.

The heavily-built and tall teenager continued to cause mayhem, breaking into cars and buildings rather than earning an honest living. He also crashed a stolen car whilst drunkenly driving it. This time he spent six months in a juvenile detention facility, after which he soon broke his parole.

The first murder

Released on 10 November 1983, he set up home with another drifter. A week later he loitered beside a vineyard near Trier, desperate to hurt someone and hoping that a female victim would come along.

26-year-old Japanese student Matsuko Ayano was simply in the wrong place at the wrong time and was attacked by the sadist. He dragged her into the vineyard and began to kick her, breaking her nose, jaw and cheekbones and fracturing her skull. He also jumped up and down on her body again and again, causing horrific internal injuries and leaving his size ten boot marks embedded in her flesh.

During the prolonged attack, he pulled down her jeans and panties. Afterwards he rifled through her handbag and stole her cash. The pretty young woman was found by a shocked winegrower and rushed to hospital where she died four days later without ever regaining consciousness.

Because there was no semen on the body, police believed that they were dealing with a simple mugging. But, like many sadists, Janusz Komar had doubtless orgasmed when his victim screamed in pain. He wanted the victim's money but the violence he used was so excessive that it clearly gave him a thrill.

The second murder

Eighteen days later his bloodlust had built again and he entered a flower shop at the gates of a Regensburg cemetery. Finding the shop owner, 68-year-old Maria Weis, alone on the premises, he kicked her repeatedly, stamping on her face and body until she was unrecognisable. During the assault she died of shock or loss of blood.

A customer found the elderly victim, her blood dripping from the walls and counter, and was so shocked that she had an angina attack. The cash register was open and its contents gone.

Komar's flatmate knew his propensity for violence so feared the worst when he came home covered in blood, but Komar paid off the drifter. Police only fathomed that he was the killer when they caught him robbing a house near the first murder scene and realised that he was also on record for committing crimes close to the second murder scene. Taken into custody, his boots matched the terrible stamp marks on both victims' flesh. He immediately – albeit very casually – confessed.

On 15 November, he was found guilty of two counts of premeditated murder and was sentenced to ten years in prison, the maximum sentence for juveniles under German law at that time.

WAYNE CLIFFORD BODEN

Like Richard Cottingham, who is profiled in the American Sadists section, the Canadian Wayne Boden fantasised about biting female breasts and put his fantasies into action again and again…

Details are scarce about Boden's 1948 birth and subsequent upbringing, but it's known that – like Jack Unterweger, Robert Rhoades, Neville Heath and Christopher Wilder – he was superficially charming and attractive to women. Indeed, he'd worked as a male model in his teens, though his career was over by 20, the age when he started to sadistically kill.

The first murder

On 23 July 1968, he went with 21-year-old Norma Vaillancourt to her Montreal apartment. It's likely that the sex play was at first consensual, as when Norma was found she had a faint passive smile on her face. But during the sex act, her lover got violently carried away and he strangled her then bit her breasts.

The second murder

The following summer, Shirley Audette talked to one of her ex-boyfriends, telling him that she was getting into something dangerous with a new lover. The 24-year-old was doubtless talking about consensual sadomasochism – she had no way of knowing that Boden wasn't satisfied with this. On their final date he raped her, bit her breasts and strangled her, dumping her body behind an apartment complex in West Montreal.

The third murder

Four months later, on 23 November 1969, he collected his latest girlfriend Marielle Archambault from the jewellery store where she worked. He'd introduced himself using a pseudonym so her workmates heard her address him as Bill. The 20-year-old was really pleased with her new beau and already kept a photograph of Bill in her room, telling friends that she was entranced by him. But all that was about to change…

Marielle must have been dumbfounded when her lover suddenly attacked her in her Montreal home. Recovering from the shock, she put up a ferocious struggle but was eventually raped, had her bra torn from her body and her breasts savagely bitten. She was cruelly strangled to death.

The fourth murder

On 16 January 1970, Boden attacked 24-year-old Jean Wray in her Montreal flat, stripping her and biting at her breasts until he drew blood. Her boyfriend had arrived during the assault to find the door locked so he understandably assumed that no one was home. He went back shortly afterwards and found the door unlocked. His girlfriend's still-warm naked and defiled body lay on the settee but the killer had fled.

The fifth murder

Aware that the authorities were hunting him, Boden now moved 2,500 miles to Calgary. There he began dating teacher Elizabeth Anne Porteous, again introducing himself as Bill. Some of her colleagues saw the immaculately dressed Bill in his blue Mercedes and noticed its distinctive window advertisement for a butcher's firm.

In the early hours of 18 May 1970, Boden attacked his girlfriend in her bedroom and a violent struggle ensued. He eventually wrestled her to the floor and raped her. He also bit her breasts. Boden strangled Elizabeth during the assault, but not before she'd torn a cufflink from his expensive shirt. It was found under her naked body the following day.

Arrested

At last the police had one of the killer's possessions, a tangible clue to his identity. With the help of Elizabeth Porteous's colleagues, they also identified his car and he was arrested on 19 May. The vampiric serial killer of five lovely young women was still only 23 years old.

Boden admitted dating Elizabeth on the night of her murder but he denied mutilating or killing her. Fortunately a local dentist was able to confirm that they were his bite-marks on her breasts – there were 29 points of similarity between

Boden's teeth and the bite-marks on Elizabeth's body. These bite-marks would later connect him with the other victims. His underpants also had the victim's pubic hair clinging to them.

At the Alberta Supreme Court, he stood trial for Elizabeth Porteous's murder and was found guilty and given a life sentence. Returned to Montreal, he was tried for three of the other four murders – he denied killing the first victim, Norma Vaillancourt, though her body bore his trademark signature.

During these trials, the man dubbed the 'Vampire Rapist' admitted all but the first sadistic killing, telling the court that he'd only wanted to restrict the women's breathing for their mutual pleasure, but that he'd got carried away. He explained that during the strangulation he'd been overwhelmed by the desire to bite their breasts.

Killing once by mistake was plausible – but killing four times wasn't, and he was given another three life sentences. He was sent to Kingston Penitentiary where he began serving his sentence on 16 February 1972. By now, psychologists believed that he was a sadistic psychopath, as he'd admitted being indifferent when the women died during his biting frenzy and breath-restricting acts.

For the next three decades, the sadist remained in the Canadian penitentiary then he began to suffer from an undisclosed illness. In February 2006 he was admitted to Kingston Regional Hospital where he remained seriously ill for the next six weeks. On 27 March, at 3.30 a.m., he passed away and the prison immediately began making funeral arrangements. He was 58 years old and had spent over half of his life in jail.

CHAPTER NINETEEN
SADISTS WHO KILL CHILDREN

The sadist who abducts a child tends to be particularly cruel because he (or she) loathes the child's innocence. Children who are loved and supported are innately happy and their carefree nature reminds the sadist of his own desperately unhappy childhood and fills him with rage. The case studies which follow are located in Wales, England and America and the victims are a 14-year-old boy, an 11-year-old girl and a two-year-old girl. (The case of a woman who tortured and killed her own child can be found in the Female Sadists chapter.)

MALCOLM KEITH WILLIAMS

Malcolm was born into a deeply dysfunctional family and had eight siblings. Two died during childhood and another two left home at the earliest opportunity, whilst one of Malcolm's sisters was removed from her parents for her own safety when she was only eight.

But Malcolm remained with his family in Glamorgan, Wales and by nine was attempting to have sex with other boys, a sign that he himself was a sexual abuse victim. At 12 he was sent to a children's home where, desperately unhappy, he ran away several times. Brought back, he began to show signs of criminality, breaking into a school and stealing a bicycle. He subsequently broke into a factory.

Moved to an approved school, he was sodomised by some of the older boys. Subsequently, on visits home, he tried to sodomise his 12-year-old brother. Sent to borstal, he continued to practise homosexuality.

Towards the end of 1960, 20-year-old Malcolm Williams was once again released from borstal and returned to his parents' house, finding work as a fitter's mate alongside his father in a power station. 29 December started off as yet another potentially unfulfilling day. He worked at the power station all morning, had his lunch at a café and tried to talk to several schoolgirls there.

But instead of returning to work after lunch, he walked to the beach at Gileston, near Barry in Glamorgan, knowing that he wanted to be masturbated by a boy. There he approached a 14-year-old named Andrew Bonnick, who had been walking by the sea with two friends.

Malcolm Williams waited until Andrew's friends left then he approached the boy and told him that another child had had an accident in a nearby concrete pillbox, a building which had been erected during the war and was now used to hold driftwood. Andrew helpfully entered the pillbox, whereupon the 20-year-old sadist attacked him, tearing at the boy's trousers so hard that he jerked the garment down to the boy's thighs but left his belt around his waist.

But Andrew fought back, grabbing at his attacker's donkey jacket. Enraged, the sadist hit him in the neck and eye then began to beat him with a notched stick. He beat the teenager again and again, aroused by his screams.

An hour or two later, realising that he'd probably been seen with the boy, Malcolm Williams concocted a story. He went to a nearby house and reported finding the lad. But the woman he reported this to was suspicious as the sadist's hands, face and clothing were covered with blood. She called her husband, Albert Bonnick, and he accompanied Malcolm Williams to the pillbox – only to find that the dying boy was his own son. He only recognised Andrew by his clothes as his face had been beaten to an unrecognisable pulp. The badly injured teenager was taken to hospital but died within hours of shock and loss of blood.

Asked to give a statement, the 20-year-old said that he'd been at work all day – but witnesses came forward who'd seen him loitering on the sand and in a nearby café. And Andrew's departing friends had noticed he was being followed by a young man.

The sadist then admitted to the murder, saying that the boy wouldn't take his jeans off so he had punched him in the neck. Holding him against the wall, he'd ripped at his trousers but the boy had refused to cooperate so he blacked his eye then began to beat him mercilessly with a branch. Eventually he'd thought the boy was dead so had made up the story about finding him.

Sentenced to life imprisonment, he was later refused the right to appeal.

ARTHUR SALVAGE

Details of this sadist's background have been lost in the annals of time as he was born in 1908 – but it's on record that at 20 he was sent to borstal for a series of petty thefts. It was noted at the time that he was of unbalanced mind.

By 1931 he was working as a poultry farmer and living with his 50-year-old widowed mother in a cottage in Upper Ruckings, Kent. He also socialised with his mother, who was in poor health, often taking her to the cinema.

But on 3 July 1931, the older woman went out for the afternoon, leaving Arthur to plant 300 cabbages. The tall, fair-haired young man did so until he saw his 11-year-old neighbour Ivy Godden playing with a ball. She'd been sent into the woods with her older brother to fetch firewood but had lagged behind, feeling bored.

The exact sequence of events will never be known, but little Ivy ended up in Arthur Salvage's bedroom where he tied her hands together and firmly bound her feet, looping the same piece of rope around her neck. He proceeded to beat her about the face, delivering a particularly savage blow to the left side of her head. He also inserted an object into her rectum in a deliberate attempt to cause pain. (He'd doubtless been sodomised by older boys whilst in borstal and had become anally fixated as a result.) During this period, Ivy's mother thought she heard her daughter screaming 'Mammy, mammy.' She searched the nearby woods in vain.

Ivy's ordeal continued. It would later be ascertained that she hadn't been sexually assaulted, Salvage doubtlessly gaining sufficient pleasure from hurting her. Eventually – though she was already dying from her rectal injuries – he strangled her to death.

A makeshift burial

The sadist put his victim's corpse in a sack and buried it in the woods that night and when Ivy's parents asked if he had seen her, he replied that he hadn't. The following day, a Saturday, he joined the local search party, telling the Goddens that Ivy was a nice little girl. On the Sunday the shallow grave was found by several of Ivy's relatives who saw that the earth had been disturbed in the clearing. They dug down a few inches and found her bound and bloodied body dressed in underwear.

On the Monday, the killer played cricket with his friends and suggested they send a message of support to Ivy's parents. He felt invincible, but, unknown to him, the police had brought in a bloodhound and taken it to the makeshift grave – and it led them straight to Arthur Salvage's cottage gate.

There, the police found sacking identical to that used to hold Ivy's body. They also found the type of rope which had been used to bind her hands and feet. Goat hair had been found on the sack – and the Salvages owned several goats. Salvage could also tie the type of reef knots which had been used to bind the child.

Confronted with the evidence, the 23-year-old admitted to the sadistic murder, saying that, for his mother's sake, he was going to be honest with the detectives. He calmly gave details of the homicide, though he wept en route to the pre-trial hearing. But by the time the case went to trial at the Old Bailey, he'd changed his mind and pleaded not guilty, saying that he'd falsely admitted to the crime in order to please the detective and get the questioning over with.

Finding him guilty after only 30 minutes of deliberation, the judge said that Salvage was 'possessed by some hideous sexual perversion'. He duly sentenced him to death. Salvage was given the opportunity to make a statement but merely stammered 'I say…' then appeared lost for words.

He refused to appeal and was questioned by three psychiatrists at Wandsworth Prison who all suggested that he be certified insane, noting that his 'sadistic impulses were sometimes uncontrollable'. His death sentence was then commuted to life imprisonment in Broadmoor.

There, the sadist admitted that six months previously he'd murdered an 18-year-old maid called Louisa Steele, attacking her at Blackheath in south-east London and biting her all over, before beating and strangling her. Detectives believed his account of the murder but he was never charged for this sadistic crime.

THEODORE FRANCIS FRANK

Sex was a forbidden subject during Theodore Frank's strict religious childhood in the USA and he understandably became obsessed by it. This obsession, combined with the beatings he received at home and at school whilst he was very young, doubtless helped inform his extreme sadism.

At 14 his parents sent him to a seminary to study for the priesthood, but he was thrown out two years later for having sex with one of his colleagues. Later he joined a monastery but was told to leave after he was found masturbating, a natural act (even animals do it) but one that many believe is forbidden by Biblical text. He then went to St Louis University to study electrical engineering but remained plagued with anger and self doubt.

Theodore Frank abandoned his studies three years later when he married at age 22. A year after marrying, he was arrested for indecent exposure. In the same year he became a voyeur, masturbating whilst staring through a girl's bedroom window. Later he was arrested again for molesting a ten-year-old girl in front of a church.

This time he spent two years at a mental health hospital in Missouri, but on his release he molested other children and spent further time in a mental facility before serving further jail time. Surprisingly, his wife had three children with him, though she was deeply perturbed by his crimes.

Throughout the 1960s, Theodore Frank was sent to prison for numerous sex offences, including raping a four-year-old Bakersfield girl and molesting an eight-year-old and a ten-year-old girl. Suspected of the murder of a seven-year-old boy in Missouri, he swiftly relocated to California.

In January 1978, he was released early from the Mentally Disordered Sex Offender Programme in Atascadero State Prison as he convinced those running the course that he was cured, this despite the fact that he admitted molesting 150 children over 17 years.

Theodore Frank found work as an engineer with a large aerospace firm, but his main reason for living remained the desire to hurt children. Yet with his silvery hair and beard, impeccable taste in clothes and cultured voice, he looked an avuncular man.

On 14 March 1978, he approached a small boy in Camarillo, Ventura County and began to lead him away from his garden, but luckily his mother saw the attempted abduction and grabbed her child back.

Within minutes he espied two-year-old Amy Sue Seitz playing in her aunt's garden. The aunt, who looked after the child every day, went upstairs for a couple of moments. Seizing his chance, the sadist persuaded the tiny child to approach the fence. When she did so, he lifted her over and abducted her.

An appalling death

Taking her to his nearby home, he used pliers on her nipples, pinching and tearing them from her body. He spent the next six hours torturing her, removing the skin from her hips and buttocks. He also repeatedly plunged and held her down in the bath, only briefly letting her up to breathe. At one stage, anxious neighbours knocked on his door asking him if he'd seen the child, but he told them no. In reality, she was alive in his living room and he was in the midst of pulling her fingers off.

The sadist returned to the child, raped her and punched her in the face. He also beat her so viciously about the head that she suffered a skull fracture and a brain haemorrhage. Eventually he strangled her to death with his bare hands. He drove 28 miles to Topanga Canyon to dispose of her corpse then put his car through the car wash to remove any forensic traces. When his wife returned from work, he behaved completely normally.

Two days later, pet dogs found the tiny corpse and dragged it home. Noticing both his dogs playing with a bloody object in their driveway, the owner investigated and found the decomposing body of the unfortunate child.

The authorities wondered what would make a man want to inflict such agonies on a tiny child. But they'd later find Theodore Frank's notebook with its bizarre rationale 'Why do I want to degrade and humiliate children? Sadism… I enjoy the humiliation. Defile the innocent. Make them scared of sex. It's dirty. I didn't have a happy childhood, neither will they… Revenge.'

But such torture murders don't make the sadist feel peaceful for very long, and four months later he kidnapped a nine-year-old girl, drove her to a remote location and tore her clothes off. He pinched her breasts and attempted to ram her panties down her throat.

Meanwhile the largest manhunt in Ventura County was well underway with police conducting door-to-door enquiries. They eventually found a mother who had stopped a man abducting her little daughter a few days before Amy was taken away. The woman was able to give them a good description of the would-be abductor and when they brought her photographs of known sex offenders she identified Theodore Frank.

Arrested for Amy Sue Seitz's torture-murder, he was sentenced to death in 1980. Four years later the State Supreme Court overturned the death penalty saying that Theodore Frank's sadistic notebooks shouldn't have been entered into testimony as this violated his privacy. A naïve attorney subsequently told the court that the sadist was a kind and loving man.

Death Row

After a public outcry, a second penalty hearing was held in 1985 and he was again sentenced to death and in 1990 the State Supreme Court unanimously voted to uphold the death sentence so the sadist remained on Death Row. He began to suffer from heart disease and had open heart surgery paid for by the taxpayer.

Like many people from abusive backgrounds, Theodore Frank was a gifted artist, but, given his sex crime, it's surprising that he was allowed to sell drawings of semi-naked children. (Paedophiles in the community feel encouraged to carry out their fantasies if they see that other paedophiles feel no guilt about their criminal actions.) He exhibited at one man shows in Las Vegas and San Francisco to considerable acclaim.

For 23 years following the murder he remained in St Quentin state prison then died there in September 2001 of natural causes – a heart attack – two months before his latest appeal was to be heard. He was 68 years old.

CHAPTER TWENTY
SADISTS WHO KILL INDISCRIMINATELY

As the previous chapters have shown, many sadists target either men, women or children, invariably choosing the gender and age group they are most attracted to. But for others, the need to cause pain and fear is paramount and they are indifferent to the victim's sex or age.

MICHAEL LEE LOCKHART

This sadist is unusual in that he dominated people from differing age and sex groups, torturing and killing two teenage girls, subjecting his ex-wife to a prolonged bondage and domination session and attacking a policeman, making him beg for his life before he shot him dead. He is also suspected of at least 20 other mutilation murders.

Born in Ohio in 1960, Lockhart would later describe his childhood as terrible and allege that he was sexually assaulted repeatedly between the ages of six and eight by two people. He grew up to become a handsome if slightly effeminate man.

By 1984, his marriage was in trouble and he was relying heavily on drugs and alcohol. He booked himself into a suicide prevention centre and they were sufficiently alarmed by his depression to refer him to the psychiatric unit of the local hospital. The admission form included the question 'What worries you most?' to which the early-stage sadist replied 'Hurting someone else.'

Lockhart's family urged him to quit the hospital and he did so but remained distraught, eventually leaving his wife and going on the road. From then on the 24-year-old caused mayhem, stealing cars, burglarising houses, committing armed robberies and even holding a woman at gunpoint. He spent various short periods in prison and in a variety of drug and alcohol abuse programmes but remained impulsive and full of hate.

The first murder

On the afternoon of 13 October 1987 he woke up in an Indiana motel feeling extremely depressed and rootless, so he determined to kill someone. He was driving through Indiana when he spotted cheerleader Windy Gallagher (her name is often misrepresented in crime reports as Wendy) leaving her school. The drifter followed her home and rang the bell, telling her that he needed to make a phone call. He was impeccably dressed and well spoken and she let him in.

When he was sure that she was home alone, the sadist pounced, overpowering the 16-year-old and dragging her into the bedroom. He tied her hands behind her back and stripped her to the waist. He then knifed her a total of four times in the neck and 17 times in the stomach, pulling her intestines out. He also savagely raped the teenager before stealing a photograph of her that he found at the scene, a trophy to remind him of the carnage. Her sister found her corpse lying in a large pool of blood.

Spousal abuse

The following month Lockhart arrived at his ex-wife's house in Ohio and bound and gagged her. For the next two days – 7 and 8 November 1987 – he terrorised and sexually assaulted her then fled, continuing to evade the police.

The second murder

The sadist continued to live by theft, then on 20 January 1988 he followed 14-year-old Jennifer Colhouer to her Florida home, gaining entry to the house by telling her that he was an estate agent who wanted to look at houses in the area. When he was sure that the teenager was alone, he stripped her down to her shoes and socks, tied her hands behind her back with strips of cloth and sodomised her. Then he cut her with a carving knife again and again. He also pulled her intestines out, an act which had formed part of his previous signature. She was found by her brother who described it as the most horrendous sight he had ever seen.

The third murder

Lockhart's next victim was a man. On 22 March 1988, Beaumont police officer Paul Hulsey tracked the sadist to a local motel and tried to arrest him in the hallway for driving a stolen vehicle. He held Lockhart at gunpoint, telling him to put his hands on the wall. But Michael Lockhart positioned himself next to a mirror and was able to see when the officer put his gun in his holster to take his handcuffs out.

He turned and hit the officer several times, also sticking a pen into his face, then shot him in the forearm when he was down. Officer Hulsey radioed for assistance then begged for mercy but the serial killer shot him again, this bullet puncturing his lungs and his heart. The killer only left the room when he was sure that the policeman was dying, but he was apprehended within hours, having hailed a taxi and fallen asleep. Lockhart was indifferent to the fact that he'd just murdered a respected police officer and family man, telling the officers, 'I killed him because he fucked up.'

Break out

But Lockhart wasn't ready to go out without a fight, and at the jury selection phase of his trial he smashed through a glass window on the third floor of the court room, cutting himself and breaking his pelvis. He was rearrested and taken to hospital.

At the triple-murderer's Texas trial, a psychologist said that he'd been molested by a neighbour at age six, and that these homosexual acts had left him conflicted about his own sexuality. He said that Lockhart had also been a victim of incest from age nine to 12.

Found guilty of capital murder, he was originally sentenced to die by lethal injection on 23 November 1993 but he kept petitioning for a stay of execution and after endless paperwork his death sentence was rescheduled for 10 September 1996. Finally it was changed to 9 December 1997 – this time it would be carried out.

Execution

During his decade on Death Row, Lockhart turned to religion and was supported by those who believed that all life was precious. We'll never know what these supporters would have said to the young siblings of Lockhart's victims, who had returned home to find their sisters dead and disembowelled.

On 9 December 1997, he enjoyed a final meal from a burger bar before being taken to the execution chamber in Huntsville, Texas. He thanked those in the prison service who had been kind to him, said that he loved his family and friends and told his murder victims' families, 'It is my hope my death will give you some kind of comfort.' Then he added, 'Warden, I'm ready.'

At 6 p.m., as the drugs were administered, he closed his eyes then gasped several times and lost consciousness. He was pronounced dead at 6.24 p.m. Anti-death-penalty supporters condemned the move but over 100 of Paul Hulsey's police officer colleagues stood outside the prison and expressed their relief at the killer's death.

CÉDRIC BELLEC

Born in the South of France in 1981, Cédric Bellec endured a life of hell with his biological family. His mother gave birth to six other children fathered by four different men. Cédric was mercilessly beaten by his father and was only six when he ran away from home. When he eventually returned his father cut open his hand with a knife by way of retribution and the authorities at last stepped in and put the deeply disturbed child into an orphanage where he remained until he was 13 years old.

At this age, he was sent to live with relatives at Montpellier, namely Philippe and Aimée Narre. Philippe was a pilot and Aimée was a schoolteacher and they were apparently kind to the boy – but it was too little too late. He began to drink and to experiment with drugs, and soon pulled a knife on Aimée Narre. He was also violent outside the home environment and tried to strangle a classmate when he was 14.

Unable to concentrate on his schoolwork, he attempted to learn mechanics and cookery but was equally inept at them. At 16 he left school and moved into a hostel where he befriended other abused youngsters who had been in care. Later still he moved into a flat with a friend in Aix-les-Bains.

But he remained full of rage and thought often of the various humiliations in his young life, including a time when Philippe Narre had slapped him in front of his schoolfriends and had criticised his lacklustre approach to life.

Premeditated murder

He decided to kill the couple and phoned them, saying that he'd like to meet up again. In turn, they invited him to their home on Thursday 14 December 2000.

Cédric now got in touch with Mickaël Catherine, a youth who worked as a drug pusher. Several of Mickaël's sisters had been sexually abused in care and he too was full of hate. The young men made their way to the Narres' house, Cédric taking along his torture kit.

They immediately tied the couple to separate chairs, stole their cash cards and went out to use them. On their return, Cédric began to beat the couple again and again. He became very excited during the torture and fetched a knife, which he inserted into one of the wounds on Philippe Narre's head. He told Mickaël Catherine (who apparently covered his ears with his hands to block out the sounds of the couple screaming) that he was enjoying hearing the bones break. He even fractured their facial bones in a very personal assault.

Later, both youths constricted the Narres' nostrils, giving them access to less and less air so that they suffocated slowly. After three hours of torture they died and the men (now joined by Cédric's flatmate) dumped their corpses in the garden shed.

They left the house but decided to return and pour acid on the victims, the latter suggestion being made by one of Mickaël's sisters, Laetitia. However, the police had got there before them so they turned the car around and fled. Two days later Cédric

Bellec was arrested and swiftly confessed to the cruel double homicide.

Standing trial at Herault Assizes in October 2003, 22-year-old Bellec admitted that he'd fantasised about torture-killing since he was a child and that he'd got a huge adrenalin rush out of beating the couple. A psychiatrist noted that the youth was unable to receive love.

An indifferent Bellec was sentenced to life imprisonment with the proviso that he serve at least 22 years. His accomplice, 25-year-old Mickaël Catherine, was also jailed for life. Meanwhile, Mickaël's 23-year-old sister Laetitia, who had suggested pouring acid on the bodies, was given eight years and Cédric's flatmate, 24-year-old Eric Tirard, who'd robbed the victims post-mortem and helped carry them to the garden shed, was given 12 years, their sentences doubtless reflecting the fact that they'd tried to cover up the crime.

CHAPTER TWENTY-ONE
FEMALE SADISTS

Statistically there are far more male sadists than female, as abused girls tend to turn their anger inwards so that it becomes depression or self-harm (everything from under- and overeating to arm-slashing), whereas boys turn it outwards onto weaker prey. But those women who *do* become criminally sadistic – often those who have suffered the most in childhood and who are highly dominant – are capable of unrelenting atrocities, as the following cases show.

AWILDA LOPEZ

Although little is known about her formative years, Awilda Lopez became a heavy cocaine user living in New York. She frequently left her two children alone for days at a time without food or warmth so when they were one and a half and two and a half years old, they were taken away from her and placed in foster care. By then she was eight months pregnant with Elisa, the child she would torture and eventually kill.

Elisa was born on 11 February 1989 with crack cocaine in her system and was immediately sent to a foster home. She thrived there for five months whilst her biological father – who

worked in the homeless shelter where Awilda Lopez resided
– attended parenting classes. He proved to be a caring man and
soon won custody.

For the next few years she remained happily with him and also
enjoyed her time at nursery school, proving to be an especially
intelligent pupil who loved to dance and was adored by the
other children and her teachers. Prince Michael of Greece met
her when he visited the nursery and was so taken with the lively
doe-eyed child that he arranged to pay for her tuition fees.

But when Elisa was almost five her mother won visitation
rights. Almost immediately staff noticed that the little girl was
bruised and increasingly withdrawn. In the same time frame,
Elisa's father realised that he had terminal cancer and began to
make arrangements to send her to relatives in Cuba upon his
death. He told everyone that he was determined to keep her
from her mother who he was convinced was abusing her.

Unfortunately, upon his death, a judge gave Awilda Lopez
custody – this in spite of the fact that Elisa's paternal relatives
begged him not to and nursery staff told of the child's changed
demeanour and many injuries. But the court was swayed by
social workers who spoke up for Awilda, saying that she was no
longer a neglectful mother and had won her first two children
back from foster care.

The reality was very different. Awilda had made a bad
second marriage to a violent man who would go on to stab
her 17 times during an argument. In turn, she was cruel to all
three offspring but she was particularly sadistic towards Elisa,
resenting her intellect.

For the next year and a half until her death, the little girl
suffered an increasing hell. She'd been offered a scholarship to
a private school but her mother turned this down and enrolled
her in a public school. She began to torture Elisa by inserting
a hairbrush into her rectum: her teachers noticed that the five-

year-old had difficulty walking and voiced their concerns but nothing was done.

Repeated whippings

Awilda also enjoyed whipping her little daughter. Neighbours frequently heard the child's screams but as corporal punishment of children was legal they said that they felt powerless to act.

Traumatised beyond measure, Elisa began to lose control of her bowels and Awilda made her eat her own excrement. She frequently wet herself and Awilda would mop up the urine with the child's hair.

The sadist also liked to stub out cigarettes over the little girl's face and body. This and similar tortures were repeated for the next year and a half, some of the beatings resulting in broken bones which didn't receive hospital care and partially healed on their own.

But in November 1995, the cruel mother went too far, slamming the six-year-old's head into a concrete wall. She lost consciousness and remained in a fugue state for up to two days, with cranial fluid leaking from her nose, mouth and ears.

Finally her torment ended in death and her mother was charged with her murder. She denied everything until she heard that her two older children wanted to testify against her: they'd seen and sometimes experienced her incredible sadism. She then admitted the sustained abuse and homicide and was given the minimum sentence of 15 years to life.

OMAIMA AREF

Born in the squatter's district in Cairo in 1968, Omaima and her seven brothers and sisters endured a desperately impoverished childhood. At six her clitoris was removed without the use of anaesthetic by her Muslim relatives. The pain was so intense that she doubtless longed for death – indeed, after this barbaric circumcision, many girls die from blood loss, infection or shock.

At ten years old Omaima was raped. This put her at risk from any future husband in her own culture who would see her lack of virginity as dishonourable and could have her stoned to death. Unsurprisingly, she grew up filled with fear and hate.

But at 19 her life improved when an American soldier married her and took her to the United States. Unfortunately the 1986 marriage was over by the end of the decade and she lurched from one unhappy love affair to the next. Her large dark eyes and dark hair made her attractive to men but her experiences ensured that she couldn't love them. And the fact that she'd been circumcised meant that she got nothing out of sex. However, like many damaged women, she used her sexuality for both sadistic and material ends – it was literally all she had.

In November 1990, she told one of her boyfriends, whom she'd been living with for three months, that she wanted to tie him up. He agreed and she bound both of his wrists to the bedposts. She then aimed a gun at him and demanded he tell her where he kept his cash. Thankfully he managed to tear himself free of his bonds, though he later found that she'd stolen one of his credit cards and run up a $1,600 bill.

Omaima fled from his apartment. Rootless yet again, she flitted from job to job, modelling clothes in a fashion store and looking after other people's children. In her spare time she went dancing and it was during one of those dance nights that she met former military pilot William Nelson, the man she would torture and kill.

Married in haste

Nelson was 33 years older than the 23-year-old Egyptian beauty and was immediately smitten with her, especially when she described herself as coming from a good family and speaking six languages. They married on 1 November 1991, though William hadn't finalised his divorce to his ex-wife so the marriage was actually bigamous.

For the first month, the newlyweds seemed happy enough, honeymooning in Texas in their new Corvette. But Omaima was already tired of sex with her new beau and had decided to avenge herself on the male species and take his cash. She also had plans to leave the town that they'd settled in, Costa Mesa, and return to Egypt to set up a business of her own.

She suggested to her husband that she handcuff him to the bed for a sex session. William Nelson apparently agreed to this and she bound his wrists and ankles to the bed. Once he was secured, she began to torture him with scissors or a knife.

But the victim struggled so violently that the cuffs left deep bruises in his ankles and he tugged so desperately at his bondaged arms that he eventually managed to break the headboard. Omaima immediately began to club him about the head with a steam iron, doing so until he lost consciousness. She battered him so often and so viciously that she bent the iron and caved his skull in. At one stage, hopefully post-mortem, she cut off his genitals and stuffed them into his mouth. (Some of the male sadists previously profiled also indulged in similar behaviour, stuffing everything from a cat's tail to excrement into the dead victims' mouths in an attempt to show their distaste for their prey and perhaps figuratively silence them.)

The new bride then spent the rest of the night dismembering the body and flushing parts of it down the waste disposal unit in the kitchen. She also cooked his hands in oil to destroy the fingerprints. The cooking may have made her hungry as she went on to barbecue her husband's ribs and ate them with a tangy sauce.

The following day she went to a male friend's house and offered him $75,000 to dispose of her husband's body parts which she'd drained of blood and put into various carrier bags. He pretended to agree in order to get rid of her then phoned the police.

At the police station, the femme fatale said that she hadn't seen her husband for days and that she missed him. Later in the same interview she said that he had raped her and two other girls. Still later she alleged that he'd tied her to the bed and hurt her and that she'd got free and killed him in self-defence.

Detectives went to her apartment and found packages of blood-drained flesh in various cupboards. There was more of William Nelson in the freezer, including his cooked and scalped head.

Court

At her trial, she admitted killing her husband but said that she had done so because he kept beating her. However, the prosecution found photos taken the day after she was allegedly badly beaten and her body showed no traces of abuse. And other scars which she showed to the courts were too old to have been inflicted by her spouse of one month. Found guilty on 12 March 1992 of second degree murder, she was sentenced to 27 years to life.

WOMEN WHO TORTURE STRANGERS

Lone female sadists, we have seen, tend to confine their cruelty to their children and adult relatives, though female sadists who work as nurses behave sadistically towards their helpless patients, female serial killers Genene Jones and Cathy Wood being prime examples. The sadistic female probably chooses victims in her domestic and work arena because she doesn't have the physical strength to abduct strangers – and taking a stranger to a forest or an outbuilding to torture them would take the female outside her home- and work-based comfort zone.

Sadly, the following case shows that when a female sadist *is* empowered to terrorise strangers within that comfort zone, she can rise to the challenge again and again...

IRMA ILSE IDA GRESE

Irma was born on 7 October 1923 to Bertha and Alfred Grese. The couple later had a second daughter, Helene, and the entire family worked on an agricultural farm in Germany. When Irma was 12 her mother died and she was left at the mercy of her father, a strict disciplinarian. The girls' lives now revolved around school and church. Irma and Helene longed to join the Nazi youth group which most of their schoolfriends belonged to, as this would allow them to enjoy a world of picnics and trips.

Alfred Grese refused to let his daughters join. In retrospect it was a sensible decision, but at the time it just seemed to emphasise his old-fashioned approach to life and the teenage Irma felt thwarted. Alfred was becoming increasingly reclusive so Irma rarely got to go anywhere.

A photo taken in her mid teens shows a somewhat overweight girl glowering at the camera, her hair scraped back tightly from her forehead, her hands lightly balled into fists. Writers who saw this snapshot years later would describe her as plain and suggest that her sadism was aimed at more attractive women – but Irma Grese blossomed after leaving home, and later witnesses described her as a beautiful blonde. These same writers simply said that she came from a 'good hard-working family' and neglected to mention that her mother had died at a pivotal time in her life and that her father was deeply conservative, very strict and physically chastised her.

A savage beating

The unhappy young woman left school at 15 and spent six months working the land before taking a job in a shop. After another six months she moved on to work as a nurse's aid in a sanatorium, telling her sister that she was desperate to escape from home.

Irma decided that she wanted to become a nurse – people who have felt unnurtured often go into nursing, believing that they can't be loved for themselves, only for offering endless care to others. She also hoped that such a job would allow her to meet and marry a doctor, but her work at the hospital was unsatisfactory and she was told to look for another job.

She took unskilled work in a dairy for a few months then turned to the local labour exchange for help. They explained that the concentration camps needed people with quasi-nursing skills (disease was rife) and in the summer of 1942 they sent her to Ravensbruck Concentration Camp for training. Thereafter, she went home for a short holiday but when her father found out that she was working at the death camps, he beat her mercilessly and threw her out of the house.

Revenge

Essentially homeless, Irma Grese returned to Ravensbruck and by 19 she'd been made a supervisor. The following year she was transferred to Auschwitz where she was in charge of 30,000 female Polish and Hungarian prisoners. All of these women were viewed by the guards as completely expendable so the beaten child could now have the ultimate revenge.

At 7.30 a.m. each morning, Grese began to patrol the grounds, terrorising the camp dwellers. She would arbitrarily target a woman and flog her until she begged for mercy. She particularly liked to hurt large-busted women, ordering them to open their blouses whereupon she cut their breasts open with her plaited whip. Afterwards she would order one of the inmates with medical training to sew the woman up without benefit of anaesthetic and would sway orgasmically and foam at the mouth.

The youthful sadist also liked to set her two Alsatian dogs – which she kept half-starved – on the prisoners. She would sometimes jump on the women's stomachs so that their intestines spilled out for the dogs to eat. During these acts she would breathe heavily and appeared to be in a sexually excited state.

Grese arranged the murders of an unknown number of women by putting a shovel outside the loosely wired fence and ordering them to retrieve it. The women were then shot by the guard in the tower who thought that they were trying to escape. She also shot many prisoners with her own pistol, sometimes carefully aiming a bullet so that it obliterated a victim's face. Like many sadists she kept souvenirs of her cruelty, having three of the victims skinned after death so that she could make lampshades of their skin.

Shortly after she was transferred to Belsen, it was liberated by the British and Irma Grese and the other sadistic guards were arrested. She was one of 44 guards indicted for war crimes by a British Military Court. Her trial took place in Hamburg, Germany in the autumn of 1945 and she pleaded not guilty, saying that she had occasionally struck prisoners but never tortured or murdered them.

But survivors from the camp spoke at length about both her legendary cruelty and homicidal actions and she was sentenced to hang. Reportage varies regarding her reaction at hearing her death sentence, with most accounts saying that she showed no emotion whilst some Holocaust deniers insist that she wept.

The famous hangman Albert Pierrepoint was sent to Germany to carry out her execution. She laughed when he had to weigh her and when he asked about her age (21).

She remained equally calm the following day as she entered the execution chamber and walked to the trap, for her defence in her own mind was that Himmler was responsible for all that had happened. She kissed a crucifix before the hood was put in place and quietly told the executioner to hurry up. Twenty minutes later her body was cut down and sent for burial, the executioner saying that he felt haunted at hanging someone so pretty and young.

The horror which Irma Grese and her contemporaries had perpetrated lived on after the camps were liberated as many of the starving prisoners tried to eat a full meal only to have their shrunken stomachs burst, leading to an agonising death.

WOMEN WHO KILL WITH PARTNERS

Female sadists who kill with a male accomplice are more likely to abduct and torture strangers: Charlene Gallego, acting alongside her common-law husband, bit her teenage victims' nipples; Judith Neelley injected drain cleaner into a 13-year-old girl whom husband Alvin Neelley had previously sexually assaulted; and Rose West violated young women with oversized dildoes whilst Fred West observed. Though young themselves, all three women lured even younger victims into their sadistic web.

Similarly, in 2001 a 46-year-old Long Island woman was arrested in conjunction with her husband for torturing an 18-year-old girl in her home. The woman had befriended the teenager online for six months before abducting her, tying her up and abusing her for a week.

In other instances, one party is more reluctant than the other to cause anguish. Karla Homolka winced as she followed her husband's instructions to insert a bottle neck into the anus of a teenage victim, and Gwen Graham – who enjoyed consensual sadomasochistic games with various lesbian lovers – showed no sadism towards her nursing charges once she ended her relationship with the manipulative Cathy Wood. Similarly, Myra Hindley showed few traces of sadomasochism in her admittedly histrionic personality, yet she allowed Ian Brady to flog her and showed off the whip marks on her buttocks for his camera.

ANGELS OF DEATH

Several female serial killers who have operated alone showed their sadistic side when dealing with the young and the elderly. Anna Zwanziger, a housekeeper turned nurse, went into paroxysms of ecstasy as her male and female victims writhed from the effects of arsenic poisoning and nurse Genene Jones appeared to have an orgasm in front of paramedics as one of her child victims died. These medical killers are euphemistically known as Angels of Death, though their primary motives are sadism and the creation of drama through euthanasia.

CRUELTY WITHOUT SADISM

But sometimes women commit acts of atrocious cruelty which aren't sadistic. For example, there have been several well-documented cases in which a female who is desperate for a baby overpowers a heavily-pregnant woman and cuts the foetus from her womb, then strangles her or leaves her to die of her wounds. The killer has caused considerable pain but the motive wasn't sadistic and she quickly diverts her energies into pretending to be a new mother and showing off the stolen infant to her delighted family.

Similarly, abused children who kill aren't always sadistic. Ten-year-old Mary Bell cut the legs of one of her toddler victims with a razor – but the cuts were made post-mortem and the motive wasn't to cause pain or terror. The unfortunate Mary had watched her prostitute mother performing picquerism on her clients and she was simply emulating this.

The final case in this chapter is unusual in that a gang was involved and the two females were the sadistic leaders. The case went to trial in November 1993 and received comparatively little publicity as this was also the month when Robert Thompson and Jon Venables were tried for James Bulger's tragic death.

BERNADETTE MCNEILLY AND JEAN POWELL

McNeilly and Powell were living lives of increasing chaos in Manchester, England long before they befriended their eventual victim, Suzanne Capper. Bernadette McNeilly, a 24-year-old mother of three, had a 16-year-old boyfriend called Anthony Dudson. Bernadette was friends with another mother of three, Jean Powell, and eventually moved in with her. Jean Powell also had sex with Anthony Dudson and Anthony had sex with 16-year-old Suzanne Capper, a polite girl who was of limited intelligence. Suzanne also briefly dated Jean's younger brother, 17-year-old Clifford Pook.

In October 1992, Suzanne spent the night in Bernadette and Anthony's bed, after which they found that they had pubic lice and blamed the teenager. They were also angry when one of Suzanne's boyfriends encouraged her to make advances towards Jean Powell. The latter was also enraged as she believed that Suzanne had stolen her pink duffle coat.

To a mature person, Jean Powell's house would have held no allure. There was virtually no normal furniture so the eight occupants of the house and the numerous hangers-on had to sit in car seats. But to Suzanne Capper it was an exciting prospect, as Powell dealt in drugs, owned a CB radio and had an interest in the occult.

Eight days of torture

Suzanne had fallen out with Jean Powell before, and Powell had beaten her. But after an argument at home on 7 December 1992, the 16-year-old returned trustingly to Powell's house. Her stepfather assumed she had remained there voluntarily so wasn't alarmed when she didn't return.

For the next few days she was to be horrifically abused by Jean Powell, Bernadette McNeilly and her teenage boyfriend Anthony Dudson. (Later in the week other gang members joined in.) They grabbed her as soon as she arrived and shaved her head and her eyebrows then held her down whilst both women took turns beating her with an enormous ornamental wooden spoon (which was at least three foot long and heavily built) and with a belt. Afterwards Jean Powell locked her in a wardrobe overnight.

The following day they took Suzanne to Bernadette McNeilly's former house, a few doors down from where she lived with Jean Powell. There they spreadeagled her to the slats of an overturned bed, binding her with electric flex. Bernadette McNeilly injected her with amphetamines and tortured her with a lit cigarette and with music played through a headset at high volume. She used the phrase 'Chucky's coming to play' (taken from a popular horror film called *Child's Play*) before each torture session and soon the words themselves were enough to make Suzanne Capper scream.

Jean Powell also took part in many of the torture sessions and the judge would later note that she, her ex-husband and Bernadette McNeilly were the ringleaders.

Halfway through the week Jean's 17-year-old brother Clifford Pook and another young man named Jeffrey Leigh called at the house and were shown the trussed and gagged teenage girl.

It's open to dispute when Jean Powell's ex-husband Glyn Powell joined in. Anthony Dudson said that Glyn Powell was involved from the first day and was responsible for shaving Suzanne's head but Glyn Powell later said in court that he was only involved from midweek. The situation was further complicated as Jean Powell later changed her story to play down Bernadette McNeilly's role as she was with her on remand in Risley jail. What's certain is that Glyn Powell became the third ringleader and played an active role in the teenager's death.

After several days of leaving the 16-year-old lying in her own excrement, Bernadette McNeilly filled a bath with disinfectant (which Jean Powell provided) and dumped Suzanne in it. She then scrubbed the screaming girl with a broom and a scrubbing brush, the action leaving numerous cuts and abrasions all over her body. Afterwards Clifford Pook pulled out two of Suzanne's front teeth with pliers.

Jeffrey Leigh would later say that he was too cowardly to help the victim – in truth he had locked Suzanne back in the wardrobe after being shown her by a happy-looking Bernadette McNeilly. He admitted that Suzanne had had a black eye, was cowering with her hands in front of her face and looked terrified. Jeffrey Leigh already had a record for violence as he had threatened his 86-year-old disabled aunt with a knife and robbed her, a crime for which he'd served three years in a young offenders institution.

Another man who visited the house and whom Suzanne begged for help said that he didn't get involved because he was afraid that Jeffrey Leigh would batter him. The man had overheard Anthony Dudson shouting 'Shut up you slag,' to someone in the back room. He asked who it was and Jeffrey Leigh had shown him Suzanne who was tied to a bed and had blood around her mouth from the extractions. Later, when he was alone in the house, she pleaded for the man to untie her but he refused because 'if I said owt, they'd of all got me, wouldn't they?'

After a week the gang had tired of torturing the 16-year-old and four of them dumped her in the boot of a car stolen by the Powells and drove her to Benfield Clough. Clifford Pook and Jeffrey Leigh remained at the house.

When they reached a brambled area, they threw Suzanne down and she curled into the foetal position. Bernadette McNeilly then poured the petrol, which Anthony Dudson had fetched in a can from a nearby garage, over her. Anthony

Dudson said that Glyn Powell started the fire but Jean Powell said that Bernadette McNeilly had initially started it. Dudson acknowledged that the first flames had gone out so Glyn Powell had started them again by using his cigarette lighter on Suzanne's back. They laughed as their victim's screams filled the air and only left the site when they believed that she was dead.

Naming her attackers

But after her tormentors had gone, the badly burned Suzanne staggered, naked, to the roadside where workmen took her to a nearby house and phoned an ambulance. The owners of the house gave her the six glasses of water she requested, though they had to hold the glass to her lips as her fingers had been burned away.

The couple were appalled by the girl's injuries – her features had been obliterated by the flames and her legs and feet were horribly charred. Her tormentors had also shaved and cut her head.

The 16-year-old remained conscious long enough to tell police that she'd been held at a house in Langworthy Road, Moston, in Manchester. She named her six tormentors and gave some details of what they'd done to her. Shortly afterwards she lapsed into a coma and three days later, on 18 December, she died.

Autopsy

Her autopsy the following month revealed the extent of her suffering, for she had been repeatedly cut, burnt and beaten. Moreover, the removal of one of her teeth had exposed a dental nerve. She had died of multiple organ failure, having suffered 80 per cent burns after being set alight.

Unrepentant

Incredibly, the gang remained indifferent to the horror of their crimes. Jean Powell even sent her ex-husband a love letter when they were in prison which said 'I love you, darling… your loving wife and best friend.' Later she'd pretend in court that she only committed some of the abuses on Suzanne because she was frightened of him.

Trial

On 16 November 1993, the trial opened at Manchester Crown Court. Bernadette McNeilly and Jean Powell admitted falsely imprisoning Suzanne Capper, as did Jean Powell's younger brother Clifford Pook who also admitted conspiracy to cause grievous bodily harm. Jean Powell's ex-husband, Glyn Powell, denied the charges as did Jeffrey Leigh and Anthony Dudson. All six denied murdering the teenager.

During the trial, each defendant tried to minimise their part in the teenager's ordeal. Glyn Powell said that he still loved Jean Powell and had only gone along with events to please her. Bernadette McNeilly admitted injecting Suzanne Capper with amphetamines but said she'd done so as an act of kindness to prevent others in the group injecting her with heroin. (In reality, one such torture session where McNeilly was alone with Capper had lasted for two hours.) Jean Powell noted that it was Bernadette McNeilly who had ordered Suzanne's teeth to be pulled out, and Anthony Dudson said that Clifford Pook had laughingly carried out the extractions and that Glyn Powell had set Suzanne alight whilst singing the song 'Burn Baby Burn'. In turn, Jean Powell said that Bernadette McNeilly had dragged Suzanne from the car boot, pushed her down the hill and set her alight.

Jeffrey Leigh said that Jean Powell often 'got mad ideas in the brain. She feels she could have people jump when she clicks her fingers.' He described Bernadette McNeilly as 'a bit weird'. Leigh admitted he'd untied Suzanne from the bed and put a balaclava over her head, knowing that some of the other gang members planned to dump her somewhere. He said that he thought 'she would go brain dead' and wouldn't be able to identify them.

Both Powells and Bernadette McNeilly were found guilty of murder and sentenced to life imprisonment. Anthony Dudson was also convicted of murder but was given an 18-year sentence because of his youth. Jeffrey Leigh was given 12 years for unlawful imprisonment and Clifford Pook was given 15 years for conspiracy and seven years for unlawful imprisonment. He was sent to a young offenders institution, the judge commenting that he'd been under the influence of his dominant older sister, Jean Powell. His counsel said that Pook was of low intelligence and that Jean Powell had introduced him to amphetamines when he was very young.

As usual, the press tried to create a moral panic, suggesting that the film *Child's Play 3* was responsible for making the defendants maim and murder. But in truth the gang didn't have a video player and a copy of the video wasn't found in the house. They had merely taped the rock music soundtrack from the original *Child's Play* film from the radio and played it during some of the torture sessions, and Bernadette McNeilly had repeated the phrase 'Chucky's coming to play' from the film whenever she abused Suzanne. It would surely have been more helpful to look at the upbringings of these women who were single parents to three children by their mid twenties, had teenage boyfriends who were barely legal and who supported themselves through drug dealing and theft.

A shorter sentence

In March 2002, Anthony Dudson's sentence was reduced from 18 to 16 years because the authorities said he'd made 'significant progress' in detention. In 2003 (now age 27) he appealed for a further reduction, his counsel arguing that the UN Convention on the Rights of the Child meant that he should have been given the lowest minimum term possible. But the High Court opted not to reduce the term served before he becomes eligible for parole.

In cases like this which involve female and male sadists, the female's role is invariably forgotten over time. This was apparent when Dudson's appeals were reported in the national press. Manchester newspapers named all of the killers involved, but most less-localised reports simply referred to the 'violent gang' he belonged to, and it probably wouldn't have occurred to newer readers that this gang included two merciless female sadists who thought that an allegedly stolen duffle coat was an excuse to torture someone to death.

But some members of the public will never forget the ordeal that Suzanne Capper suffered, and, when Dudson's appeals were being highlighted, a woman who'd served on the jury at his trial wrote to the newspapers reminding them of this mixed-gender gang's atrocities.

PART FIVE

BOUNDARIES

CHAPTER TWENTY-TWO

SAFE AND SANE: CONSENSUAL SADOMASOCHISM

The burnings, tooth extractions and starvation highlighted in the previous cases are a world removed from consensual sadomasochism – yet the law often fails to make a distinction between forced and consensual BDSM (bondage, domination and sadomasochism) activities. Similarly, the psychiatric profession classifies sadomasochism as a paraphilia (deviant desire), ranking it alongside immoral practices such as paedophilia. In this climate of distrust, consensual sadomasochists understandably prefer to remain underground, so I'm indebted to respected erotic artist Lynn Paula Russell for speaking to me so freely about her sexuality.

Lynn Paula Russell is equally well known in the BDSM community as Paula Meadows, editor and illustrator of the adult corporal punishment magazine *Februs* and a contributor to numerous associated publications. She prefers to be called Paula, her middle name.

Paula became interested in punishment for pleasure at the start of the 1980s. She explains: 'I began to appreciate from my own personal experiences how the power of sex underpins most of what we do; also I realised that sexual relationships are rarely built on equality, but on power dynamics which are often quite unconsciously followed.'

She continues: 'My first inkling of my own propensity for masochism came about when I read *Story of O* and later a book called *A Taste for Pain* by Maria Marcus. Both these books drew attention, in different ways, to the problem of how otherwise strong women come to terms with the fact that they need to be dominated, and sometimes experience pain in order to obtain sexual pleasure and liberation. It was this paradox that intrigued me.'

Unsurprisingly, Paula's entry into power-play eroticism had its difficulties. 'At the beginning there was confusion. I remember a specific occasion when my interest started to come to the surface – it was quite unexpected. I recall being aware of a strong impatience with my partner at the time and a desire to wake him up and get him going. Suddenly I found myself saying *I'd like to whip you!* He suggested I get on with it. This was one of those moments when you leap across an imaginary abyss… but it brought no immediate satisfaction. After giving him a few half-hearted whacks with a belt I began to feel bad. However, when I let him spank me in return it was arousing, helped me overcome inhibitions and seemed to clear away emotional detritus. This was a turning point.'

Nevertheless, it took time for her to come to terms with sexual submission. 'When you decide to act out a masochistic fantasy for the first time, you take a big step – you are confronted by the reality and harshness of real pain and this is a good thing. It wakes you up, shows you what you are really doing and leads you away from the more unconscious gratifications of emotional masochism. Then, as you repeat the treatment you become more used to it and begin to enjoy that warm feeling and the adrenaline high it gives you. But the fact that you need pain or humiliation or whatever to achieve that erotic high means there is a problem somewhere inside the psyche which is trying to be resolved. If we just accept our submissive role this is not the answer, it is merely acknowledging that this is a symptom that needs attention. So we act out the problem (hopefully in safety and with controls), in the hope of fulfilment and resolution. I call it a problem, but in a way, you know, it is more like the grit in the oyster that helps to make your own unique individual pearl.'

Slowly Paula began to meet like-minded people and explore her limits, even making an adult video in which she was spanked. 'This all led to meeting a different set of friends. Some of these new friends were open about their interests in sadomasochism (SM) and I found myself involved in a network of people who met up regularly to enjoy themselves in a very uninhibited fashion. I can't tell you how surprised I was to discover that the interests I had tentatively explored privately with my partner, thinking we were the only ones, were actually shared by hundreds of others! But at first, I didn't know this was part of a worldwide scene.'

Like many females who choose to experiment with sexual submission, Paula is a strong woman who is confident and articulate. The same is invariably true of male submissives. It tends to be the headmaster and headmistress of a school – or company directors – who opt for sexually submissive roles in private, choosing to hand over their power for erotic delight. That said, a percentage of women who are attracted to sexual submission have low self-esteem.

Like many of her contemporaries, Paula had struggled to find a suitable name for her sexual choice. ' I always had trouble calling myself submissive because that label never seemed to fit. I couldn't allow myself to be controlled by another and always disliked bondage, however much I trusted people, but neither could I begin to control someone else. Let's just say I was submitting to the experience – not the person. I was playing at being submissive because I found it impossible to initiate happenings for myself. I liked to be egged on to do things that normally I wouldn't dare to suggest. That way I wouldn't have to take responsibility for them. I've heard many other submissive types describe it like this. This meant I had a nature that had a strong tendency to be led and people looking for a submissive partner would have picked that up subliminally as soon as they met me.'

At first she was swept away on a tide of erotic bliss. 'When you are susceptible to a dominant person you don't observe the techniques they use to get their effect; you fall under their spell. When you realise how they press buttons in you this is a big step forward. It is then possible to look out for these behaviour patterns with other people in your ordinary everyday life and practise resisting.'

This understanding has doubtless fed into her erotic books, the first being *The Illustrative Art of Lynn Paula Russell* which includes scenes from her own life, *Story of O* illustrations and a series of sensuous drawings called 'Bodyscapes'. It was followed by *A Sexual Odyssey*, concentrating more on Paula's illustrative work for corporal punishment (CP) magazines. Later she produced *Sexcitement,* a sex manual with a much more personal touch. It covered areas usually avoided by other manuals, like CP, bondage, and exploring submission and domination role play, the object being to encourage couples to be honest with each other, build trust and safely experiment. Her other titles include *Painful Pleasures* (a large collection of CP illustrations originally published in Februs) and *The Illustrated Book of Corporal Punishment*, all published by The Erotic Print Society.

So what was the general public's reaction to her work and chosen lifestyle? Paula admits that 'as a rule I don't discuss BDSM with people who aren't in the circle so I don't often get to hear outsiders' views. Certainly, in the media there's an assumption that SM enthusiasts are perverts who get off on cruelty (if they are dominant) and sad, pathetic victims if they choose to be on the receiving end. I can't help feeling that it's impossible to explain otherwise to those who have an ingrained view. Devotees just have to carry on speaking about it in open-minded books such as this, and use any other opportunities that arise.'

That said, she recognises that 'the message will take a long time to permeate but some methods of achieving self knowledge, such as this, have to be discovered and fostered in private. Bringing them to the surface and making them more acceptable to the general public only serves to diminish their meaning, as can be seen in the adoption of fetish ideas as fashion statements. Personally, I find ignorant people's negative attitudes towards what I choose to do completely irrelevant. It is simply none of their business. If they want to come in and try for themselves that's fine but if they don't then there's no way of explaining to them.'

Paula has realised that there are different kinds of consensual sadist and masochist. 'There are different sorts of sub. As I said before, some women are susceptible to certain buttons being pressed and then the right kind of man can manipulate her. These women are often suffering from feelings of low self-esteem. However, there are certain women who wish to play in the same way as some men play – we've all heard of the powerful managing director who arranges to be caned by a fantasy headmistress – meaning that they are dominant characters with a strongly defined sexuality who wish to experience the thrills of the submissive role. There are many perks for the submissive – being on the receiving end of all the attention is one of them, and feeling free of any obligation to make decisions is another. These kind of women are dictating exactly what they want and are not to be confused with the weak and easily led.'

She has now reached the stage where her own physical interest in BDSM has been satisfied. 'At first I was fulfilling a buried desire to exhibit myself. I submitted to whippings, like 'O', and experienced her satisfaction... sampled group sex. I know I allowed myself to be used on occasions but it doesn't matter now – I learned a lot from it. I challenged myself to try new things and overcome taboos. I found out for myself what was good and beneficial and what was not so good. I learned when to trust and when not to. There were difficult moments, things that didn't work, but mainly it was an adventure. Obviously I needed this extra experience though I can't tell you exactly why. I needed to get in touch with something in myself.'

She notes that 'Nowadays I don't feel driven any more. I have found out the things I needed to know. Something happened when I was about 50... the desire for lustful adventures died down and my sexuality seemed to be differently centred: it was as if it had moved from the genitals to the heart. I suppose when all is said and done, all that matters is our ability to live and love abundantly and whatever helps us to this end is good.'

It should be clear by now to even the most anti-BDSM reader that there's absolutely no connection between Paula's life-affirming exploration of sadomasochism and the kind of forced sadomasochism described in the previous chapters. As such, can she give a positive message to any reader trying to come to terms with their erotic power-play sexuality?

'First of all,' she says, 'if you find yourself fantasising about any sort of SM situation, don't start worrying about it. Initially you aren't really responsible for what arises in your imagination, the ideas pop up spontaneously and are a sort of pointer towards something in you that needs to be acknowledged. So don't ever be ashamed of what you fantasise about. On the other hand, what you decide to do about it is another matter – that is under your control. It's always best to find someone sympathetic to talk to about these things, then you don't feel so isolated and alone. It certainly isn't good to brood and keep things inside – that way they fester and become obsessions.'

She continues 'Be aware and always respect others. There are very strict rules and protocols to be followed. The SM scene is not a free-for-all where anything goes. Trust and understanding must be built up, friendships made, before any physical activity can take place. When this happens you can establish a secure environment for letting your hair down safely. All this sounds a bit serious – actually it isn't, once you find the right friends. I remember much hilarity and amusement, as well as some more deeply erotic moments.'

CREATIVE SADOMASOCHISTS

Paula's deeply erotic moments illuminate her work – but there are many other consensual sadomasochists in the creative professions who are less at ease with their fantasies. Indeed, creativity and an offbeat sexuality often exist in the same individual, as the kind of unhappy childhood which tends to create a sadomasochist can also trigger an artistic temperament, probably because the humiliated and beaten child survives by creating a powerful imaginative life. The brief biographies which follow – of a composer, critic, poet and cartoonist – are just four examples of respected artistes with a strong interest in erotic sadism.

PERCY GRAINGER

The late composer Percy Grainger – considered by many to be one of the world's finest concert pianists – was a well-known flagellation enthusiast. Whipped frequently and severely by his otherwise doting mother until he was 15, by his twenties he'd become an obsessive self-flagellant. He took a selection of whips with him on his worldwide sell-out tours and would beat himself until he bled. His doctor noted that 'by accepting himself as he was, biologically and sexually, he defused, so to say, a sizzling time bomb within him which otherwise might have blown his personality to bits'.

Grainger was fortunate that, as a life-long atheist, he had no qualms about masturbation or non-procreative sex. He wrote: 'The world of modern doctoring, modern machines, modern art, modern amorality would be just paradise if we could only shed the blight of religion.'

He was also fortunate in finding several girlfriends and later a wife who were happy to be whipped. He and his spouse Ella even put together a document which said that if one of them died whilst being flagellated by the other, the whipper was not to be held responsible. (In reality, the law does not recognise such documents, a fact explored later in this chapter.) The Graingers' union lasted for 32 years until his death in 1961.

KENNETH TYNAN

The theatre reviewer Kenneth Tynan – the illegitimate child of a deeply religious mother and already married father – was a confirmed flagellant by the time he went to Oxford, but, unlike Percy Grainger, he felt great shame at his sadomasochism and tried to sublimate it by entering into a vanilla marriage. He later tried to coerce his first wife into submitting to the rod, something which she loathed. The marriage broke down and she later said in her biography that he'd beaten her up.

Tynan embarked on a second marriage but couldn't resist starting a sadomasochistic affair with an equally avid masochistic young woman. They brought in a third party to watch and participate in their erotic spanking games and he was in heaven. Yet he ended the affair and, when a friend asked him what his abandoned lover was supposed to do, he snapped 'Remember.'

Tynan was at his best when he had lots of creative work (he wrote books and newspaper and magazine columns as well as numerous reviews) and occasional SM diversions. But as his work dried up – largely because of his vituperative attacks on people – he became more and more frantic to live out his sexual fantasies, and took to hiring escort girls and masseuses to beat him and submit to the whip.

Beleaguered for years by chronic emphysema, made worse by his addiction to smoking, he died in the summer of 1980 age 53.

PHILIP LARKIN

Widely regarded as one of Britain's best post-war poets, Larkin grew up both admiring and fearing his father. The older man had a quick temper – his colleagues described him as ferocious – and was increasingly irate with his wife. Larkin developed a stutter and later said 'I never left the house without the sense of walking into a cooler, cleaner, saner and pleasanter atmosphere.' Visitors rarely called uninvited at the Larkins' and Philip grew up having nothing to do with girls – he did have a sister, but she was ten years his senior so inhabited a different world.

The teenage Philip had a strong sex drive but it was laced with unhealthy levels of derision and rage. He flirted with the idea of homosexuality but decided that he really wanted to be a schoolgirl, a role he saw as a mixture of enviable passivity and games-based fun.

At Oxford University, the young poet wrote two sadomasochistic lesbian novels for his own and his friends' delectation, *Trouble at Willow Gables* and its sequel *Michaelmas*

Term at St Bride's. In the first book, a prefect forces a black-stockinged schoolgirl over a desk and removes her tunic for the headmistress to beat her. The girl is caned swiftly but inexpertly until she collapses on the floor. The rest of the sadomasochism in *Willow Gables* is latent, with girls lightly bullying each other and one tying another up in order to play a prank.

The sequel, where the girls are older, is even more tame, though two of the 18-year-old former pupils wrestle each other until one collapses into the other's lap. Another girl stretches to show her silk stockings and yet another has to strip in front of a former prefect who openly admires her naked body. This same girl is threatened with a good thrashing by an older woman.

Though he attempted and failed to find a publisher for both novels, Larkin's interest in sadomasochism remained, and in his poem *Administration* he talks of pulling down girls' pants.

As he matured, he became enamoured of pornography and amassed a hall cupboard's worth of magazines. He was loitering outside a sex shop one day when the owner came out and asked discreetly, 'Bondage was it, sir?' But the poet was terrified of police censure and would only buy milder pornographic mags. It's likely that the tension between the type of sex he enjoyed and the sex of his most secret fantasies added an extra frisson to his writing, though he didn't intend to tell the world of his sadomasochistic novels and wanted them to be destroyed after his death.

ROBERT CRUMB

The celebrated cartoonist Robert Crumb – honoured in 2005 with an exhibition at Bonhams in New Bond Street – is one of the finest examples of personal sexual confusion being sublimated into fascinating art.

Crumb and his siblings endured numerous cruelties at the hands of their tyrannical father, a quartermaster in the UK marines. Unable to cope, their mother retreated into a world of her own and became addicted to amphetamines.

Unsurprisingly, the children grew up into deeply troubled adults. His brother Charles, a brilliant artist who remained at home with his mother, eventually committed suicide. And his brother Maxon took to pulling down women's panties in public places, resultantly becoming a registered sex offender. He now lives in a Skid Row hotel and practises bizarre religious self-purification rituals, including sleeping on a bed of nails. Meanwhile Robert Crumb describes one of his sisters as 'a really negative lesbian'.

Crumb himself was deeply withdrawn for many years and admitted that he was full of hostility, especially towards women whom he liked to ride as if they were ponies. He dealt with this in his numerous drawings whose subjects included everything from incest to animal sex. But as his success grew, so did his sexual allure and he began to have relationships, including a second marriage which has lasted for over 30 years.

Insightful about the importance of his work as a release mechanism, he admitted in a 2005 interview with journalist John Preston that 'If I hadn't been a cartoonist, I might have been a psychopathic killer. Or else I might have killed myself.'

The law

Robert Crumb is not the only man (or woman) from a damaging background to come to terms with his sexuality and go on to lead a fulfilling life. Numerous consensual sadomasochists have spoken of their journey as a way of curing childhood hurts. Mark Ramsden, who has edited two fetish magazines and written several humorous and offbeat sadomasochistic novels, told this author 'Some people find it therapeutic and liberating to confront childhood traumas in a sexual context,' though he adds that 'there's no reliable data as to whether such sex enthusiasts are any better at relationships than anyone else'.

Mark notes that 'exploring the dark side with a sympathetic partner can heal some deep wounds and enable personal development – or at least provide a temporary respite from the pain of being human'.

As to the motivations of each party in a consensual sadomasochistic encounter? 'It's likely that the authoritarian personality seeks power to compensate for what they perceive to be their own weaknesses or imperfections.' He believes that many of us are control freaks who lack the power to control anything, and adds 'Seeking transcendence through role play is one way out.'

Ramsden also stresses that the mainstream notion of the submissive as doormat is totally wrong: 'Most supposed submissives are seeking to control their dominants and in consensual play they actually are in control. As the submissive gets most of the action in return for a little pantomime of letting the dominant feel powerful it is a tempting option, particularly as you get to lie down while other people fuss over you.'

So a carefully controlled consensual situation is arguably a win-win situation, yet it's still illegal in Britain for a recreational sadist to leave any but the most trifling marks on a consenting partner and they can be imprisoned for a maximum of five years under the charge of causing actual bodily harm.

In December 1990, 16 consenting gay sadomasochists were found guilty of this very charge and some of them were sent to prison for terms of up to four and a half years. Following a public outcry about this decision, the Law Commission produced a consultation paper on Consent in the Criminal Law. They found that sadomasochism was 'surprisingly widespread' and provisionally proposed that minor injuries should not be regarded as criminal 'if the other person consented to the injury of the type caused.'

This proposal has yet to be enshrined in law, which makes for endless confusion. As the situation stands, sadomasochism itself is legal, but leaving the kind of marks that it necessitates can be illegal and lead to prosecution, regardless of the submissive's consent.

Undoing the damage

Understandably given such legal censure, the consensual sadomasochist is often conflicted about his sexuality. Meanwhile, the public's perception of the criminal sadist is that he remains indifferent to his crimes. But is this always the case? Patrick Byrne's chronic insomnia, Christopher Wilder's stomach upsets, Richard Cottingham's ulcer and Dayton Rogers' extreme weight loss and migraines suggest otherwise. And if these men are capable of feeling guilt about their crimes, they can probably benefit from therapy.

An irate public justifiably doesn't want these sadists treated for their own sake – but a prison system which could calm such dangerous men would be a system which was much safer for prison officers and prison tutors, as well as the numerous medical and dental staff who have to spend time with such killers. As such, the final chapter explores a treatment model which has had impressive results.

CHAPTER TWENTY-THREE

CHANGING THINGS

Only six per cent of British killers are considered insane – which leaves 94 per cent presumably capable of some form of legitimate communication. Many of these men are psychopaths and the psychiatric profession has always maintained that they are untreatable. As such, they are simply locked away without therapeutic help.

But this approach can have its dangers and lead to acts of violence in jail, as occurred with prisoner Darren Blancheflower. Sentenced to life imprisonment for armed robbery, he took offence when his carpentry tutor criticised his work and attacked the unfortunate man with a hammer, ignoring his pleas. During the assault, another prisoner shouted to Blancheflower and he looked over at the man then calmly continued to rain crushing blows upon his tutor's head. His victim died, after which Blancheflower told his fellow prisoners that he wanted to kill again.

A therapeutic approach

He believed that he was born evil and would die evil, so was initially resistant to therapy, threatening to strangle prison psychiatrist Dr Bob Johnson with a pyjama cord. For a while the sessions were halted, then Dr Johnson resumed his work, eventually exploring Blancheflower's childhood. At this stage the typical abused upbringing of the sadist emerged.

The prisoner initially refused to talk about his mother, simply making dark statements about how he wanted to hurt her. But slowly he gave details of what he'd been through. Later, he talked about his childhood abuse of animals which included starving his pet rabbit for several days then cutting it in half. He'd also put numerous live frogs through a crushing machine when he was only ten years old, taking pleasure from seeing their flesh and blood squirt out.

Responding to Johnson's therapy, the psychopath became much more relaxed, the change noticeable in his voice tone and body language. He eventually acknowledged that he might be able to resolve issues through talking, that he didn't have to use violence.

Bob Johnson treated 18 such psychopaths in Parkhurst Prison between 1991 and 1996 at the invitation of the then governor. He recorded 700 hours of interviews with these men, finding that they had invariably become evil after suffering childhood trauma which left them with repressed toxic memories. They tended to see themselves as being faultily wired, but the doctor made clear that they were only faultily programmed and therefore salvageable. (Sceptics believe that such violent men merely invent an abusive upbringing but the cruel childhoods of numerous prisoners has been well documented.)

Dr Johnson found that it was often two years into treatment before these damaged individuals could talk about certain aspects of their childhoods. They initially said that they were indifferent to their toxic parent or that they'd like to get their own back by inflicting hellish tortures – but further sessions revealed that subconsciously they were still afraid of them.

And these men had good reason to be afraid. One killer told Dr Johnson about being abused from the age of four by a close relative. Widely regarded as an unfeeling hard man, he broke down and wept, admitting, 'I've been hurt too much.' Another murderer told the psychiatrist that he'd been multiply abused by his father, being sodomised from the age of eight and made to cross-dress by age ten. He went on to molest his friends at school – and in adulthood he shot dead his pregnant girlfriend. Talking at last about his violent parent, he admitted, 'I was terrified of him... he was a nutter.' He began unravelling the past.

This man too visibly relaxed after being treated by Bob Johnson – and Johnson himself noted similar changes in his other psychopathic patients. 'They changed visually... stopped hitting each other... showed a more relaxed body language and began sleeping better. They also stopped having stomach pains.'

It was obvious to everyone that his approach was paying dividends – after all, the bell which signalled a violent incident had rung numerous times prior to the psychiatrist's arrival, whereas after several months of treating these killers, it didn't ring at all.

But in 1996, Parkhurst decided to close its C-Wing so all of Dr Johnson's patients were moved to different prisons, despite the fact that some were at critical stages of their therapy. Aware that his newer patients would regress, the psychiatrist resigned in disgust.

Only a naïve or foolish prison service would have released these men early because they self-reported that they no longer felt violent and because they now behaved peaceably in a community setting – after all, many sadists wise up and become model prisoners. But a prison service which denies prisoners a seemingly effective treatment, knowing that they will eventually serve their tariffs and be released back into the community, is foolish in the extreme.

The following year, the BBC programme *Panorama* decided to publicise Johnson's impressive work, but all information about prisons had to be cleared by the then Home Secretary Michael

Howard. He favoured a 'born evil' explanation of prisoners so applied to the High Court to prevent the programme being aired. Thankfully the judge allowed *Panorama* to be broadcast and it was shown on the BBC in March 1997.

Emotional Health

Subsequently, Johnson co-founded the James Nayler Foundation, a charity which researches and treats all types of personality disorder. The Foundation has begun to produce videos exploring how frozen terror from childhood makes people violent or afraid and they are training other therapists to carry on their work.

The psychiatrist has had great success in treating everyone from persistent thieves to agoraphobics by unlocking their hidden trauma. (Some abused children turn their anger inwards and become self-destructive adults – 170,000 self-harmers a year are presented at casualty departments in Britain whilst numerous others blot out the pain with alcohol, food and drugs. Others turn the anger outwards and become violent parents and spouses or indiscriminately violent criminals.)

Dawn, who features in one James Nayler training video, had tried everything from counselling to acupuncture to hypnotherapy in an abortive attempt to rid herself of crippling panic attacks, but it was only when she sought therapy from Dr Johnson that she realised that her symptoms had arisen 'because my dad used to hit me when I was little'. She also became aware that she'd been terrified of both of her parents, and by taking her back to the point where she first got frightened, the psychiatrist was able to free her from her fears.

To expound his theories, Johnson has written a book, *Emotional Health*, subtitled *What Emotions Are And How They Cause Social And Mental Disease*. Aware of the sadism that violent upbringings can produce, he states on the title page that 'nothing written here excuses, nor remotely justifies, any atrocity'. He adds that it's nevertheless vital that we look at the reasons for such atrocities if we are to prevent them from happening again.

Johnson explains that all adult emotional disease has its roots 'firmly based in the remnants of an infantile strategy'. He notes that we need truth, trust and consent in order to enjoy emotional health and writes that 'In their absence there is not the remotest chance of controlling aberrant emotions, however destructive or even self-destructive they may become.'

So why were prison hospitals such as Ashworth so resistant to his work? Dr Johnson told this author that 'Patients, nursing management, hospital board and NHS executives all desperately wanted me to stay, but the consultant psychiatrists had the power to block learning something new, and did so.'

Sadly, the prison system has yet to embrace his therapeutic model, so are violent prisoners now given a chemical cosh? 'Not so much sedation, but sadism and deracination and control and solitary confinement.'

He's convinced that sexually sadistic men can benefit from his therapy in the same way as more generally violent men, though acknowledges that 'it could take longer – certainly it has worked well with those I have treated successfully'.

Young psychopaths

Other institutions have had success with child and teenage psychopaths when they are removed from their home environment. For example, the normal repeat offending rate is 40 to 45 per cent but when Professor Pamela Taylor worked with teenage psychopaths in Broadmoor in the 1990s, she got the recidivism rate to under 20 per cent. In the same time frame, Odenkotte Special Hospital in Holland also trained young psychopaths to cope in the community.

SADISTIC KILLERS

School's out forever

Ironically, those sadists who end up in community institutions have often been ill-treated in their previous institution, that of the schoolhouse. Abuse in schools also had a deleterious effect on several of the sadists profiled here with Neville Heath, Richard Cottingham and Colin Ireland being caned – and watching other children being caned – in class. The removal of corporal punishment from state schools will have lessened the chance of future sadists being formed through such practices, though private schools are still allowed to beat their pupils. In the main, only parents who approve of corporal punishment send their children to schools which administer it, so these children are also likely to be beaten at home.

Cruelty also occurs in schools abroad: in 2003, a 17-year-old Japanese schoolboy who fell asleep in class was handed a knife by his teacher and told to slice open his index finger. He did so, whereupon the teacher ordered him to write a punishment essay in his own blood.

Hell house

But being repeatedly and inconsistently chastised in the home is the strongest indicator that a child will go on to become sadistic or masochistic, with working class men the most likely to become violent. Anthropologist Elliot Leyton has noted that this is because working class parents are the most likely to resort to physical punishment in the home so that 'their children are exposed to violent and aggressive role models; they mature with fewer inhibitions – and more positive associations – towards aggressivity.' (11 out of the 15 sadists profiled in this book were working class, as were most in the case studies which form the themed chapters.)

At the moment, hitting a child is legal, though since the Children's Bill came into effect in Britain on 15 January 2005 it's illegal for a parent to hit a child and cause swelling, bruising or grazing of the skin. It's also illegal to shake a child or hit them about the head or with an implement, and parents guilty of such excessive chastisement can now face a jail term of up to five years.

But the National Society for the Prevention of Cruelty to Children has pointed out that there shouldn't be an *acceptable* way to hit children, that the guidelines still leave them vulnerable to abuse. They've stated: 'The law needs to send out a clear message that it is as wrong to hit a child as it is to hit an adult.'

Because of the current confusion about so-called legitimate hitting, far fewer people report child cruelty than animal cruelty – yet there's often a crossover between the two as adults who abuse their pets are also much more likely to abuse any children living in the home.

Removed from their violent carers and given significant therapeutic help, many of these children blossom into considerate teenagers. Rex Krebs went from child sex offender to model citizen after being taken away from his cruel father and put into a supportive environment. But he was eventually returned to his father, regressed and went on to commit two terrible homicides.

And Rex Krebs' body count was statistically low, as the average sadistic American serial killer claims eight known victims before he is caught. And as we've seen, some account for even more victims – Robert Hansen privately admitted to murdering 17 women and Robert Rhoades is suspected of up to 50 unsolved homicides.

These sadists cause widespread emotional suffering as the relatives, friends, workmates, neighbours and acquaintances of the victim are all affected by their horrific torture-murder. And many of these outwardly charismatic men continue to manipulate others within the prison environment.

Ironically, the victims' families often call for these sadists to be birched or whipped, not realising that the corporal punishment received during childhood fuelled their very first revenge fantasies: beaten on the soles of his feet by his parents, Dayton Rogers went on to beat and cut the feet of numerous prostitutes. Whipped by his father, Victor Miller went on to bind and whip other boys.

The punitive treatment of offenders is similarly counter-productive, as illustrated by Christopher Wilder who was given electroconvulsive therapy after raping a classmate. Already deeply disturbed through being physically and sexually abused, he simply fashioned a torture device from an electric cable and gave his unfortunate victims electric shocks.

Such nightmarish childhoods explain why these men want to mutilate and kill but can't excuse them. Many other people have suffered repeatedly throughout their formative years but have chosen not to pass that suffering on. Moreover, almost every sadist profiled in this book was loved at some stage by a partner or spouse and most of them had children who would initially have loved them unconditionally. They had the option of making a life based on shared respect but made the active choice to denigrate and destroy.

The final word goes to Viktor Frankl who saw many men cope with extreme adversity at Auschwitz. 'We who lived in concentration camps can remember the men who walked through the huts comforting others, giving away their last piece of bread; they offered sufficient proof that everything can be taken away from a man but one thing, the last of the human freedoms, to choose one's attitude in any given set of circumstances, to choose one's own way.'

APPENDIX: USEFUL ADDRESSES

Organisations change premises (and occasionally close due to lack of funding) so check out their websites whenever possible to confirm their current status and locale.

Emotional Wellbeing

National Association for People Abused in Childhood, 42 Curtain Road, London, EC2A 3NH – their website at www. napac.org.uk includes a booklist with sections for survivors, their relatives and professionals. Their national helpline for survivors is 0800 085 3330.

James Nayler Foundation, PO Box 49, Ventnor, PO38 9AA – a charity co-founded by Dr Bob Johnson to expose the link between childhood trauma and adult mental health difficulties. Website www.TruthTrustConsent.com

The Samaritans offer confidential emotional support by telephone 24 hours a day to anyone in distress. You'll find your local branch number in the phone directory or call their national number 08457 90 90 90. Website www.samaritans. org.uk or you can contact them by post by writing to Chris, PO Box 9090, Stirling, FK8 2SA. The Samaritans also run a campaign to encourage people of all ages to e-mail them if they prefer not to use the telephone. E-mail jo@samaritans.org

Erotic Powerplay

www.lynnpaularussell.com is the website of erotic artist Lynn Paula Russell which includes a free gallery of her adult art.

Spanner Trust, BM 99, London, WC1N 3XX exists to defend the rights of sadomasochists of every sexual orientation. Website www.spannertrust.org

Preventing Child Abuse

Children Are Unbeatable, 94 White Lion Street, London, N1 9PF. Send a stamped self-addressed envelope marked 'free leaflets' to receive information about positive childrearing practices. Website www.childrenareunbeatable.org.uk

National Society for the Prevention of Cruelty to Children, Weston House, 42 Curtain Road, London, EC2A 3NH – if you suspect that a child is being abused, telephone them on 0808 800 5000 or e-mail help@nspcc.org.uk. Website www.nspcc.org.uk

www.there4me.com is a website run by the NSPCC for children aged 12 to 16. It gives advice on bullying, difficulties in the home and exam worries so that no child need feel alone.

SELECT BIBLIOGRAPHY

Arnett, Jeffrey Jensen *Metalheads: Heavy Metal Music & Adolescent Alienation* (1996, Westview Press Inc)

Begg, Paul & Fido, Martin *Great Crimes and Trials of the Twentieth Century* (1993, Carlton/Simon & Schuster)

Begg, Paul *Jack the Ripper* (1998, Robson Books)

Bird, John *Percy Grainger* (1982, Faber & Faber)

Britton, Paul *Picking Up the Pieces* (2000, Corgi Books)

Busch, Alva *Roadside Prey* (1996, Pinnacle Books)

Church, Robert *Accidents of Murder* (1989, Robert Hale Ltd)

Cole, D.J. & Acland, P.R. *The Detective and the Doctor* (1994, Robert Hale Ltd)

Davis, Barbara *Suffer the Little Children* (1999, Pinnacle Books)

Douglas, John & Olshaker, Mark *Mindhunter* (1996, Heinemann)

Du Clos, Bernard *Fair Game* (1993, St Martin's Paperbacks)

Eskapa, Roy *Bizarre Sex* (1995, Parallel Books)

Fowles, John *The Collector* (1998, Vintage)

Furneaux, Rupert *Famous Criminal Cases 6* (1960, Odhams Press Ltd)

Gekoski, Anna *Murder By Numbers* (1999, Andre Deutsch)

Gibney, Bruce *The Beauty Queen Killer* (1984, Pinnacle Books)

James, Mike (edited) *Women Who Kill Viciously* (1999, True Crime Library)

James, Oliver *Britain On the Couch* (1998, Arrow Books)

James, Oliver *They F*** You Up* (2003, Bloomsbury Publishing)

Johnson, Bob *Emotional Health* (2002, James Nayler Foundation)

King, Gary C. *Blood Lust* (1992, Onyx)

Lane, Brian *The 1995 Murder Yearbook* (1994, Headline)

Larkin, Philip *Trouble at Willow Gables* (2002, Faber & Faber)
Leith, Rod *The Prostitute Murders* (1983, Lyle Stuart Inc)
Leyton, Elliott *Men Of Blood* (1995, Constable & Company Ltd)
Linedecker, Clifford *Thrill Killers* (1998, Futura)
Lucas, Norman *The Sex Killers* (1988, W.H. Allen & Co)
McCrary, Gregg *The Unknown Darkness* (2003, HarperCollins)
McLagan, Graeme & Lowes, Nick *Killer On the Streets* (2003, John Blake Publishing)
Michaud, Stephen & Hazelwood, Roy *The Evil That Men Do* (1998, St Martin's Press)
Mitchell, Corey *Dead and Buried* (2003, Pinnacle Books)
Motion, Andrew *Philip Larkin: A Writer's Life* (1993, Faber & Faber)
Pincus, Jonathan H. *Base Instincts* (2001, W.W. Norton & Company)
Ramsden, Mark and Randall, Housk *Radical Desire* (2000, Serpent's Tail)
Selwyn, Francis *Rotten to the Core?* (1988, Routledge)
Tate, Tim & Wyre, Ray *Murder Squad* (1992, Thames Mandarin)
Vronsky, Peter *Serial Killers* (2004, Berkley Publishing Group)
Whittaker, Mark & Kennedy, Les *Sins of the Brother* (1998, Pan Macmillan Australia)
Wilson, Colin *The Mammoth Book of Murder* (2000, Robinson Publishing)

Magazines and newspapers
Marriner, Brian 'Britain's Cruellest Murder Ever?', *Master Detective* (April 1994)
Preston, John 'Crumb's Comforts', *Sunday Telegraph* (13 March 2005)

Spencer, Matthew 'Murder and Sadism in the Kent
Countryside', *Master Detective* (March 2005)

Filmography

Curing Childhood Traumas 1: How Dawn Taught Unbrainwashing,
produced by the James Nayler Foundation (November 2004)
Curing Crime 1: Tony's Story, produced by the James Nayler
Foundation (April 2004)
FBI Files: Christopher Wilder, produced for the Discovery
Channel and broadcast on Britain's Channel Five
FBI Files: Killer Abroad, produced for the Discovery Channel
and broadcast on Britain's Channel Five
Manhunt To Kill and Kill Again, produced by Folio and
broadcast by BBC1 (September 2004)
Murder Detectives: The Ties That Bind, produced by Medstar
and broadcast on Britain's Channel Five
Panorama: Predators, produced and broadcast by BBC1 (March
1997)
Real Crime: Girlsnatcher, produced by Yorkshire Television and
broadcast on ITV (March 2004)

INDEX

Adams, Christine 127, 130

AIDS/HIV 57, 59, 244, 245, 249, 250

Altiery, Andrea 147, 157

American serial killer victim count 325

amyl nitrate 247

Anderson, Anthony 45, 46, 47, 48, 49, 63

animals, cruelty towards 16, 52, 66, 71, 73, 79, 170, 174, 222, 223, 225, 234, 251, 320, 325

Archambault, Marielle 267

Aref, Omaima 288, 289

arson 46, 52, 53, 135, 136, 154, 155, 220, 242

Audette, Shirley 267

Ayano, Matsuko 265

Baird, Stephanie 34, 35, 36, 37

Beart, Paul 64, 65

Beggs, William 81–7

Bell, Mary 297

Bellec, Cédric 283, 284, 285

Birnie, Catherine and David 232

bisexuality 119, 242, 243

Bittaker and Norris 188

Blancheflower, Darren 319

Bockova, Blanka 258, 263

Boden, Wayne 266–269

Bonaventura, Sheryl 213

Bonnick, Andrew 271

borstal 17, 18, 40, 46, 53, 271, 272, 273

Bournemouth 23, 24

Bradley, Perry 58, 59

British National Party 67

Brown, Margaret 35, 37

burglaries 40, 46, 53, 150, 220, 256

Burns, James 245, 246, 249

Byrne, Patrick 30–8

cannibalism 35, 162, 165

Catherine, Mickaël 284, 285

Catherine, Laetitia 284, 285

Capper, Suzanne 298–304

Carpenter, David 155

Carr, Maryann 185, 186, 192, 194

Child's Play film soundtrack 299, 303

Children's Bill 324

Clarke, Caroline 226–9, 231

Cervantes, Nondace 126, 130

Cole, David 248, 249

Colhouer, Jennifer 281

Collier, Andrew 59, 61

Consent in the Criminal Law 317

Connolly, Anthony 246, 247, 249

Copeland, David 65–71

corporal punishment
    of children 134, 288, 324
    adult erotic 306, 309
    adult, healing childhood hurts 326

Corll, Dean 242

Cottingham, Richard 9, 181–96, 266, 318, 324

Coutts, Graham 87–93

Crawford, Aundria 113, 114, 115

cross-dressing 10, 32, 240, 321

Crumb, Robert 315–6

Cummings, Anita 173–180

Cummings, Jesse 170–80

Cummings, Sherry 172–9

Cunanan, Andrew 243, 250–4

depersonalisation of victim 25, 88, 212

depression 45, 67, 121, 130, 199, 200, 280

Denyer, Paul 232–40

DeVore, Cynthia 126, 130

Dinsdale, Peter 242

Dodge, Beth 216

Douglas, John 11, 155, 159

Dudson, Anthony 298–304
Dunn, Christopher 58

Easland, Roxanne 145
Eberle, Danny 166, 167, 168
Eklutna Annie 143, 144, 157, 158, 160
electroconvulsive therapy 326
Emotional Health 322
Ergolo, Karin 260
Everist, Deborah 223
Exley, Shannon 224

Faversham, Raymond 46, 47
Fearn, Donald 193
Februs 306, 309
Feddern, Angela 150, 159
female circumcision 289
Ferguson, Theresa 150, 159
Fitt, Yvonne 74
foot fetish 100, 117, 119
Frank, Theodore 275–8
Frankl, Viktor 326
Fream, Debbie 236, 237
Frey, DeLynn 151, 156, 159
frontal lobe dysfunction 130, 233
frozen terror 322

Furrell, Lisa 145, 159

Gacy, John Wayne 242
Gallagher, Windy 280
Gallego, Charlene 295
Gardner, Margery 21, 22, 23, 26–29
Gauguin, Paul 9
Geiger, Susan 186, 187, 194
Gibson, James 223, 224, 229
Godden, Ivy 273, 274
Goodarzi, Deedeh 187, 195
Gonzales, Rosario 207, 208
Gough, Stuart 43, 44
Goulding, Paula 151, 152, 156, 157
Graham, Gwen, 296
Grainger, Percy 312, 313
Grese, Irma 292–5
Grober, Linda 209, 210, 211
Gyles, Reatha 126, 130

Habschied, Anja 225, 226, 228
Hall, Archibald 141
handkerchief fetish 16, 18
Hansen, Robert 133–61, 325
Hammerer, Heidemarie 259, 263
Heath, Neville 15–29, 63, 266, 324

Henley, Elmer Wayne 242

Hillside Stranglers 188

Hindley, Myra 296

Hitler 49

Hodges, Maureen 125, 130

hog-tying fetish 110, 112, 113, 114, 124, 167, 215

Holden, Richard 42, 44

Homolka, Karla 296

Horveth, Marcia 256

Howard, Michael 321

Hulsey, Paul 281, 283

IQ 31, 65, 119, 134, 163

incest 48, 282, 316

Ireland, Colin 50–62, 63, 245, 324

Jack the Ripper 28, 181

James Nayler Foundation 322

Johnson, Dr Bob 319–23

Jones, Genene 291, 296

Jones, Ricky Lee 100

Joubert, John 162–9

Kemper, Edmund 233

Kenyon, Elizabeth 208

Komar, Janusz 264–6

Konrad, Elsa 48

Korfman, Michelle 213, 214

Kosminski, Aaron 28

Krebs, Rex 105–16, 325

Lake, Leonard 207

Lamont, Marcus 47, 48

Larkin, Philip 314, 315

Larsen, Malai 146, 159

Leigh, Jeffrey 299, 300, 302, 303

Leyland, Mark 247, 248

Leyton, Elliot 324

Lockhart, Michael 279–82

Logan, Suzanne 212

Long, Sherri 262

Longhurst, Jane 89–93

Lopez, Awilda 286–8

Lopez, Elisa 286–8

Lucas, Henry Lee 67

Luna, Sue 148, 149, 157, 159

Lupo, Michele 243–50

MacDonagh, Kevin 245, 246

Madson, David 252

Marshall, Doreen 24, 25, 26, 28, 29

Maslow's hierarchy of needs 10

Masser, Brunhilde 258

masturbation 31, 52, 88, 90, 107, 114, 119, 123, 136, 147, 156, 164, 167, 183, 184, 199, 202, 234, 245, 248, 259, 271, 275, 313

Maybury, James 28

McClusky, Damien 248, 249

McNeilly, Bernadette 298–304

Messina, Joanne 144, 145, 157, 158,

Miglin, Lee 252, 253

Milat, Ivan 188, 218–31

Miller, Victor 39–44, 63, 326

Mock, Lisa 126, 130

Moitzi, Sabine 260

Moody, Judy 175–9

Moody, Melissa 175–80

moral panic 303

Morrow, Sherry 147, 156, 157, 158

Narre, Aimée 283, 284

Narre, Philippe 283, 284

Nazi propaganda 53

nail bombs 63

necrophilia 9, 35, 63, 88, 89, 242

Neelley, Judith 295

Nelson, Omaima 289–90

Nelson, William 289, 290, 291

nervous breakdown 40, 42, 233

Neugebauer, Gabor 225, 226, 228
Newhouse, Rachel 112, 114, 115
Nilsen, Dennis 242
Noblett, Anne 77
NSPCC 51

O'Dell, Leslie 190, 191, 192, 194
Oldham, Barry 82, 83
Onions, Paul 224, 225, 228, 229, 230
O'Sullivan, Deborah 64, 65

Paulson, Cindy 152–5
paedophilia 41, 52, 53, 91, 96, 97, 103, 170, 175, 199, 243, 278, 306
Panorama 321, 322
parole 40, 92, 105, 111, 112, 114, 123, 131, 136, 141, 158, 239, 240, 255, 257, 265, 304
Patrician Brothers 219
Peacher, Trevor 41, 43, 44
Pederson, Tamara 149, 157, 159
pet shop sex 246
Petrov, Stasys 48
picquerism 63, 297
Pierrepoint, Albert 295
Pook, Clifford 298, 299, 300, 302, 303
Porteous, Elizabeth 268, 269

Powell, Jean 298–304

Powell, Glyn 299, 301, 302

Prem, Regina 260

Preston, John 316

psychopaths 18, 22, 27, 28, 37, 40, 44, 45, 49, 64, 65, 80, 175,
    236, 257, 263, 264, 269, 316, 319, 320, 321, 323
    and repeat offending 323

Ramsden, Mark 316, 317

razor fetish 63, 81

Reese, William 253

Reyner, Jean 190, 192, 195

Rhoades, Robert 9, 96–104, 266, 325

Rifkin, Joel 155

Rimer, Lindsay Jo 74

Risico, Tina 214–7

Rodriguez, Irene 262

Rogers, Dayton 117–32, 318, 326

Russell, Lynn Paula 306, 309

Russell, Natalie 237, 238

Salvage, Arthur 272–5

Sanders, John 28

Schefer, Margaret 256

Schilt, Karen 186, 194

Schmidl, Simone 225

Schrempf, Elfriede 259

Seitz, Amy 276, 277

self-harm 286

sex change 239, 240

sex offenders programme 64, 121

Smith, Jennifer 127–30

sodomy 81, 99, 114, 115, 153, 183, 184, 187, 189, 191, 192,
    222, 271, 273, 281, 321

Spiteri, Emanuel 60, 61

Starkweather, Charles 155

Steele, Louisa 274

Stetson, Ricky 165, 168, 169

Stevens, Elizabeth 235

Story of O 307, 309

Street, Valorie 189, 191, 192, 194, 195, 196

stuttering 133, 134, 145, 155, 314

suicide 24, 36, 67, 97, 195, 222, 254, 264, 280

survivalism 53, 54

Taste For Pain 307

Taylor, John 71–80

Taylor, Professor Pamela 323

The Collector 206, 207

Thill, Mary 140

Thompson, Robert 297

Tierney, Leanne 76–80

Tirard, Eric 285

Toth, Roszsa 236, 239

Trail, Jeffrey 251, 252

transvestism 201, 204, 205

Tynan, Kenneth 313, 314

unsolved murders 74, 80, 103, 200, 230, 325

Unterweger, Johann Jack 255–64, 266

Vaillancourt, Norma 267, 269

VanZamen, Celia 138

Venables, Jon 297

Versace, Gianni 253, 254

voyeurism 32, 275

Vronsky, Peter 188

Walden, Terry 211

Walden, Christopher 167, 168

Walker, Peter 56–58, 60

Wallace, Barry 84, 85, 86

Walters, Joanne 226, 228

Walters, Regina 100–3

Watson, Tereasa 150, 159

Weis, Maria 266

Weisenfeld, Pamela 190, 194

West, Rose 295

Wilder, Christopher 68, 155, 198–217, 266, 318, 326

Williams, Malcolm 270, 271, 272

Wilt, Dawnette 215, 216

Wray, Jean 268

Weston-super-Mare 28

Wood, Cathy 291, 296

Wood, Deborah 74

Worthing 23, 28

Zagler, Sylvia 259

Zwanziger, Anna 296

Other titles from Summersdale

REAL
CRIME SCENE
INVESTIGATIONS
Forensic Experts Reveal Their Secrets
CONNIE FLETCHER

Real Crime Scene Investigations

Connie Fletcher

£9.99

ISBN-10: 1 84024 530 1
ISBN-13: 978 1 84024 530 1

Forensic science is increasingly important in solving crime, and millions of people all over the world are captivated by the TV programmes *CSI: Crime Scene Investigations*, *CSI: Miami* and *CSI: New York*.

Just what secrets can a decomposed corpse reveal? It's not just fingerprints and DNA, it's also blood spatter patterns, footprints, minute indentations, dust patterns – every contact leaves a trace.

Discover how an investigator found grounds for conviction in a single fibre as long as a fingernail. In this compelling book, experts such as homicide detectives, forensic scientists and crime lab specialists reveal the real stories behind their most challenging cases. The result is more fascinating than fiction.

Connie Fletcher is the author of What Cops Know, a bestseller that is used in FBI training; Pure Cop, which was also published as an audiobook narrated by Jerry Orbach of Law and Order; and Breaking and Entering, adopted as a 'must-read' by the International Association of Women in Policing.

KILLERS

The Most Barbaric
Murderers of Our Times

nigel cawthorne

Killers
The Most Barbaric Murderers of Our Times

Nigel Cawthorne

£9.99

ISBN-10: 1 84024 485 2
ISBN-13: 978 1 84024 485 4

'*On 24 February 1994, the police turned up at 25 Cromwell Street, an ordinary three-storey house in central Gloucester, with a warrant to dig up the back garden. The door was answered by Stephen West, the 20-year-old son of the householders Fred and Rosemary West. The police told him that they were looking for the body of his sister Heather, who had disappeared in May 1987 at the age of 16.*'

The world's most depraved murderers were somebody's neighbour, someone else's father. What turns a person into a killer? Enter the dark world of true crime…

With sixteen chilling chapters on notorious killers including Harold Shipman and Charles Manson, those less well known such as Albert DeSalvo and Dennis Nilsen, and the massacres at Hungerford and Columbine, this book examines how and why these people became the most barbaric murderers of our times.

EXECUTION

A GUIDE TO THE ULTIMATE PENALTY

'Essential reading for all gore junkies' *Sunday Express*

GEOFFREY ABBOTT

Execution
A Guide to the Ultimate Penalty

Geoffrey Abbott

£9.99

ISBN-10: 1 84024 433 X
ISBN-13: 978 1 84024 433 5

A gruesomely fascinating catalogue of methods of judicial execution from around the world and through the ages

In his own darkly humorous style, Geoffrey Abbott describes such hair-raising categories as death by cannibalism, being sewn into an animal's belly and a thousand cuts, and reveals the macabre origins of familiar phrases such as 'gone west' or 'drawn a blank' as well as the jargon of the underworld.

A former Beefeater at the Tower of London, writer and TV personality Geoffrey Abbott has his own collection of vintage torture instruments and is the author of 19 books including *The Executioner Always Chops Twice* and *Lipstick on the Noose*.

www.summersdale.com